Fascism: Essays on Europe and India

George Grosz, *Cross section* (1920)

Fascism
Essays on Europe and India

Second Edition

ENLARGED AND UPDATED

Edited by
Jairus Banaji

Three Essays
COLLECTIVE

Second Edition January 2016
First Edition April 2013

ISBN 978-93-83968-12-1

Three Essays
COLLECTIVE

B-957 Palam Vihar, GURGAON (Haryana) 122 017 India
Phone: 91-124 2369023, +91 98681 26587, +91 98683 44843
info@threeessays.com Website: www.threeessays.com
Printed and bound at Chaman Offset Printers, New Delhi

I must clear up once and for all a fundamental error: that we dead are somehow dead. We are full of protest and energy. Who wants to die? We speed through history, examining it. How can I escape the history that will kill us all?

Alexander Kluge, *Die Patriotin*

George Grosz, *Pandemonium* (1919)

Preface

In the last three years before the Nazis took power in Germany their share of the vote expanded from some 6½% in the Reichstag elections of 1930 to over 17% in 1933. The combined vote share of the two leading Left parties remained more or less stable between 1930 and 1932 and fell slightly in 1933, but the tragic fact is that 'the conflict within the Left was stronger than the will to offer joint resistance against the Right' (Peukert, *Inside Nazi Germany*, p. 103). This was not all, however. In Germany the Left failed not just because it was hopelessly divided against itself but because it failed to oppose antisemitism in a concerted and systematic way, and almost certainly underestimated the potential of fascism to capture a mass base. The exception to this was Arthur Rosenberg's essay, written in exile in 1933, which argued both that fascism was more widely based than just the middle class or any particular section of it, and that ideology or an assortment of ideologies played a fundamental role in harnessing whole sectors of the civilian population to the Right. The groundwork for the eventual and rapid victory of the Nazis in the early thirties lay in the active existence of a powerful nationalist Right that was unreconciled to the German Republic (deeply hostile to democracy) and wedded to authoritarian, racist and militaristic subcultures. Since these arguments are laid out in the essay itself and also summarised in the introduction to it below, this is not the place to rehearse them. But they have a major resonance for us in India where communal ideologies play a major role in shaping the politics of the extreme Right and, as the essays on India suggest, function as our counterpart of the nebulous common sense that was pivotal in the formation of a Nazi mass base. Kannan Srinivasan demonstrates the purely subaltern nature of Indian fascism in the classic period when the Nazis and Mussolini ruled Germany and Italy respectively and the Indian national movement overshadowed the more extreme versions of nationalism being forged by Savarkar and the Hindu Mahasabha. Sumit Sarkar's classic essay was published soon after the catastrophic events of December 1992/January 1993 which saw major and frontal assaults by the Sangh Parivar and its political allies, including mass pogroms against Muslims in Bombay. It was one of the first pieces of writing on the Indian Left to return to the category of fascism in order to understand the nature of the movement that had brought about those catastrophes. Dilip Simeon expands the perspective to show how the idea of a nation state with a homogeneous ethnic or religious community at its core is intrinsic to the fascist project, whichever part of the religious spectrum it comes from. The essays in this book are an attempt to situate Indian communalism in the wider frame of fascist political cultures and their role in creating/consolidating a mass base for the extreme Right, and of course of the debates about fascism which have grown considerably since the sixties.

Simeon also underlines the illusory nature of majorities and minorities. In the Indian version of fascism the Nazis' ethnic definition of nationhood is replaced by a religious one, and the 'mobilizing force of antisemitism' (Kershaw, *Hitler*, p. 138) by a manic obsession with Muslims and other religious minorities. If the German defeat in the First War was, as Sartre says, 'transcended as a revolt against the defeated fathers and as a wish for revenge among young Germans *through the practice of Nazism*'

(Sartre, *Critique of Dialectical Reason*, t. 1, p. 667), in India it was the abject humiliation of being what seemed like a permanently colonised, dominated people that the Hindu Mahasabha sought to transcend by its targeting of 'the' Muslims and real Muslims. (See Srinivasan on Savarkar.) The targeting of minorities as a means of mobilising the 'majority' is a manipulation of seriality, both because 'the' Jew or 'the' Muslim does not exist except as a racial/religious stereotype and because the majority does not exist *except as seriality* and, in the action of the group on the series, as what Sartre calls the pure 'illusion of totalised seriality'. (See the way Sartre analyses these relationships in *Critique of Dialectical Reason*, vol. 1, p. 642ff.).

Mass mobilisations by the extreme Right and state complicity in communal violence have *both* left Indian democracy profoundly battered over the last two decades especially. There is a slower version here of the collapse of Weimar democracy, one staggered over the fateful years since the gruesome mass crimes against the Sikhs in Delhi in 1984. Those crimes remain a shameful indictment of the extent to which state complicity in mass violence has become an endemic feature of India's political system. Having said that, the pogroms against the Sikhs were not part of a conscious agenda to remould the nature of the Indian state. In India the Rosenberg perspective on fascism is best demonstrated by the pogroms that engulfed Gujarat in 2002 – a spate of organised 'spontaneous' violence that was *calculated* to generate mass support through communal mobilisation, with the violence concentrated in very specific constituencies. (This is shown by Dhattiwala and Biggs, *Politics & Society*, 40/4 (2012) pp. 483–516, e.g., 'Violence was worst in districts or constituencies where the BJP faced the greatest electoral competition', p. 501). The Chief Minister had actual or 'constructive' knowledge of the crimes being committed and would, in any international criminal jurisdiction, be facing trial for command responsibility for them. And as with Hitler's growing acceptability in wider social circles after 1924, his sordid image has since been refurbished to transform a hardened RSS functionary into prime-ministerial material, thanks to the Washington-based PR and lobbyist firm APCO, hired at taxpayers' expense to obliterate the memory of 2002. The forces aiding this image makeover include major sycophants in India's business community, leaders of industry who have chosen to make Gujarat and Modi the platform for a regroupment around their authoritarian vision of a state fanatically committed to capitalism ('development') and brooking no interference from an effete and ostensibly corrupt bureaucracy; all this powerfully aided of course by the media with its own culture of sycophancy and unbelievable prostration in the face of power. Given all that has happened subsequently (*post* 2002) to contain and undermine the judicial system there and actively subvert the course of justice, to consolidate a mass base around hideous communal prejudices and around the ghettoisation of a whole community, also to win the support of industrial capital with lavish grants of land and unhindered access to the leader himself, the trajectory of the new fascism in India is almost certainly best studied in the context of Gujarat. At the heart of this story lies the issue of 'mass' support for deeply authoritarian political forces and cultures, of civilian compliance with communal persecution behind the semblance of democratic forms. The public culture of democracy is so radically hollowed out and degraded that in the end it yields a mere mask, a form of legitimation, for a regime immersed in criminality.

A word finally about the reading list at the end of this book. The literature on fascism has grown by leaps and bounds and is so massive that any bibliography that doesn't call itself 'select' would be impossible to fathom. For example, in the LSE library in London the non-periodical literature that deals more or less directly with Nazism alone (shelfmarks DD240–DD256) straddles 8 stacks, each comprising 8 shelves with roughly 40 titles per shelf, i.e. over 2500 titles. Tim Mason, 'Whatever happened to "Fascism"?', *Radical History Review* 1991, was an early attempt to assess the impact of this humongous proliferation of scholarship on the more classic, left-dominated 'theories of fascism' literature that held the field in the sixties and seventies. And interestingly, racism and genocide were among the themes that Mason saw emerging in a big way, which Marxist theories had tended to ignore. Rosenberg is an exception to this, not in the sense that he lived to witness the full horrors of the Nazi genocide or its impact but because the racism that culminated in genocide was central to his narrative and to the way he explained the 'mass' element in the success of fascism. For Rosenberg, next to the more immediate complicity of the state in tolerating the activity of the fascist squads, it was ideology and its inert grip on the masses that explained the apparent ease with which Nazism transformed itself into a mass movement in the late twenties. That ideological incubus (cf. Marx, 'The tradition of all dead generations weighs like a nightmare on the brains of the living') was itself complex, an amalgam of the rabid nationalism of the late nineteenth century, the age-old antisemitism of Bloch's 'non-contemporaneous' classes, the newer antisemitism of the white-collar groups, and of course the traumatic responses to the birth of democracy in 1918, following a war that literally traumatised millions of Europe's citizens. The reading list mobilises some of this literature, e.g., Kauders' excellent monograph on the rapid escalation of antisemitism after 1918, Claudia Koonz's argument in *Mothers in the Fatherland* that through their normal routine commitments to domesticity German women contributed to the stability of the Nazi regime, or Ruth Birn's devastating review of Goldhagen and his view that a genocidal racism was somehow innate in German culture and society, to which Goldhagen reacted with the threat of a defamation lawsuit! Not included there is Walter Benjamin's classic 'Artwork Essay' (1936) that looked only obliquely at fascism but grasped a central feature of its control and manipulation of 'technological art forms', viz. that 'mass movements present themselves more clearly to the camera than to the human eye. Cadres of hundreds of thousands are best captured in bird's-eye view. And if that perspective is as accessible to the human eye as to the camera, the image that the human eye carries away from the scene is not amenable to the kind of enlargement that the recorded image undergoes.' (Benjamin, *One-Way Street and Other Writings*, p. 279, n. 33).' (See the brilliant discussion of these ideas in Esther Leslie, *Walter Benjamin. Overpowering Conformism*, pp. 162–67).

The first two chapters are reprinted from *Historical Materialism*, 20/1 (2012), pp. 133–89. I'm grateful to the editors of *Historical Materialism* for permission to reprint these from the pages of their excellent journal. Sumit Sarkar's essay is reprinted from *Economic and Political Weekly*, XXXVIII/5, January 30, 1993. My thanks to him and to EPW for permission to publish it here. The chapter that concludes this collection is an expanded version of a lecture I gave at Jamia Millia Islamia, New Delhi, on 18 March 2013. It was the fifth lecture in the Walter Sisulu Memorial Lecture series. My thanks also to Asad Zaidi for agreeing to have this collection put together.

March 2013

Contents

Notes on contributors

Jairus Banaji is associated with the Department of Development Studies, SOAS, University of London. His book *Theory as History* won the Isaac and Tamara Deutscher Memorial Prize for 2011.

Sumit Sarkar is a well-known historian of modern India. Until recently he was Professor of History at the University of Delhi. His books include *Modern India, 1885-1947*, *Writing Social History* and *Beyond Nationalist Frames*.

Dilip Simeon is a Delhi-based historian and writer. His publications include an academic monograph on the labour movement in Jharkhand and the novel *Revolution Highway*.

Kannan Srinivasan (kannansrinivasan.org) is an Adjunct Research Fellow of the School of Political Inquiry at Monash University and was for many years a journalist.

PART ONE

Arthur Rosenberg on fascism

George Grosz, *Toads of property* (1921)

Fascism as a mass-movement

TRANSLATOR'S INTRODUCTION

Jairus Banaji

Arthur Rosenberg was a major historian and Communist Reichstag deputy best known for his books *The Birth of the German Republic, 1871–1918* (1928) and *A History of Bolshevism* (1932). The three broad phases of his life as a Marxist are the years from 1919 to April 1927, when he played an active part in the KPD-Left, the period from May 1927 to March 1933, following his resignation from the KPD (the years that best define him as a 'Communist without a party'), and the tragic final decade of his life when he fled Germany along with his family, would find himself stripped of German citizenship, and lead an impoverished life as a tutor in Brooklyn College, New York, having failed to find any sort of academic position in England. All of Rosenberg's major works stem from the last period of his life, except for *The Birth of the German Republic*, which he published in 1928.

As a member of the left wing of the USPD, Rosenberg found himself joining the German Communist Party in October 1920. The hallmark of the Left-current within the KPD was of course its intransigent opposition to any sort of front with the SPD in the intensely volatile political climate of Weimar, but unlike Fischer and Maslow (more substantial leaders of the 'Berlin Left', as the KPD-Left was called), Rosenberg himself was deeply resentful of excessive Comintern interference in the affairs of the German party. By 1925 the KPD-Left was split wide open, lost control of the party-leadership to Thälmann, and saw a major purge of the Left-elements, including Korsch and Werner Scholem, all denounced as 'anti-Bolshevik'. Rosenberg seems to have survived this purge but resigned from the party in April 1927. He remained a Reichstag deputy for about a year, but was doubly ostracised both within the academic establishment and by the orthodox Left in Germany. Thanks to the implacable hostility of Eduard Meyer and Ulrich Wilcken, he was denied a proper appointment in Berlin University. By now, the eve of the massive expansion of Nazism among the electorate, he wrote exclusively for publications run by the SPD. In *A History of Bolshevism*, the last book he published before his exile, he characterised Stalin's Russia as 'state-capitalist' (this in 1932). On 30 January 1933, Hindenburg appointed Hitler Chancellor and the German Communists frantically appealed to the SPD for a 'united front' when the terror started in February. By the end of March Rosenberg had fled to Zurich with his family, in September he moved to London where he failed to land a job at the LSE, and then four months later got a one-year fellowship at the University of Liverpool where he wrote *Democracy and Socialism*. *Fascism as a Mass-Movement* appeared as a booklet ('Broschüre') in 1934 under the pseudonym 'Historikus' and published by the Karlsbad publisher Graphia, which was run by SPD refugees and German-speaking Social Democrats in Czechoslovakia. Rosenberg left for the States in late October 1937 and eventually died of cancer in 1943.[1]

The abbreviated version of Rosenberg's fascism-essay that runs to 65-odd pages in Abendroth's collection *Faschismus und Kapitalismus* is the one translated here.[2] It divides into three portions, the first mapping a general vision of the history and politics of Europe in the later-nineteenth century, and the second and third dealing with Italy and Germany respectively. The distinctive feature of the argument is summed up in the title itself, namely, the conception of fascism as a *mass*-movement. Written in 1933, this contrasted *both* with the Comintern's official line that fascism was 'the power of finance-capital itself',[3] a sort of political incarnation of capital, and with the contrary theories that saw fascism mediating between capital and labour on the model implied in Marx's analysis of Bonapartism.[4] Rosenberg seems to have steered clear of this whole debate, which as a historian he may well have found superficial. The crucial point for him was to know *where fascism came from, not what it resembled in the past*. He rejected the view that fascism was somehow primordially or quintessentially connected with the petty bourgeoisie in particular – either driven by it or largely founded on it – suggesting that it had a much wider social appeal and was more widely based than that view implied. If fascism was a product of its own ideology, then that ideology was already widespread by 1914. Throughout the main countries of Europe, liberalism was either stillborn or successfully contained and defeated. This was as true of the Hapsburgs as it was of Germany or Britain for that matter. The crux of the new 'authoritarian conservatism', as he called it, was its ability to win mass-support, popular conservative majorities, by encouraging a new breed of nationalism that was ultra-patriotic, racist and violently opposed to the Left. This took different forms in different parts of Europe but its essential features were the same – a 'demagogic nationalism' that targeted minorities (in Europe, mainly Jews) to build a mass-support. The powerful surge of antisemitism that swept through Europe in the last quarter of the nineteenth century was a fundamental part of this radical nationalism.

Thus Rosenberg's key argument here is that '*the ideology which is today called "fascist" was already fairly widespread throughout Europe before the War*, and exerted a strong influence on the masses.' He goes on to say, 'However, with one exception, what was missing then was the peculiar tactic of using stormtroopers which is thoroughly characteristic of modern fascism.

The sole exception was formed by the Black Hundreds of Tsarist Russia and their ability to stage pogroms' (p. 34).

> Legally, the stormtroopers *should* be tried and sentenced to jail. But in fact nothing of the sort happens to them. Their conviction in the courts is pure show – either they do not serve their sentence, or they are soon pardoned. (p. 35)

The important insight here is that *stormtroopers work with the connivance of the state*, a theme he returns to repeatedly. As for the pogrom itself, he claims '*the rage of the patriotic masses has to be manufactured*' (ibid.). This is what happened in the Tsarist pogroms of 1905.

Rosenberg saw Italian fascism as a modernising force that broke the power of the Southern cliques to pave the way for Northern industrial capitalism. In Italy, 'Fascism was and remained the party of the advanced North' (p. 61), smashing the working class but also 'breaking the dominance of the backward feudal cliques of Central and Southern Italy' (ibid.). 'Mussolini was the leader of the modern Italian North, with its bourgeoisie and its intelligentsia.' (ibid.)

> The state-capitalist concentration of the country in the so-called 'corporatist system' facilitated control of the country by the most efficient groups of capitalists. Heavy industry, chemicals, automobiles, aircraft, and shipping were all systematically developed. Where in all this is the 'petty-bourgeois' spirit that is supposed to form the essence of fascism? (p. 64)

In the German case, it is the sheer weight of the nationalist Right that is so striking. Nazism emerged from this background, survived its fragmentation in the years of stability between 1924 and 1929, and retotalised both its ideologies as well as much of the German past – the massive weight of militarism and the widespread latent antisemitism that survived into the Weimar period. Rosenberg starts the German analysis by drawing a key distinction between households dependent on wage-employment (*die Arbeitnehmerschaft*) and industrial workers in the narrower sense. For example, he included government-employees and office-workers in the proletarian camp because their jobs involved some form of paid employment. Of a total of around 25 million paid employees and proletarians in this broad sense, 'at most only 11 million were factory-workers in the true sense' (p. 67). Those workers, say, roughly a third of Germany's population, remained loyal to the Left down to the bitter end,[5] but other sections of the general mass of paid employees (the majority) consistently voted for the bourgeois parties throughout the Weimar years. The huge Republican majority of January 1919 soon crumbled. The November Revolution left the state-machinery intact – that is, in the hands of the old bureaucracy, a bastion of reaction – and the middle-class, 'large sections of the white-collar and government-employees who had greeted the Republic in November with enthusiasm', 'would soon stand aloof from it in sheer disappointment' (p. 68). In fact, the percentage of the wage-earning population that was *opposed* to the Left (including the Catholic Centre Party) increased dramatically in the crucial early years of Weimar. Rosenberg claims that by March 1933, when the Nazis polled a stunning 17 million votes against 12 million for the Social Democrats and KPD, something like 11.5 million votes of the 'other wage-earners' category went to the parties of the Right.

Fascism as a Mass Movement is an essay about the origins and growth of fascism, not fascism in power. Though much of the humongous bibliography that has grown up around the subject particularly since the late sixties deals overwhelmingly with the latter (with Neumann's *Behemoth* as an early and outstanding example of the kind of issues that would dominate subsequent historiography), the essential themes of Rosenberg's argument stand fully vindicated by recent scholarship. 'The error of the Italian Communist Party lies mainly in the fact that it sees fascism only as a military-terrorist movement, *not as a mass movement with deep social roots*', Clara Zetkin warned in 1923.[6] It is *this* conception – of the capacity of the Right to mobilise mass-support – that forms the central thread of Rosenberg's essay, where the key to its interpretation lies *both* in the political defeat of liberalism and its rapid retreat across most of Europe in the nineteenth century *and* in the virulent nationalisms that emerged to buttress the rule of traditional élites against the threat of democracy and Marxist socialism. If the singular brutality of the Nazi genocide remains a watershed in the history of the modern world,[7] one that Rosenberg could scarcely have anticipated in 1933, the racial myth of the *Volksgemeinschaft* that paved the way for it was far from novel, its roots firmly embedded in the 'integral nationalism' of Treitschke and Maurras and the visions of national redemption preached by Schönerer and Lueger (against both Slavs and Jews) to Pan-German constituencies in Austria that Weiss has described as 'one of the most anti-Semitic publics west of Russia'.[8] Thus the argument, cited above, that 'the ideology which is today called "fascist" was already fairly widespread throughout Europe before the War' is thoroughly convincing. It is a major insight into why the fascist movements could expand so rapidly, both in Italy and in Germany (in the early and late twenties respectively), against the background of war-hysteria and assaults on the Left (in Italy) and of a powerful nationalist Right in Germany that prepared the ground for the Nazis. The centrality of racism to Nazism in particular emerges more forcefully in Rosenberg's essay than any other Marxist writing of the twenties and early thirties. So does the argument that the success of the fascists depended crucially on the connivance or active complicity of the existing state-authorities, many of whom would of course have been active members of the PNF and NSDAP. This was starkly obvious in Italy where the *squadristi* 'succeeded because they could always count on the state', (p. 54) but no less so in Germany where, as Neumann noted, not one of the conspirators in the right-wing Kapp Putsch of 1920 had been punished even 15 months later, 'the Weimar criminal courts were part and parcel of the anti-democratic camp', and the 'courts invariably became sounding-boards for [Nazi] propaganda';[9] and where, as Rosenberg points out, 'a whole series of government-officials, especially in the army, maintained close contact with the

Freikorps and [other] counter-revolutionaries' (p. 74). Finally, a major part of the essay sets out to discredit the so-called 'middle-class theory' of fascism. Rosenberg was convinced that fascism was not a petty-bourgeois movement nor was the mass-base of the fascist parties confined to the petty bourgeoisie. Of course, Trotsky saw fascism 'raising itself to power on the backs of the petty bourgeoisie', and then putting the middle-classes 'at the service of capital'. 'Through the fascist agency, capitalism sets in motion the masses of the crazed petty bourgeoisie.'[10] Reich, too, made the middle-class central to fascism, seeing submission to or 'identification with' 'authority, firm, state, nation, etc.' as peculiar to the mass-psychology of the lower-middle-class. 'The middle class was and continued to be the mainstay of the swastika.'[11] But of course none of these characterisations prove that fascism was a movement *of* the middle-classes, at least in the stronger sense in which Luigi Salvatorelli had argued this for Italy in 1923.[12]

What *is* true, on the other hand, is that the middle-class was particularly susceptible to Nazi propaganda, and that, whereas 'working-class milieus dominated by the parties of the Left...remained unyielding terrain for the NSDAP', a major share of the Nazi vote in the electoral landslide of September 1930, at least 40 per cent, came from the middle-classes.[13] That a further 25 per cent of Nazi voters was drawn from the working class suggests first that the German workers were far from homogeneous either socially or politically, and second that the appeal of fascism was not class-specific but rather, as Neumann suggested, more widely spread over 'the most diverse social strata'.[14] These are both points that come through with remarkable clarity in *Fascism as a Mass-Movement*. Rosenberg's distinction between the general mass of wage-earners/salaried employees and industrial workers in particular crucially explains the difference in political behaviour between workers who stayed with the Left down to the end and workers who supported the Nazis. Kershaw notes that, down to the Reichstag election of May 1928, the Nazis' 'concentration on the industrial working class had not paid dividends',[15] yet

Mühlberger, analysing branch-membership data for various periods between 1925 and 1933, claims that the Nazis secured 'significant support' in predominantly lower-class areas.[16] Anywhere between 28 per cent and 46 per cent of Nazi branch-members might consist of workers, both skilled and unskilled.[17] The contradiction is only apparent. First, the 'rush to the swastika' occurred chiefly *after* 1928, following the winter of 1928–9 and against the background of worsening economic conditions. But, just as important, if workers living in heavily industrialised urban centres such as Hamburg remained immune to Nazism, those who lived in small communities and villages were more vulnerable. 'It was residence in a rural environment that was decisive.'[18] And not just residence, of course, but age, gender, religion, and whether one retained a job at all. Workers were on the whole significantly underrepresented in the hard-core Nazi ranks, except for the SA where, at least in Western and Southern Germany, the rank-and-file was largely 'lower class'[19] (mainly unemployed, as Rosenberg notes), the white-collar groups, or 'new middle-class' more broadly, dramatically *over*represented, as were 'the élite', including students and academic professionals. Certainly the most balanced assessment of this still largely controversial issue remains the one Noakes offered years ago in his study of Lower Saxony and electoral districts that saw some of the highest Nazi votes in 1930–3. He concluded that the Nazis 'could appeal to a whole range of classes and interests', even if 'it was the lower middle class which was most attracted to the party'.[20] This, broadly, is Rosenberg's position, since he makes repeated reference to the white-collar element and civil servants being a decisive part of the Nazi social base, while refusing to characterise either the party or the movement as middle-class. White-collar workers in particular showed a bizarre affinity for the racist (*völkisch*) organisations that were striking precursors of the Nazi movement, above all the Deutscher Schutz- und Trutzbund (DSTB) and its successor the DVSTB.[21] That the SPD white-collar union failed to organise more than a handful of these employees who preferred to join 'professional' organisations[22] suggests that, more than *material* interest or the immediate perception of one, these (white-collar elements, lower- and middle-ranking civil servants, the self-employed, etc.) were strata of the *Mittelstand* that drew their identity or their sense of one from their family-backgrounds and the deeply nationalist and authoritarian traditions interiorised there.[23] Describing his own experience of visiting large factories and managements in 1934 and 1935, Sohn-Rethel wrote:

> As a rule the hard core of the workers, but to a lesser extent the younger ones and the new apprentices, were not Nazi and did not pretend to be Nazi...But the middle and lower white-collar workers (*Angestellten*) were those for whom the party-badge was a symbol of faith and who assumed unmistakeable Nazi bearings...The members of the 'new intelligentsia' were the most inflexible of these – the real rabid fanatics [who] seemed so passionately committed to the interests of capital without having any personal share in its profits.[24]

'Symbol of faith', 'rabid fanatics' – these are not characterisations that could apply to the mass of 'ordinary Germans', those who were neither direct perpetrators nor hate-campaigners. Yet this is where the real problem of fascism lies. As Christopher Browning notes in his extraordinary book *Ordinary Men*, 'the vast majority of the general population did not clamor or press for anti-Semitic measures', yet they allowed a gulf to open up between the Jewish minority (and of course other minorities) and themselves.[25] Thus we have a paradox or seeming paradox of what Browning in another work calls a 'widespread receptivity to mass murder',[26] or what, less dramatically, has been called 'German public support for Nazi rule',[27] including the fact that knowledge of the concentration-camps (and deportations, mass-shootings of Jews, etc.) *was* available and 'fairly widespread',[28] coupled, on the other hand, with the sharp and obvious distinction between the overtly Nazi element of the population and a civilian population, the so-called 'Mitläufer', that could show repeated disgust at overt acts of brutality and violence *even as it accepted* 'the broad principles of legal discrimination and exclusion on racial grounds' and harboured discriminatory attitudes.[29] Brecht's own ambivalence about the distinction between the German people and the National Socialists would of course survive to dominate postwar Germany and appear repeatedly in Fassbinder's work and in films such as *Germany, Pale Mother*. As Anton Kaes says, 'Those born in 1945, like Fassbinder, were given the German past as an unwanted legacy'.[30] Fassbinder himself had an acute sense of the continuities between the bourgeois values of the nineteenth century and the ideology of the Third Reich, the ferocious culmination of German/bourgeois nationalism in the horrors of the Nazi state.[31] This is a perspective close to Rosenberg's view that it was the bourgeoisie that formed the chief bearer of this redemptive conception of German power in the decades before 1914 (p. 96). But the problem of civilian compliance remains. 'O Germany, pale mother! / What have your *sons* done to you.' The Nazi movement was almost exclusively male,[32] yet millions of women voted for the Nazis in 1932, and in 1936 'eleven million out of thirty-five million women in Germany were members of the *NS-Frauenschaft*'.[33] To suppose that women were 'peculiarly resistant to National Socialism'[34] is to espouse a strangely essentialist feminism that fails to confront the issue of fascism in any serious way, and just as David Bankier's work broke new ground in exploring the issue of compliance head-on, showing the complex ways in which passive and genocidal forms of racism interacted,[35] Claudia Koonz's books *Mothers in the Fatherland* and *The Nazi Conscience* are both important pointers to some of the ways in which socialists and the Marxist Left should restructure the terms of the debate about fascism, neither exaggerating the extent to which workers (for example) were integrated into the fascist state[36] nor shying away from the harder issue of the type and degree of complicity of large masses of the population in the régime's criminality, however we choose to characterise that – as 'genocidal consensus',[37] 'passive complicity',[38] or just plain 'moral indifference'.[39]

Finally, even if fascism today is not and will not be the return of old-style fascism but more eclectic and variegated versions of extreme-Right politics, Rosenberg's essay loses none of its relevance for us. In particular, the increasing support drawn from the working class by parties of the extreme Right in countries such as France, Austria, Denmark and Norway,[40] or the ability of the Sangh Parivar in India (the RSS/BJP combine) to create mass-mobilisations based on hate-campaigns and strategies of tension should be some of the more pressing reasons why the Left needs to return to the issue of fascism in a central way.

Endnotes

1 Biographical data from Lorenzo Riberi, *Arthur Rosenberg. Democrazia e socialismo tra storia e politica* (Milan, 2001), and Mario Keßler, *Arthur Rosenberg. Ein Historiker im Zeitalter der Katastrophen (1889–1943)* (Cologne/ Weimar/ Vienna, 2003), both of which (Keßler especially) have full bibliographies of Rosenberg's writings. Eduard Meyer was Germany's leading ancient historian at the time but also a staunch nationalist (a supporter of the Deutsche Vaterlandspartei) and a resolute opponent of Weimar, e.g., Keßler, *Arthur Rosenberg*, pp. 48–9.

2 Arthur Rosenberg, 'Der Faschismus als Massenbewegung. Sein Aufstieg und seine Zersetzung', in Wolfgang Abendroth, ed., *Faschismus und Kapitalismus. Theorien über die sozialen Ursprünge und die Funktion des Faschismus* (Frankfurt, 1967) pp. 75–141.

3 Dimitroff told the Seventh Congress of the Comintern: 'Der Faschismus – das ist die Macht des Finanzkapitals selbst'.

4 Notably August Thalheimer, 'Über den Faschismus', in Abendroth, ed., *Faschismus und Kapitalismus* (reprinted from *Gegen den Strom. Organ der KPD (Opposition)*, 1930).

5 The KPD was a solidly working-class party, cf. Michael H. Kater, *The Nazi Party: A Social Profile of Members and Leaders 1919–1945* (Oxford, 1983) p. 37: '[in 1927] more than 80 percent of the KPD members belonged to the working class'.

6 Zetkin cited in Nicos Poulantzas, *Fascism and Dictatorship: The Third International and the Problem of Fascism*, tr. Judith White (London, 1974) p.

84. She refers to 'broad social layers, large masses that reach even into the proletariat', cf. John Riddell, 'Clara Zetkin's Struggle for the United Front', http://johnriddell.wordpress.com/2011/05/03/clara-zetkin%E2%80%99s-struggle-for-the-united-front/

7 Enzo Traverso, *Understanding the Nazi Genocide: Marxism after Auschwitz*, tr. Peter Drucker (London, 1999).

8 John Weiss, *Conservatism in Europe 1770–1945: Traditionalism, Reaction and Counter-Revolution* (London, 1977) p. 119, with Chapter 6 on Heinrich von Treitschke, and Chapter 8 on Maurras.

9 Franz Neumann, *Behemoth: The Structure and Practice of National Socialism* (London, 1942) pp. 27ff., and his striking observation that '[i]n the centre of the counter-revolution stood the judiciary'.

10 Leon Trotsky, *The Struggle Against Fascism in Germany* (New York, 1971) pp. 405, 406, 155.

11 Wilhelm Reich, *The Mass Psychology of Fascism* (London, 1972) pp. 40ff., and the statement 'fascism, viewed with respect to its mass basis, was actually a middle-class movement' (p. 42).

12 Luigi Salvatorelli, *Nazionalfascismo* (Turin, 1923).

13 Ian Kershaw, *Hitler 1889–1936: Hubris*, (Penguin Books, 2001) p. 334.

14 Neumann, *Behemoth*, p. 37: the NSDAP was '*composed of the most diverse social strata* but never hesitat[ed] to take in the dregs of every section, supported by the army, the judiciary, and parts of the civil service, financed by industry, utilizing the anti-capitalist sentiments of the masses and yet careful never to estrange the influential moneyed groups'.

15 Kershaw, *Hitler 1889–1936*, p. 303.

16 Detlef Mühlberger, *Hitler's Followers: Studies in the Sociology of the Nazi Movement* (London and New York, 1991) p. 203.

17 Mühlberger, *Hitler's Followers*, pp. 37, 77, 115, 139.

18 Kater, *Nazi Party*, p. 36.

19 Mühlberger, *Hitler's Followers*, p. 180. 'Workers' formed 58 per cent of all SA recruits prior to 1933 (p. 177).

20 Jeremy Noakes, *The Nazi Party in Lower Saxony, 1921–1933*, (London, 1971) pp. 79, 19.

21 Noakes, *Nazi Party in Lower Saxony*, pp. 9–11; Peter H. Merkl, *Political Violence under the Swastika: 581 Early Nazis* (Princeton and London, 1975)

p. 56. Uwe Lohalm, *Völkischer Radikalismus. Die Geschichte des Deutschvölkischen Schutz- und Trutz-Bundes 1919–1923* (Hamburg, 1970) calls the Bund a 'Wegbereiter des Nationalsozialismus'.

22 Herman Lebovics, *Social Conservatism and the Middle Classes in Germany 1914–1933* (Princeton, 1969) p. 37.

23 Merkl, *Political Violence under the Swastika*, based on the Abel biographies.

24 Alfred Sohn-Rethel, *Ökonomie und Klassenstruktur des deutschen Faschismus. Aufzeichnungen und Analysen*, second edition (Frankfurt, 1975) pp. 195–6; Sohn-Rethel, *Economy and Class Structure of German Fascism*, tr. Martin Sohn-Rethel (London, 1978) pp. 135–7, translation modified.

25 Christopher R. Browning, *Ordinary Men: Reserve Police Battalion 101 and the Final Solution in Poland* (Penguin Books, 2001) p. 200.

26 Christopher R. Browning, *The Path to Genocide: Essays on Launching the Final Solution* (Cambridge, 1992) p. 64.

27 Hedley Bull, ed., *The Challenge of the Third Reich: The Adam von Trott Memorial Lectures* (Oxford, 1986) p. 5. Of course, as Tim Mason never failed to point out, '[t]he Nazi regime set out to obliterate the German Left', arresting anywhere between a hundred to two hundred-thousand socialists and murdering 'tens of thousands' of them, Mason, 'The Third Reich and the German Left', in Bull, ed., *The Challenge of the Third Reich*, pp. 96–7.

28 Ian Kershaw, 'German Popular Opinion and the "Jewish Question", 1939–1943: Some Further Reflections', in *The Jews in Nazi Germany 1933–1943*, edited by Arnold Paucker, Sylvia Gilchrist and Barbara Suchy (Tübingen, 1986) pp. 378ff.

29 Kershaw, 'German Popular Opinion and the "Jewish Question"' (n. 28).

30 Anton Kaes, *From Hitler to Heimat: The Return of History as Film* (Cambridge, MA., 1992) p. 76.

31 Rainer Werner Fassbinder, *The Anarchy of the Imagination: Interviews, Essays, Notes*, edited by Michael Töteberg and Leo A. Lensing, tr. Krishna Winston (Baltimore, 1992) pp. 115ff.

32 Mühlberger, *Hitler's Followers*, p. 90: 'It was almost exclusively a male movement...'

33 Adelheid von Saldern, 'Victims or Perpetrators? Controversies about the Role of Women in the Nazi State', in *Fascist Italy and Nazi Germany: Comparisons and Contrasts*, edited by Richard Bessel (Cambridge, 1996) pp. 219, 217.

34 Stephenson, *Women in Nazi Germany* (1981), cited in Saldern, 'Victims or Perpetrators?', p. 218.

35 David Bankier, *The Germans and the Final Solution: Public Opinion under Nazism* (Oxford, 1992).

36 See, for example, the excellent paper by Tobias Abse, 'Italian Workers and Italian Fascism', in Bessel, ed., *Fascist Italy and Nazi Germany*, which argues that 'a tradition of class-conscious militancy established in Italy in particular pre-Fascist circumstances was not broken under Fascism' (p. 53), and that Italian Fascism 'never really gained any widespread consensus of support amongst the industrial working class of northern and central Italy' (p. 42).

37 Claudia Koonz, *The Nazi Conscience* (Cambridge, MA., 2003) p. 221.

38 Otto Dov Kulka and Aron Rodrigue, 'The German Population and the Jews in the Third Reich', *Yad Vashem Studies*, 16 (1984) pp. 421–35.

39 Kershaw, 'German Popular Opinion and the "Jewish Question"', discussing his own earlier assessments in *Popular Opinion and Political Dissent in the Third Reich: Bavaria 1933–1945* (Oxford, 1983).

40 Paul Hainsworth, *The Extreme Right in Western Europe* (Abingdon, 2008).

George Grosz, *Pillars of society* (1926)

Arthur Rosenberg, 1889-1943

Fascism as a mass-movement

Arthur Rosenberg (1934)

Abstract

Arthur Rosenberg's remarkable essay, first published in 1934, was probably the most incisive historical analysis of the origins of fascism to emerge from the revolutionary Left in the interwar years. In contrast to the official Comintern line that fascism embodied the power of finance-capital, Rosenberg saw fascism as a descendant of the reactionary mass-movements of the late-nineteenth century. Those movements encompassed a new breed of nationalism that was ultra-patriotic, racist and violently opposed to the Left, and prefigured fascism in all these ways. What was distinctive about the fascists in Italy and Germany was not so much their ideology (a pastiche of motifs that drew on those earlier traditions of the conservative and radical Right) as the use of stormtroopers to wage the struggle against democracy in more decisive and lethal ways. After the broad historical sweep of its first part, the essay looks at the factors that were peculiar to the Italian and German situations respectively, highlighting both the rôle of the existing authorities in encouraging the fascists and the wider class-appeal of the fascist parties themselves, beyond any supposed restriction to the middle-class or 'petty bourgeoisie'.

1. Forerunners and pogroms

The touching story of Hitler and his first six disciples, the story of how jointly they founded the party and how after that these seven men became first a million, and then 6 million, and then 30 million, 40 million, the whole German people, belongs to the permanent inventory of National Socialist speeches. Behind Mussolini there is a similar story. But just as the *Duce*'s grand and imposing qualities surpassed those of his jaded imitation, the Führer, so did the founding of his party outstrip that of Hitler's in sheer stateliness. There were no fewer than 145 participants at the First Congress of the Italian Fascists that assembled on the premises of the commercial school in Milan on 23 March 1919. Yet here too the ascent was utterly dizzying: from those 145 individuals to as many thousands, then to millions and finally, if you believe the official spokespersons and statisticians, the entire Italian nation.

This expansion from tiny handfuls to a mass-movement of millions overrunning entire nations is indeed puzzling. Not only the supporters of fascism but even many of its opponents felt that they were confronting a riddle. Many of those who would write about fascism had heard something, at one time or another, about sociology or about the 'class-theory' of Marxism. Thus began the search for that class, or, more vaguely, for that layer of people, that made this miracle possible. Unfortunately, the theory of social classes is not quite as simple as it appears at first glance. Anyone seated in front of a piano can start thumping the keys, but that does not make him a musician. Likewise, juggling around with social classes does not amount to a social analysis, and least of all to a Marxist one. Sociological dilettantes generally came to the conclusion that the mysterious class that helped Hitler and Mussolini to power was the petty bourgeoisie. The greengrocer Fritz Schulz became a truly demonic power. With one hand he kept the working class in check and, with the other, capitalism. Schulz is the very epitome of Germany and master of the new century. Now as a person Schulz may well be a true hero, he may well have won all possible distinctions of war through his rôle in the trenches, and could well be the champ in his borough. But here we are not dealing with Schulz as a person, but with Schulz the greengrocer, the petty bourgeois. It is really remarkable that the petty bourgeoisie as a class should have overrun Germany, Italy, Poland, Austria and half a dozen other countries, and that the rest of the world was likewise threatened by the prospect of going 'petty bourgeois'.

There was a period in the history of Europe when the petty bourgeoisie as a class, that is, master-craftsmen and small traders organised in their respective guilds, actually did play a major rôle in economic life and production. This was the case during the later middle ages. At that time there existed neither a proletariat nor capitalism in the modern sense. This was the golden age of the guild-master. But not once in those days, when the guild-masters had all the trumps in their hand, economically and ideologically, could they succeed in governing any of the large European nations. In Germany, it is true, the guilds did wield power in a number of cities, but on the national scale they lived in wretched submission to the nobles of the countryside. And wherever the cities themselves emerged as real political and military powers, as in the Hansa, there the leadership lay not in the hands of master-craftsmen but in those of the big merchants. Starting in the sixteenth century, every new generation of Europe saw a further reduction in the social weight of the petty bourgeoisie. Thus five-hundred years ago when craft-production encountered fertile soil and unmechanised manual labour formed the chief source of all values, the petty bourgeoisie was, even then, too weak to capture political power. And today, in the age of assembly-line production, aircraft and electricity, how has this petty bourgeois suddenly become insuperable simply because he puts on a brown shirt or a black one, and Hitler and Mussolini scream out at him? You may as well say that a properly-lit wax-candle gives more light than the most powerful electric lamp.

But several contemporary writers see the causes of fascism not in the petty bourgeoisie so much as in the youth, or even in both at once. The theory of the youth as the basis of fascism is even more remarkable than the one about the petty bourgeoisie. The distinction between young persons and the older generation has existed for as long as humanity itself, and will continue to do so as long as beings of our constitution inhabit the planet. Yet youth as such has never formed itself into a political movement; for, all the specific forms in which mankind as such is divided within itself are likewise forms that divide the youth. Is it conceivable that there will come a time when the sons of bank-directors will decide to unite with the sons of engineering workers to jointly smash all the privileges enjoyed by the bank-directors and all the organisations of engineering workers, and, on their ruins, establish the brilliant fascist 'League of Youth'?

The debate about theories of fascism is not simply a pastime for people who sit at desks and speculate about sociology. In reality, it is a bitter and serious affair of extraordinary practical and political importance for the working class. If you want to smash your enemy, you must first have a precise knowledge of him. The fantastic and utterly illogical explanations that circulate regarding fascism have created the strange conviction among democrats and socialists that there is something quite irrational about their main enemy – something that defies argument. The emergence of fascism is then comparable to a natural phenomenon, for example, to an earthquake, a sort of elemental power that bursts from the hearts of humans and tolerates no resistance. And often enough the fascists themselves promote such conceptions, especially in Germany, where they proclaim that the reign of reason and of mechanical logic has now finished, that today the emotions and primal instincts of the nation are again supreme. Sometimes socialists and democrats feel they have finished with political opponents of the usual sort, but they despair of ever stemming the onslaught of this 'new religion'. Desperately, people search for the means by which the fascist offensive can be fought back. People break their heads thinking up ways of winning over or at least neutralising this petty bourgeois, who has suddenly become the arbiter of the fate of whole nations. Others want to adapt the level of their own party or movement to that of the youth. In spite of all that, sometimes these people doubt whether it is at all possible to withstand the new political cataclysm. The fascists cunningly exploit this mood of panic, as they did particularly when it appeared among the democratic and socialist supporters following the German elections of 1933. Such demoralisation is designed to make it possible for any more-or-less bankrupt reactionary politician to overthrow the most deeply-rooted conceptions of freedom and the most solid workers' organisations simply by donning a coloured shirt, training a band of immature youth, and dishing out public speeches on the 'rights of youth' and on 'national redemption'.

Today it is more necessary than ever for workers *not* to let themselves become confused and demoralised. When the fog that fascism creates in all countries clears away, behind it one sees an all-too-familiar figure. This character is, of course, neither marvellous nor mysterious, he brings no new religion and certainly no golden age. He comes neither from the ranks of the youth nor from the mass of the petty bourgeoisie, even if he is an expert at deceiving both these groups. He is the counter-revolutionary capitalist, the born enemy of all class-conscious workers. Fascism is nothing but a modern form of the bourgeois-capitalist counter-revolution wearing a popular mask. Strictly speaking, it is not entirely correct to apply the same term 'fascism' to movements as disparate in character as Mussolini's party in Italy and Hitler's party in Germany. To see this one has only to recall that the very cornerstone of Nazi ideology, the Jewish and racial question, are very largely ignored by Italian fascism. However, the usual political terminology of today calls all capitalist counter-revolutionary movements 'fascist', once they acquire a mass-character and simultaneously rely on an active party-force specifically trained for civil war.

Ever since the modern form of production emerged, capitalism has dominated all civilised countries. However, it is not difficult to see that the capitalist class was never in a position to force its will on the mass of the people directly through any violence of its own. It is a comical idea to imagine factory-owners and bankers taking to arms and subjugating the rest of the population with rifles and sabres! The old feudal aristocracy could still govern by relying on its own physical power. In the middle ages, knights in heavy armour were actually superior to the other classes of the population in terms of military strength. So too in a country where power lies in the hands of the mass of workers or peasants, the exercise of physical force will lie directly in the hands of the ruling class.

By contrast, the capitalists are compelled to rule indirectly. Just as they do not hammer and forge their own commodities, and do not stand behind the counter and sell those commodities to their customers, so they cannot themselves constitute their own army, police and electorate. They need assistants and servants to produce, to sell and to govern. In every country the capitalists rule only so long as decisive sectors of the population feel at one with their system, are ready to work for them, to vote for them, to shoot others on their behalf, all in the conviction that their own interests demand the preservation of the capitalist economic order.

The assistants and servants who, consciously or otherwise, work on behalf of capitalism in Europe today are as numerous as they are variegated. In the first place, in almost all countries where the capitalist system prevails, it has, in one form or another, put up with representatives of the traditional, pre-capitalistic, feudal order. Monarchy and nobility, church and army, and the upper bureaucracy have all evolved from the feudal period into modern capitalist times. At first, of course, the bourgeoisie had to establish its claim to power against the aristocracy in a revolutionary way. It came forward as the representative of the entire nation in the latter's struggle against a privileged feudal minority. It united all of the middle and lower strata around its banner and in this way forced the feudal lords to capitulate. But as soon as victory was won in this struggle, the capitalists quickly sought a compromise with the feudal elements, so as to present a joint front with them against the democratic and even socialist aspirations of the mass of the poor. From the feudal tradition there sprang the ideologies of authority, discipline, and of military virtues and forms of life, which are so crucial to the understanding of fascism.

Likewise, the estate of the intellectuals emerged out of the old feudal order into the modern bourgeois period. It resigned itself to the new form of society exactly as it had earlier to the aristocracy. But because the intellectual does not stand directly within the process of production, does not himself create surplus-value, but only lives off surplus-value, and that, too, indirectly, he retains a special position (*Sonderstellung*) even under capitalism. In general he is quite convinced that he represents not the commercial interests of the capitalists, but the general interests of the nation. However, because 'unfortunately' private property is essential to the prosperity of 'the nation', the average European intellectual finds himself compelled to support capitalism and reject socialism – reluctantly, of course. Because the intellectual estate is professionally involved in representing 'general' interests and 'general' conceptions, it is especially well positioned to extract the sweet pap of national self-sacrifice from the bitter reality of the class-struggle.

Finally, below the capitalists in the social pyramid come the peasants and craftsmen. Their social weight varies from country to country depending on the special conditions of development. Even lower in the scale, at the bottom, comes the enormous army of wage-earners. They are all more-or-less vulnerable to the enticements of capital. This is true not simply of the peasants and craftsmen. In Germany, even before Hitler's rise to power, a significant proportion of wage-employees (*Arbeitnehmer*) voted for the bourgeois parties, and in England even today a substantial section of the working class supports the Conservatives. It follows that the political dynamics of the capitalist countries of the nineteenth and twentieth centuries has always been a hugely complicated affair. The peculiar equilibrium of capitalist society has always depended on a multiplicity of distinct and seemingly opposed forces.

The great bourgeois mass-movements of more recent European history belong to two specific types – the liberal and the anti-liberal. *Fascism is the most recent example of this second category of anti-liberal bourgeois mass-movements*. The bourgeois liberalism of the nineteenth century was founded on free competition. It demanded freedom and peace. In domestic politics, 'freedom' meant the removal of state-compulsion, above all, a wide-ranging economic autonomy that delegated to the state the notorious rôle of night-watchman. Free trade and peace were the complements of this system in foreign policy. They promised humanity a golden age where, for the first time, the free play of economic forces could unfold without hindrance, throughout the face of the globe. This liberal gospel of 'Freedom, Free Trade and Peace' inspired the popular masses, the middle-classes and often even the workers. In England, Liberalism was dominant in the years following the electoral reform of 1832 – at first without challenge, or almost so, up to 1866, then down to the World-War, both alternating and competing with a restructured Conservative Party. In Germany it attracted the mass of people from 1848 to about 1878 – thereafter, down to the War, it commanded the support of a minority. Clearly, in Germany liberalism could never flourish quite as smoothly as it did in England. Its brief dominance was never founded on its own strength; on the contrary, it had to be satisfied with the crumbs of political power thrown to it by the feudal monarchy. In France, the liberal era lasted from 1830 to 1848, under the bourgeois monarch Louis Philippe. Then came the period of the dictatorship of Napoleon III, which lasted until 1870 and was followed once again by the liberal Republic, which clearly found it hard to keep itself going against the onslaughts of the anti-liberal movements of the decades preceding the War. From its inception, the Italian monarchy bore the appearance of a liberal state, although behind this façade all manner of other, far-from-liberal forces lay concealed. In Russia, in the period before the War, the bourgeoisie likewise professed liberalism. Obviously, under Tsarism its political power was even more tenuous than the influence enjoyed by its counterparts in Germany.

In all the major European countries mentioned above, liberalism encountered other tendencies that naturally shared with it its firm support for the capitalist form of economy, but wanted to have nothing at all to do with liberal principles. These tendencies rejected the purely 'night-watchman' rôle of the state and demanded in its place strong intervention from the public authority in economic life. To liberal free trade they contraposed protectionism, to liberal pacifism, an aggressive imperialism. They cared little for international harmony, and put the 'nation' above everything else. They rejected democratic notions of equality and instead put the main emphasis on traditional forms of hierarchy. They aspired to being purely indigenous (*bodenständig*) and sought to restore respect for authority.

The economic background to this change from liberalism to a new, authoritarian, conservatism is, as was understood quite some time back, an internal transformation in the capitalist process of production. Capitalism evolved from the period of free competition to the new era of massively concentrated giant enterprises with their drive to monopoly. This new monopolistic capitalism insulates its national economic sphere by protective tariffs. It uses violence and territorial expansion to try and win new countries for further exploitation. It finds the sedate, pacifistic ideology of the liberal era quite useless for its purposes. It demands *authority, centralism and violence*.

It is precisely the biggest and most powerful capitalists, the owners of giant monopolistic enterprises and of the financial institutions linked to them who were the first to abandon the hackneyed soil of liberalism and turn to the new imperialist methods. The vast majority of middling and small capitalists remained faithful to the liberal tradition for much longer. To capture state-power, the capitalists opposed to liberalism are compelled to enlist allies in other sectors of the population. The most astute leaders of the new imperialism manage to outdo even the liberals and the bourgeois democrats in their demagogy. Sometimes, under the slogan of national defence of the poor, they even fight the 'narrow-minded monied interests' of liberalism. There is scarcely any doubt that *modern fascism belongs with this type, and that it has developed the nationalist propaganda characteristic of this kind of politics to perfection*.

In England it was the Conservative Party, renovated by Benjamin Disraeli on imperialist foundations, that gave the franchise to urban workers in 1867, to draw them away from liberalism. The result was that in 1874 the Conservatives for the first time won a majority in the House of Commons, thanks to the electoral support they received from workers. In England under Disraeli, and later, under Chamberlain, the Tories were supported by the bulk of the aristocracy, the big City financiers, the owners of heavy industry, the great mass of the intelligentsia, and major sections of the industrial working class. All these elements were brought together behind the slogan of 'national greatness'. On the other hand, broad strata of the middle and small capitalists, the petty bourgeoisie and even the countryside remained faithful to liberal ideals. In France the right-wing was financed, after 1871, by the big banks and by heavy industry. The French 'national Right' proclaimed revanchism – the idea of a victorious war of revenge against Germany for the restoration of France's 'national honour' lost at the battle of Sedan. A general attempt was made to revive the militaristic and monarchist traditions of the past. Nobility and church enlisted in the service of this patriotic movement. The liberal Republic was denounced as 'cowardly' and 'unpatriotic', and there was a longing for the dictatorship of a national redeemer. In the 1880s this rôle devolved on General Boulanger, who, as the voting-patterns would show, did temporarily enjoy the support of the majority of the French people. Around the turn of the century the French Republic was again seriously confronted by the threat of a military *coup d'état* which had some popular backing. The French Right based itself on the upper classes of French society, on sections of the petty bourgeoisie and on groups of workers who had been duped by them, whereas the socialist workers and large masses of the petty bourgeoisie fought passionately for republicanism and democracy.

In Germany, after 1878, the old-style liberals lost their majority in the Reichstag. Heavy industry turned to protectionism and evolved a programme of colonial, military and naval expansion in league with the aristocracy. The intelligentsia drew its inspiration from military discipline and the Prussian spirit. Democracy was a despicable 'un-Germanic' intrusion. The bourgeois *Lebensideal* was modelled on the figure of the reserve-officer. After 1878, in the Protestant areas of Germany, the rural masses were followers of the Conservative Party (DKP). Likewise, significant sections of the petty bourgeoisie swung to the Right. Heavy industry and its intellectual lackeys transformed the old National Liberals so radically that, of 'liberalism', only the name survived. The liberal banner was bequeathed to the tired hands of the pure liberals. In the Reichstag elections of 1887, under Bismarck's leadership, the Conservatives and the National Liberals bound up with heavy industry together won the majority. Of course, Social Democracy expanded rapidly under Wilhelm II, but the old-style liberalism was so emasculated by now that in the Reichstag the Conservatives, together with the National Liberals and the Catholic Centre Party, controlled a secure majority. And so, in Germany too, as in England and in France, the last third of the nineteenth century and the early-twentieth century saw the retreat of a traditional liberalism and its displacement by newer, nationalist/imperialist forces. In Germany, too, the imperialists formed an alliance with the army, the church and the intelligentsia. However, prior to 1914, Germany did not see any grand or unified nationalist mass-movement; the different wings of German nationalism remained divided. The reason for this is not hard to understand. The Kaiser's régime was so strong that it could survive *without* the support of popular votes and parliamentary majorities. It sufficed if national imperialism (*der nationale Imperialismus*) in Germany could control the Imperial régime – on that basis it could get whatever it wanted, and it could afford to dispense with the bother of demagogic campaigns to win votes and so on. The ruling classes of Imperial Germany did not need the expedient (*die Mittel*) of democracy to the same degree as the upper classes of France and England clearly did in those years. Court-chaplain Stöcker's attempt to assemble a populist, anti-liberal and anti-socialist mass-movement in the towns and cities was discouraged by the Imperial government itself. For any movement of this kind would have forced the ruling circles in Germany to make definite concessions to the 'greedy masses', and they had no inclination to this sort of policy. The Kaiser and big capital felt safer with the protection afforded by the Potsdam Guard than with the good graces of Stöcker's mass-congregations.

This interplay of liberal and anti-liberal bourgeois forces that largely shaped the development of England, France and Germany from 1871 to 1914 appears to be missing in the corresponding period of Italian history. But this is merely a semblance. The various tendencies described earlier were present here as well. Here, too, liberalism of the old style was gradually pushed back by the imperialism of big capital (*großkapitalistischen Imperialismus*), which, in the decade preceding the War, led directly to the Tripolitan War of 1911–12 and to active involvement in the Balkans. A drummed-up nationalism directed its sharpest attacks against Austria, demanded the emancipation of its 'unredeemed' Italian brothers in Trento (Trentino) and Trieste, and used every conceivable means to catch up with the more prosperous superpowers in Northern Europe. However, the official party-politics of Italy was completely immersed in the swamp of semi-feudal corruption, with its breeding-ground in the backward districts of the central and southern parts of the peninsula. The truly active social forces of the country found in its parliamentary system either no expression at all or only the most imperfect one. In Russia too, in the period just before the World-War, the big bourgeoisie deserted to imperialism and geared itself for the conquest of Constantinople and other rapacious projects formulated by the Tsar's ministers. These were also years when the Tsar's police-agents attempted to create a mass-movement loyal to the Tsar as a counterweight to the Revolution. They bought up the dregs of the *lumpen* proletariat with liquor and money, and created 'true Russian' trade-unions led by the police, as alternatives to the banned socialist unions. Yet, Russia did witness a significant mass-movement, the Union of 'True Russian Peoples' or 'Black Hundreds', which showered itself in glory with the pogroms it conducted.

In both parts of the Austro-Hungarian Empire, it was liberalism that initially dominated the Constitution of 1867. The so-called 'liberals' of Hungary clearly belonged to a category apart. They came from the landed aristocracy and monied bourgeoisie, and they suppressed the broad mass of people with unsurpassed violence. Thus Hungarian liberalism did not, strictly speaking, need to accomplish a transition to specifically imperialist methods. Hungary's brutal political régime came wrapped in the cloak of a wildly over-excited Magyar nationalism.

At first, in the decade following 1867, Austria was dominated by a liberalism of the usual kind, comparable to contemporary German liberalism. But towards the end of the 1870s, this regnant liberalism collapsed in Austria as well. Indeed, down to the very end, Hapsburg feudalism got along excellently with the capitalists in heavy industry and finance. The firms that supplied the Danube monarchy with weapons and financial loans were unconditionally loyal to the Emperor, and sufficiently powerful as long as they used the necessary backstairs in Vienna. The influence of the middling liberal bourgeoisie of German extraction was systematically pushed back in Austria. Supported by a small and monarchist middle-class and by the Catholic Church, Lueger founded the mass-party of Christian Socialism. He was a first-rate agitator and mass-organiser. He captured a majority in Vienna, allowed himself to be elected mayor of the Imperial capital and would eventually become leader of the strongest faction in the Austrian parliament, one on which the Imperial régime was permanently dependent. Lueger was a leader of the 'common man' (*der kleinen Leute*). Finance-capital had no direct connections with his party. But in the later part of his life Lueger became a key supporter of the Hapsburg monarchy, whose existence was in turn decisive to the fortunes of big business. It was a game with a clear allocation of rôles – Lueger and his populist party, the Kaiser and his aristocratic ministers, and the big Vienna bankers all basically shared the same goals.

The German intellectuals who lived in Austria, especially the younger ones, were deeply dissatisfied with their social position in the generation before the War. Longingly, they looked across the borders into Imperial Germany where, under Hohenzollern dominance, young students had come to have a stake in Germany's drive to become a world-power. In Austria, however, the régime generally favoured Slavs to the detriment of ethnic Germans. Moreover, the Christian intelligentsia felt threatened by the lively competition of the considerable number of Jewish intellectuals. Austria's German youth would only too willingly have placed themselves in the service of a big-power 'national' imperialism, but the régime had no use for them. The Austrian régime was anything but German-nationalist (*deutschnational*) and Austrian high finance even less so. Thus young people of German extraction who lived in Austria began to develop feelings of neglect and exclusion; at least some sections of them. Their German nationalism and their hatred of anything non-German was all the more virulent. The remarkable phenomenon of a whole layer of young German academics who, in the years leading up to 1914, felt part of a subjugated and oppressed nationality was, of course, inconceivable in Wilhelmine Germany, with its student-clubs and reserve-officers. But this 'type' existed in Austria in the Pan-German and German-nationalist student-circles. Their ethnic romanticism and their sour racial resentments rubbed off on to sections of middle- and working-class youth. It was from this background that Adolf Hitler came over to Germany, and in the new conditions that prevailed there after 1918 he certainly needed no lessons in nationalism.

A demagogic nationalism spontaneously seeks an object through which it can daily demonstrate its own superiority and onto which it can release the delirium of its racial frenzy. Poor white people in the southern states of America hated the blacks. But at the same time they needed them, because without their persecution of black people they could not develop their own instincts. The same was true of the Turks in the period of Abdul

Hamid's maltreatment of the Armenian population. The German youth of Bohemia stood in a position of equal strength vis-à-vis the Czechs, and the young Czech nationalists repaid the German nationalists in the same coin. However, a specially useful and convenient object for such racism were the Jews. In the anti-liberal and nationalist mass-movements of prewar Europe described above, the Jewish Question played an extraordinarily important rôle. The Russian *lumpen* proletariat could be as easily incited against the Jews as some of the intellectuals and middle-class elements in Central Europe.

The Union of True Russian Peoples basically survived on Jew-baiting. Lueger built his Christian Social Party in the first instance by using antisemitic propaganda. When Reverend Stöcker wanted to arouse a monarchist and Christian mass-movement in Berlin, it was the Jews he attacked. French nationalism around the turn of the century was likewise sharply antisemitic. Here a contributory factor was the quite accidental circumstance that the struggle between diffferent parties was passionately fought over the question of the guilt or otherwise of the Jewish captain, Dreyfus. One can therefore conclude that already before the War, in at least four of the six major countries of Europe, nationalist mass-movements opposed to liberalism were bound up with hostility to the Jews. Moreover, in Austria the German nationalists and Christian Socialists vied with each other in their hatred for the Jews. By contrast, in prewar Hungary no strong antisemitic mass-movement ever developed: the wealthy Budapest Jews were friends of the ruling oligarchy. In Italy, where the number of Jews has never been significant, it was precisely Jewish families who were among the most active supporters of modern imperialism. Here, as in England, there was no purely political antisemitism.

Concerning the form of state, the reactionary mass-movements of Russia, Austria, Hungary and Germany were unconditionally for the defence of the existing authoritarian monarchies and of all the values bound up with them. In France the Right was opposed to democracy, and at best put up with the Republic as an unavoidable evil. The most extreme groups of French nationalism longed for a *coup d'état*, and therefore either for a military dictatorship or for a restoration of the monarchy itself. In Italy the constitutional question was never actually posed prior to 1914. In England the vast mass of workers and of the middle-class were unconditional supporters of the parliamentary order. Here any political group that toyed with the idea of a dictatorship would have met with immediate political extinction. The Conservative Party was thus compelled to work within the parliamentary framework. Men such as Disraeli and Chamberlain were actually proud of winning parliamentary majorities.

As you can see, *the ideology which is today called 'fascist' was already fairly widespread throughout Europe before the War*, and exerted a strong influence on the masses. However, with one exception, what was missing then was the peculiar tactic of using stormtroopers which is thoroughly characteristic of modern fascism. The sole exception was formed by the Black Hundreds of Tsarist Russia and their ability to stage pogroms. The stormtrooper-tactic peculiar to fascism is really quite a curious social phenomenon. It appears to contradict all political logic. Of course, the use of violence by ruling classes against the classes they rule over is as old as the history of human civilisation itself. In particular, the capitalist classes of Europe never hesitated to use the utmost harshness and mass-bloodshed whenever their position of power was threatened by socialism or even just by popular movements for democracy. In 1848 and again in 1871, the French capitalist class suppressed the Parisian workers with a series of bloody massacres. From 1878 to 1890 Bismarck kept the German workers' movement shackled by his anti-socialist laws. Now, it goes without saying that the ruling class uses its state-apparatus for the exercise of force, for the state-apparatus is there precisely for that purpose – the authorities, police and judicial administration are there to combat subversion, and when those do not suffice, the army is brought in. In special emergencies the ruling class can reinforce its state-power by calling in volunteer-forces or mercenaries, but even in those cases it is the official state-power itself that struggles directly against the revolution with its own weaponry and laws. When the oppressed masses are weak, they put up either no resistance at all or weak resistance to the ruling class and state-violence. When they feel stronger, then they too take up arms and a civil war results. Popular uprisings disrupt the normal functioning of the state-apparatus – both sides take to arms and struggle to the very end. The picture is familiar from the English Revolution of the seventeenth century, the French Revolution of the eighteenth century, and the Russian Revolution in our own century.

Stormtroopers of the fascist kind appear to match none of the normal permutations of the political struggle. Their very existence signifies that normal conditions no longer prevail. On the other hand, they do not form part of a state of open civil war either. Rather, political opponents of the government have become disagreeable to the authorities but are not strong enough to pose the question of power in a frontal assault. The government and the ruling groups do not deploy the standard or regular state-authorities against the opposition, but volunteer-corps are recruited from the mass of the population to handle this job. They attack, ill-treat or murder all persons who have become unpopular, destroy or plunder their property, and unleash a wave of persecution and terror calculated to drown all opposition. The activities of stormtroopers of the fascist type are in complete violation of the laws. Legally, the stormtroopers *should* be tried and sentenced to jail. But in fact nothing of the sort happens to them. Their conviction in the courts is pure show – either they do not serve their sentence, or they are soon pardoned. In this way the ruling class shows its stormtrooper heroes how grateful and sympathetic it is.

Now, under what conditions is the political activity of stormtroopers possible? In the more recent history of Europe the pogroms conducted by the 'Black Hundreds' in Russia in October 1905 form the first clear and significant example of this phenomenon, which is today so familiar to us. The first condition of their appearance is a complete disintegration of the normal state-power. As a rule, the ruling class does all it can to strengthen the official authority of the state. In its view the state forms an embodiment of the general, public interest. The judiciary is an expression of 'impartial' justice. Respect for the state and its authorities, belief in the power of law, is one of the strongest weapons in the hands of the ruling class. It is only when a country is totally shaken by a crisis of revolutionary proportions, and when the ruling groups can no longer hope to survive with the help of the law and police-administration alone, that they begin to look around for other means.

The government and authorities themselves avoid any direct attack on the revolutionaries, democrats, socialists and Jews. But one day the 'anger of the people' explodes, the upright citizen who still believes in God, King and Country emerges, smashes the wicked rebels and restores the power of legitimate authority. Yet if the anger of the people had been real, there would never have been a crisis. Thus *the rage of the patriotic masses has to be manufactured*. In October 1905, faced with a powerful revolutionary upsurge of the masses, the Russian government did not dare to assemble its police and Cossack forces and order them to liquidate the Jews and the socialists. On the other hand, with police-help, a popular movement of a patriotic, anti-liberal, antisemitic nature was created, and these stormtroopers were then let loose on Jews and revolutionaries. In this way a certain division of labour emerged: the Tsarist régime was not directly and officially responsible for the shameful actions of the pogroms' heroes. One could thus retain a certain distance, at least in the image projected abroad and in the press, even as many officials and police-chiefs openly defended the Black Hundreds. On the other side, there were many straightforward conservative supporters of the Tsar who wanted nothing to do with the pogroms. There were officials and even ministers who took a clear stand against the pogroms.

It is by no means necessary that at any given moment the entire ruling class has to accept the stormtroopers and their methods of struggle. As a rule, there will be differences of opinion. The liberal bourgeoisie and certain fastidiously authoritarian conservatives will condemn the stormtroopers and the methods of fascism. But it would be a disastrous mistake for the working class to suppose that such differences mean very much. Despite all tactical differences, the fascist stormtroopers belong with the ruling capitalists and feudal landlords as the flesh of their flesh. It is not true that in such periods there are three distinct forces in the state – ruling capitalists, fascists, and socialists who stand for democracy. Rather, there are always only two forces – the capitalists and the fascists on one side, the democrats and socialists on the other. One damaging drawback of the theory of a 'petty-bourgeois' fascism is that it obscures this simple fact in the eyes of workers. For then the world looks like this: first there are the capitalists in power, next there is the petty-bourgeois fascist opposition, finally, there is the proletarian socialist opposition. With this threefold division, every conceivable trick and manœuvre becomes possible, for example, an alliance of socialists with fascists against the ruling bourgeoisie, or a coalition of socialists with the liberal and upright conservative capitalists against the fascists, or some other soap-bubble of this kind. Illusions of this sort have been disastrous for the working classes of Germany, Italy and other countries.

In 1909 Trotsky wrote about the pogrom-mobilisations of October 1905:

> For this crusade the Russian government had enlisted its troops in every conceivable nook and cranny, from liquor-joints to brothels. Here you saw the petty shopkeeper and the tramp, the publican and his regulars, the house-servant and the police-spy, professional crooks and casual thieves, small craftsmen and brothel-attendants, and the starving and intellectually desolate small peasant who had perhaps abandoned his home-village only yesterday and whose head had been thoroughly confused by the din of factory-machines.

Initially, at the start of the Russo-Japanese War, the police had undertaken trial mobilisations of obscure masses, and these staged street-demonstrations in favour of the government's war-policy. Trotsky continues:

> From this time onwards the consciously planned and organised mobilisation of the scum of society witnessed an extraordinary development, and even if the greater mass of participants in the pogroms – if one can speak of 'mass' here – remained a more-or-less fluctuating element, the core of this army was formed on a disciplined and organised military basis. This hardcore received its slogans and watchwords from above, and passed them on into the ranks below. It was also this core that decided the timing and the scale of any murderous action that had to be organised.

Here it is sufficient to draw out only those features of the Russian pogroms and the Black Hundreds that are relevant to a history of fascism. The Black Hundreds prepared their actions by first circulating their newspaper in the localities they hit upon. This was soon followed by the 'experts' turning up on the scene, sent there from other cities. Now the crucial rumours would start circulating – the Jews are planning an attack on all law-abiding Christians, the socialists have desecrated a holy image, the students have torn a picture of the Tsar to shreds. Then proscription-lists would be posted up, with the names of individuals and the homes earmarked for plunder and demolition on a priority-basis. On the notified day the Black Hundreds would assemble, initially at the churches for some special service. This would be followed by a procession of fluttering national flags, during the whole of which a military band would play patriotic tunes without interruption. Slowly the first window-panes would be smashed, the first passers-by manhandled. Then some shots would ring out, supposedly fired by the socialists or Jews on 'peace-loving' national demonstrators. A cry for revenge would resound loudly at this point, and a mayhem of unrestrained looting, assault and murder would then erupt.

The police are there, but they remain passive and are in no position to defend the victims of the 'people's' pogrom. But as soon as the Jews or the socialist workers mount an organised resistance, the police move into action immediately, and, if they think it is required, even the army intervenes. Every attempt by workers to defend themselves is crushed, and the pogrom can continue. In the autumn of 1905 the Black Hundreds committed some

4,000 murders in hundreds of Russian towns, to say nothing of all their other crimes. As far as its scale is concerned, this movement of the 'true Russian peoples' can certainly be compared with the more recent actions of the Blackshirts and Brownshirts. At a time of enormous revolutionary tension, when millions of workers were on strike in Russia, when in innumerable villages there were peasant-rebellions, and the soldiers and sailors were starting to mutiny, it was still possible for the ruling class to enlist hundreds of thousands of impoverished elements as stormtroopers of the counter-revolution. Hatred of Jews, a stupid, fanatical nationalism, bribery and alcohol all combined to draw together such masses of the petty bourgeoisie, *lumpen* proletariat and occasionally even the right-wing workers. The possibility of stealing and plundering with total impunity drove hordes of professional criminals into the storm-troops. However, there was an additional factor – the powerful temptation for all impoverished individuals who had come down in the world to join the stormtroopers, for as members of these fascist bands that were tolerated by the authorities they were suddenly wrenched from being non-entities to becoming powerful elements in whose hands lay the fate of their fellow human beings. On this point, too, Trotsky writes with fine psychological insight:

> Now this man without shoes has become king. An hour ago he was a trembling slave hounded by the police and by hunger. Now he feels like an absolute despot, he can do anything he likes, everything will pass, he is master of life and death. If he feels the urge to do so, he throws an old woman from the window of the third floor to the pavements below, he smashes the skull of a baby with a chair, he rapes a small girl in front of a crowd of people. He shrinks from none of the tortures which only a brain driven mad with liquor and frenzy could contrive. For he can do anything he likes, everything will pass. God bless the Tsar!

Once the counter-revolution triumphed in Russia, the pogroms became unnecessary, and the ruling class returned to 'law and order'. But the Russian example shows us that a ruling class or a régime that can only keep itself alive through the terror spread by the storm-troops is finally doomed to extinction. The systematic destruction of all existing notions of justice, order and legality that the pogroms and stormtroopers bring about is something no-one can forget. The next revolutionary wave brings with it a ruthless collapse and retaliation. After that bloody autumn of 1905, Nicholas II was no longer Tsar of all Russians 'by God's grace'. He was only the dirty little chieftain of the Black Hundreds. The heroes of bygone pogroms could not save Tsarism.

In no other European big power outside of Russia had the disintegration of state-power, prior to 1914, advanced to such a degree that the nationalist, anti-liberal movements would actually want to promote stormtrooper-terrorism. It was the impact of the World-War and the general social crisis that dominated its aftermath in Europe that finally secured renewed space for the methods of the pogrom.

2. Italy

Throughout Europe, at first, the World-War signified a triumph of national authority. The parties of the prewar period disappeared in the shadows of a civil truce. The censor took care to establish a complete unity of what the papers carried and of public opinion. Scientists, artists, associations and groups were all, without exception, pressed into the service of the 'national cause'. Above all, a wave of economic centralisation swept through the countries of Europe as the War imposed its own demands on the economy. Capital, organised in trusts, took over control of state-policy and those companies imposed their stranglehold over the production of whole branches of industry. All the belligerent big powers were now transformed into 'total' states (*'totale' Staaten*).

It is easy to see that everywhere the anti-liberal, nationalist tendencies gained the upper hand. In Germany, Austria-Hungary and Russia, at least in the early part of the War, the autocracy stood more solid than ever. In the coalition-régimes that led the war-effort, the Conservatives in England, and the parties of the

Right in France, soon came to occupy the leading position. In Germany, Austria-Hungary and Russia, the key decisions that led to war were made by the ruling monarchs and their counsellors, ministers and General Staff. The masses were not asked how they felt about the War, they simply had to obey and to show the expected national enthusiasm. In these circumstances, in July 1914 the big powers that lived under autocracies were under no compulsion to promote a policy of war by using nationalist mass-hysteria. As for France, she had to put up with a war that Germany had declared on her. In England, finally, the House of Commons debated the question openly and decided in favour of war by a free vote.

The course of development was quite different in Italy. Here the régime itself and the majority of the people were initially in favour of neutrality, and it was only the nationalist mass-movement that actually drove Italy into the War in 1915. The methods by which Italy was hustled into the War are of extraordinary interest. The Italian war-movement of 1915 – whose most popular leader, already, was Mussolini – is the historical link between the anti-liberal mass-movements of the prewar period and the fascism, strictly so-called, of the 1920s. The prospects of those who supported Italian involvement in the War appeared bleak in the autumn of 1914 and even early the following year. Italy's national interest could obviously be served just as well by preserving a stance of neutrality, as long as she could extract a good price for it from the belligerent powers. The socialist workers were for peace, so too were the Catholics and the traditional liberals. The great mass of the middle-class and the rural population simply wanted to be left alone. They had no special yearning for blood-stained laurels. Even the large majority of professional officers were against this war, because their sympathies lay with Germany and they were quite reluctant to become involved on the side of the Entente. In spite of all this, the big capitalists who were bent on imperialist expansion tied up with the younger intellectuals and succeeded in pushing Italy into war. Monarchy, government and the parliamentary system had scarcely any weight in Italy, even when combined. The state-apparatus was weak and no match for a stormy mass-movement, even if the movement started only with a minority of the population.

The events of 1915 and Mussolini's subsequent capture of power both have their roots in the peculiar history of Italy in the nineteenth century. The country was divided, economically and socially, into two parts, which, apart from their common Italian nationality, had little to do with each other. The North was dominated by a modern bourgeois culture, represented chiefly by the cities of Turin, Milan and Genoa. In terms of education and economic activity, the provinces of the North were comparable to the countries of Central Europe. By contrast, in Central and Southern Italy, in the area previously controlled by the church and in the ex-kingdom of Naples, the prevailing relations were still almost medieval in character. Here the mass of the population consisted of petty producers and impoverished peasants who could neither read nor write, and who were deeply sunk in superstition. The unification of Italy found its point of departure in the advanced North. But the great liberal statesman Cavour, who laid the cornerstone of Italian unification, intended originally to embrace only the Northern provinces. He had no inclination to incorporate Central and Southern Italy directly into the unified state. Cavour was perfectly aware that the North was in no position to be able to digest the South.

However, the patriotic youth of Italy, full of bourgeois ideas of freedom and national greatness, cared nothing for Cavour's moderation. Cavour was Prime Minister of the North-Italian state of Piedmont, which has been described as the Prussia of Italy. In fact, the small and weak political apparatus of Piedmont was scarcely comparable with the powerful war-machine of Prussia. There is no battle of Königgrätz or of Sedan in the history of Piedmont. The Piedmontese dynasty had won the royal throne of Italy not through its military strength, but simply through skilful exploitation of the circumstances. When Bismarck founded his German Empire, the German bourgeoisie could rely on the enormous power of the Prussian army and Hohenzollern autocracy. The Italian bourgeoisie could expect no help whatsoever from the Piedmontese dynasty and its officer-corps.

So the nationalist youth of Italy did not rely on the military services of Piedmont. On the contrary, they formed her volunteer-corps (*Freikorps*) which moved into action independently to defeat the King of Naples and the Pope. In Garibaldi this volunteer-corps of Redshirts found its perfect leader. In a celebrated campaign, Garibaldi threw the feudal monarchy of Naples on the rubbish-heap. The Redshirts had triumphed where the official national State of Piedmont had simply vacillated nervously.

In a certain sense one might say that Garibaldi's Redshirts were the forerunners of Mussolini's Blackshirts. Yet one could never describe Garibaldi's following as fascist. For Garibaldi himself was a sincere national democrat, and his supporters never staged any pogroms. They never beat up defenceless people behind police-protection. On the contrary, they enlisted voluntarily in the battle against Italy's foreign enemy. They took up the tasks before which the official, 'national' government of Italy shrank back. Garibaldi's Redshirts were recruited from the best and most self-sacrificing section of the country's bourgeois youth. The Garibaldini were of course inspired enough to succeed in uprooting the feudal régimes of Central and Southern Italy and could thus accomplish the country's unification. But they could not change the real social forces within Italy. 1870 represented the first stage in the national unification of Italy. But this Italy looked completely different from the one Garibaldi and his fighters had dreamed of.

In the decades that followed, the bourgeoisie of the North proved incapable of assimilating the feudal South. The dominant social groups of the South were formed by the big landowners who ruled over an impoverished mass of small tenants, by the priests and by secret societies composed of corrupt political cliques. Milan and Turin were too weak to drain the marshlands of the Mafia and Camorra. Meanwhile, in the last third of the nineteenth century, Italian history would witness not a dramatic struggle between North and South, but a wretched compromise. The so-called 'liberal' politicians of the North reached an understanding with the ruling groups of the South. While the Northern ministers left the South alone, the country south of Rome supplied them with a couple of hundred thoroughly pliant deputies to vote down any possible opposition. In the South the traditional barbarism thus managed to survive. Whenever the half-starved and illiterate peasantry rebelled against the landlords, the gendarmerie of the 'liberal' state intervened and shot them down. In the parliamentary elections the local authorities colluded with the landowners. But in Rome the persons whom the masses elected in this way belonged to the 'liberal' or even to the 'radical' camp.

So Italy's parliamentary democracy was a dismal comedy, a mask for semi-feudal barbarism and repression. The first person to take charge of this new system was the Prime Minister Crispi, himself a southerner. His more intelligent successor, Giolitti, came from the North, it is true, but he dominated the Southern machinery of voting and corruption with exemplary skill. Under these conditions, it is not difficult to see that the country's revenues were in the first instance used to finance purely local interests, that the state was incapable of pursuing a consistent policy aimed at cultural and economic development, and that, compared with the other big powers, Italy remained both poor and backward. In the period before the War the Socialist Party of Italy fought courageously against these conditions and the general state of exploitation, but its base was formed by only a small minority of the population.

It is also not hard to see that this rut of self-styled 'liberalism' that Italy had got itself into scarcely appealed to the modern big capitalists of Turin and Milan. They wanted an overhaul of the country that would enable her, finally, to catch up with the more advanced countries of the West. The young intelligentsia was likewise seething. Still immersed in the traditions of Garibaldi, they longed for a strong, superior and prosperous Italy and fought the politicians of the day. There was a whole host of patriotic youth-organisations, which were designed basically to help the 'unredeemed brothers', viz. Italian nationals who lived in Trento and Trieste under Austrian domination. When these young students became somewhat older and entered paid positions in the state-bureaucracy, their nationalist fervour cooled down. However, the patriotic traditions of the Garibaldini that characterised the youth of Italy's upper classes survived and continued to penetrate newer generations at school and university. Sometimes out of disappointment with the shortcomings of the monarchy, this patriotic youth inclined towards republicanism. In the years leading up to the War the rulers of Italy lived in a constant double fear – on the one hand, they feared the prospect of revolutionary action by the radical workers, syndicalists, anarchists and socialists, on the other, the possibility of a putsch by the radical nationalists. Of course, the ruling groups enjoyed the confidence of the King and could rely on a parliamentary majority. But this hardly mattered, because the obedient electoral mass was composed of a stolid peasantry and petty bourgeoisie that could in any case never rush to the help of the government if any radical activists moved into action in the bigger cities. Moreover, it was doubtful whether one could rely completely on the troops themselves.

These peculiar social conditions made it possible, precisely in Italy, for the imperialistic big bourgeoisie to appear in a certain sense revolutionary. They made it possible for the ruling parties with their half-bourgeois, half-feudal support, to declare war and for 'the people' to be incited against parliament and, if it came to that, against the King. As I said earlier, the growing weight of modern imperialism in Italian politics is clearly discernible in the decade before the World-War. The outbreak of the World-War formed the litmus-test of the strength of imperialism in Italy. That was when the radical Socialist Mussolini abandoned his old party and put himself at the head of the pro-war movement. In her biography of Mussolini, Margherita Sarfatti gives a vivid description of the mass-movement that swept through Italy at the time:

> 'Down with Austria/ And with Germany,/ And with Turkey/ In their Company!'. Bands of youth sang these lines, arm in arm, with slow, rhythmic passion and the resounding beat of marches. A strange instinct had united them in such serious, war-like discipline for the first time. These words formed the *leitmotiv* of the Interventionists [supporters of Italian intervention in the War]. The Interventionists overflowed through all the streets and piazzas of Milan and slowly this flood drained across the whole of Italy, embodiment of the inflexible will of a nation that would no longer tolerate limits to its heroism. The thick-set worker with fluttering scarf, the small, bespectacled government-official who had outgrown his jacket, the lanky athletic student with his collars turned up – now all of them lined up together as one fraternising mass. They were the youth pure and simple, the eternal youth, idealists. It was to these young elements from the factories and high schools, young in years and in spirit, that the editor of *Popolo d'Italia* [Mussolini's new newspaper] hurled forth his summons with unerring instinct. They burned to make history, these young elements whom Mussolini later, in the years of nascent fascism, again gathered around himself with the cry '*A noi!*'

If you discount its official fascist flourish, this description is a nice reflection of the ideology of the Italian war-movement of 1915. Young intellectuals supported the war-programme of the big bourgeoisie, because they longed to 'make history', that is, to establish through struggle both their own greatness and the greatness of the fatherland. Youth from the bourgeoisie and petty bourgeoisie and, to some extent, even from the working class managed to break loose from their own background. In the Italy of 1915 the so-called 'Garibaldi tradition' exerted an especially confusing influence. One really did seem to stand before a struggle for 'fatherland and freedom', as their forefathers had in 1848–9 and 1859–60.

The youthful fervour of the interventionists filled the streets of the major cities of Italy, assisted by the money of Italian capitalists and of the Entente. The din was so deafening that the liberal peace-camp was forced into retreat, despite the support of the Catholic Church and of the Socialists. This is not the place to describe all the diplomatic manoeuvring that preceded Italy's entry into the War. The foreign minister Sonnino, personally an honest man but a resolute imperialist, lobbied for war. Still, as late as the middle of May, old Giolitti's influence seemed to have secured the prospects of peace once more. At that time Mussolini wrote:

> As for me, every day I become more firmly convinced than ever that the salvation of Italy demands that we shoot a dozen or so deputies, shoot them in the back, I say, and throw a couple of ex-ministers into jail. I have become thoroughly convinced that parliament in Italy is a plague-boil that poisons the blood of the country. We have to cut it out. The honour and the future of our fatherland are in danger, the fatherland stands at the most terrible juncture in its history. People, the word lies with you – either war or a Republic.

The danger of peace breaking out soon passed, however, and the Italian imperialists saw their dream of war fulfilled towards the end of May. In Italy this formed the first real triumph of those ideas and that class-combination (*der Klassenkombination*) that would later be called 'fascist'. Both the term 'fascist' and an organisation of Fascists were already in existence in the movement of 1915. Mussolini founded a league of radical supporters of involvement in the War. Their individual local groupings were called *Fasci di azione rivoluzionaria* [combat-groups for revolutionary action]. However, in January 1915 they had only five thousand members throughout Italy, and the pogrom-type stormtrooper-tactic that would later characterise fascism had still to be developed. The first *Fasci* confined their goals to dragging the country into the War. When that objective was achieved, they were dissolved. Only in 1919 was the Fascist organisation re-established.

Mussolini went to the front as a war-volunteer, but he and the other interventionists were destined to have quite remarkable experiences in the trenches. By this I mean not the usual hardships of soldiers in modern warfare, but disappointments of a quite different nature. In the editorial office, the popular mass-meeting, the street-demonstrations, early in 1915, Mussolini had put himself at the head of enthused masses. But in the trenches he and his political collaborators experienced the bitter hatred of the great mass of their fellows against the war-instigators, and many active officers thought exactly like the men under them. Now it was time for the other side of the coin to show itself. In the demonstrations in the big cities, tens of thousands of impassioned young patriots could palm themselves off as 'the' nation. But in the trenches they found the real people. The trenches had brought together the great masses from the countryside and small towns, as well as the organised working class of the big cities, and all of them hated the War. Mussolini's most enthusiastic collaborator in conducting war-propaganda had been an ex-syndicalist, [Filippo] Corridoni. Corridoni had likewise gone to the front. But there he died. Mussolini later recounted how he got news of his friend's death:

> I'd just knocked off from labour-duty and was resting a while, when some chap came up to me and asked, 'Are you Mussolini?'. I said, 'yes'. 'Good,' said the other fellow, 'I have some good news for you – Corridoni has kicked the bucket! Serves him right, if you ask me! To hell with all you interventionists!'.

As a people the Italians are at least as brave, resolute and self-respecting as the other peoples of Europe. The extraordinary mediocrity of the Italian army during the World-War is therefore all the more remarkable. After three whole years the Italians still could not defeat a mere section of the Austrian army, and when some German divisions mounted an offensive, it entered a complete crisis and could only be propped up by urgently dispatched English and French auxiliary troops. The history of Italy's performance in the War only makes sense when you consider that the great majority of the Italian soldiers hated the War and put up passive resistance to the army-leadership. This example could be of the greatest significance, should any of the present-day fascist countries again become involved in war.

While the Germans, French and English entered the War of 1914 convinced that their very existence was at stake, and while in those countries at least ninety per cent of the people consciously and firmly demanded involvement, Italy fought the War in a style that was already fascist, that is, the War was forced on its people by a noisy, well-organised minority. It is inevitable that a fascist state at war will be a state in crisis, because modern warfare can only be carried on with the cooperation of the entire people. In war the fascist régime has to appeal precisely to people whom it has trampled under foot, and it is bound to encounter their passive (and later also their active) resistance.

The imperialist government of Italy linked with the name of Sonnino would have collapsed miserably in the winter of 1917–18 without the help given to it by the Allied powers. Thanks to the efforts of the American, British and French bourgeoisies, Italy would likewise belong to the victorious camp at the close of 1918, and in the peace it obtained roughly the goals for which it had entered the conflict. But the Italian people were not happy with their victory – for three-and-a-half years they had suffered the absolute wretchedness of life in the trenches and deprivations at home. Now, on top of that, there was the mass-unemployment bound up with the transition from a war-economy to a peacetime economy. Italy's economic structure, inherently precarious, simply could not take the shattering blows of the crisis. The spectre of inflation spread through the country, and impoverished masses watched as profiteers speculated shamelessly in currencies and commodities.

In the year 1919 the overwhelming majority of the Italian people were filled with savage hatred against the policy of war and everything connected with it. On this question workers, peasants and the middle-class all thought absolutely alike. The nationalist intoxication of 1915 passed into its hangover. True, Trento and Trieste had been forcibly taken and were now part of Italy. But what use was that compared with all the suffering and sacrifice that the people had had to put up with? The mood in the country was such that the pro-imperialist faction lost its grip on the government-machinery and the liberals of the prewar period returned to power. Thus the irrepressible Giolitti re-emerged from decline. When Mussolini went to the front in 1915 he had left behind the bluster of a triumphalist mass-movement. When he returned with the rank of an under officer (he was destined to obtain no higher position in the army, so great was the aversion of his superiors to the interventionists), he was alone and despised. In 1919 he continued to come out with his paper in Milan but no-one ever took him or his tendency seriously at the time.

The bitter hatred of the vast majority of Italians against the policy of war, and against its instigators and beneficiaries, produced an extraordinary strengthening of socialism. For the Socialist Party of Italy (PSI) had consistently opposed Italian participation in the War, and in its aftermath this position appeared totally justified. In the elections of 1919 the Socialists won over 150 seats. The number of Left-voters was far greater than the size of the industrial working class in the country. Indeed, a very substantial part of the urban petty bourgeoisie came around to supporting the Socialist movement, and, something of even greater significance, possibly, socialism even gained a foothold among the peasantry and tenants of the South. Next to the Socialist deputies in numbers came the representatives of a large Democratic-Catholic party, while the leftovers of the old liberal or conservative groups watched the future with anxiety.

In the years 1919 and 1920, Italy appeared to stand on the brink of a proletarian revolution. The PSI decided to join the Third International. Strikes and demonstrations were a daily occurrence. In hundreds of municipalities, the PSI won a majority and took over the local administration. The influence of the trade-unions increased. Poor peasants no longer submitted to the authority of their landlords. The high-point of this whole revolutionary movement was formed by the famous factory-occupations in the autumn of 1920, when workers in all the major cities and industrial areas took over the factories and ran them for some time.

In fact, if there *had* been a determined revolutionary party to unify the movements of workers and poor peasants, a successful proletarian revolution may well have occurred in Italy at that time. Such a party could have given the masses leadership in the decisive battles. Given the mood of the people and the extraordinary weakness of the so-called liberal government, the armed forces would not have put up any substantial resistance. However, the great majority of Italian Socialists were not serious about revolution; they simply lacked the will. The working masses had no previous experience of revolutionary struggle, and most of their leaders had no idea what they should do in this critical conjuncture. Moreover, the socialist movement was internally disunited and torn by divisions, and in 1920 it dissolved into three distinct tendencies that engaged in a sharp mutual fight. In this situation, the Italian Socialists chose the worst possible course: they projected the appearance of being revolutionary without actually being so. They appeared radical enough to inject panic-stricken terror into the ruling and propertied classes, but they were not radical enough to deliver the really decisive blow. The two years 1919 and 1920 passed without the Socialists either taking power or doing anything of any significance. The revolution, however, is not something you can put into cold-storage. When the proletariat let the most favourable period pass, it made itself the sacrificial lamb of its enemy.

In March 1919 Mussolini had refounded the organisation of the different *Fasci di combattimento* that had existed in 1915. He began with a couple of hundred supporters. At that time his radical-nationalist programme was about as unpopular as you could get. In the parliamentary elections of that year the Fascists suffered a complete rout. The mass of soldiers had returned from the front full of bitterness against the war-instigators, but the prevailing mood against the War, shared by the liberal government, sometimes took the wrong forms. Hardly any care was taken of those disabled in the War and, more generally, of those who had participated in the War. Sometimes it happened that officers were beaten up simply because they had uniforms on, or a furious popular mob would strip veterans of their decorations. None of this would have had much importance if the socialist revolution really had developed out of the revulsion against the War. But the revolution did not come, and the many thousands of now-unemployed veterans felt neglected and betrayed. This was true both of the rank-and-file elements of the former army and of the demobilised officer-corps, which felt completely deracinated. Slowly, in precisely these circles, the old activist nationalism now gained a new lease of life. However, its first prophet was not Mussolini but the poet Gabriele D'Annunzio.

In the huge nervous tension that the Italians lived through in the years 1919–21, not only did they experience economic hardships, but they came to feel that their former allies had done them down in the peace-treaties. Ignoring the advantages and possessions that the peace had brought Italy, attention tended to focus on the little that Italy had *not* succeeded in getting. Thus Fiume, an Adriatic seaport inhabited by Italian nationals, had not been allotted to Italy as part of the peace-treaties. Many Italians got excited over the fate of Fiume. D'Annunzio assembled a volunteer-corps, transgressed national boundaries against the will of the government and occupied Fiume. The poet had acted in the manner of Garibaldi. While the government dithered, D'Annunzio had gathered the patriotic youth and marched at their head.

Mussolini realised the extraordinary significance of this expedition to Fiume. He mobilised his party for the action and did everything he could to sustain the propaganda for D'Annunzio. This was the first time national stormtroopers were again deployed against the socialist and pacifist wave that swept through Italy in those years. Gradually, Mussolini's own stormtroopers attracted the largest following, and by 1921 fascism had again become a major political force in Italy. The party expanded thanks less to the standard methods used by political movements than to the violent offensive opened by the stormtroopers, this time not against an external enemy, as under Garibaldi and D'Annunzio, but against the enemy at home, the organised socialists and communists.

The liberal government felt the ground shaking under its feet. The workers and poor peasants rejected the ruling system, yet even among the capitalists of the North and the powerful Southern landowners there was growing disillusionment with the régime for doing nothing about the Red Flag. The so-called 'liberal' governments of the prewar epoch had kept themselves alive through electoral manipulation in the central and southern parts of Italy, where the local administrations had colluded with the landowners and political cliques of the area in mobilising votes for the Right. These breezy days of the old-style liberalism were now over: since the World-War it had simply melted in the heat of the class-struggle. The liberals returned to power in 1919 only because the mass of the population hated the imperialists, while the Socialists, on the other hand, were not powerful enough as yet to take over the government. The liberal prime ministers of 1919– 22 were mere stop-gaps in whom no-one put any confidence at all. For this reason they made no daring decisions during their term of office and wished to preserve good relations with all parties and classes.

Mussolini again appealed to the younger intellectuals and, in particular, to the veterans to rally around himself. The liberal prime ministers and the Socialists had ruined the victory, they had pushed the country into disaster, they had insulted and neglected the soldiers, veterans and the war-disabled. Now fascism would draw the necessary conclusions from the victory and build a new, proud and prosperous Italy. The unemployed students, traders and workers whom the Socialists had not been able to help came to Mussolini. When his stormtroopers won their first skirmishes, demolished union-offices, beat up militants, sometimes assassinated them, the capitalists realised that a new star was rising for them. The industrialists now began to finance fascism, and even the landowners willingly joined the new movement to suppress the small tenants under their control. The Fascist punitive expeditions moved outwards into the villages where, by violence and murder, they completely smashed the local organisations of agricultural workers and small peasants. The landowner could again sleep safely at last.

In the course of 1921 Mussolini became the much-admired protagonist of the bourgeoisie and big landowners. The younger intellectuals and the veterans rushed to him *en masse*. Everywhere the Italian workers put up the most courageous resistance to the Fascists and their terror-squads. Of course, there was no nationally coordinated campaign of defence against the white terror, one that mobilised the full strength of workers throughout the country. But in all places the workers fought the terror-squads with heroism, even if from isolated and losing positions. If one looks closely at the history of the Italian working class in the years 1921–2, at the endlessly long series of essentially similar events – arson, assaults, demolitions, murders – one comes to the conclusion that despite all the unfavourable circumstances, the working class *would* have destroyed fascism if the state-power had shown even the slightest element of neutrality or objectivity. But wherever the proletariat successfully resisted fascism, the state-gendarmerie or the army immediately intervened. The workers may well have been a match for the Fascist stormtroopers, but they were no match for the organised armed power of the state. The police simply shot the actively fighting workers, or jailed them, and the Fascists would then re-emerge to complete their work of destruction in triumph.

The Italian experience repeated a pattern discernible in the Russian pogroms. *The terrorist-squads succeeded because they could always count on the state*. The liberal politicians of 1919–20 had not dared to provoke the workers in those years. When the socialist wave ran high and they had to reckon with the coming proletarian revolution, the liberal government had proclaimed a sort of political neutrality vis-à-vis the different classes in struggle. Even during the occupation of the factories, in the autumn of 1920, the government had withheld permission to fire on the workers, and contented itself with diplomatic interventions. But once Mussolini began his re-emergence, the bourgeoisie recovered its nerve, and the new mood now infected the bureaucracy, the police-chiefs and the army-officers. When the Fascists showed such bravado in attacking the Red trouble-makers, the police could hardly hold themselves back. The remarkable contradictions in Italian society in 1919–20 had undermined the legal administration of the state so profoundly that no respect was left for it any longer. In a purely technical sense, the regular army and police were still vastly stronger than the Fascist gangs. But the Fascists had the uncompromising will to smash the workers' organisations. It was always the Fascists who launched the attacks, and only then would the state move into action with its massive machinery of repression, tailing after them. If the situation became critical, the state would take on the main job and the Fascists would take the credit for the victory.

Imagine a fight where there are five people on one side, armed only with sticks, and a group of ten persons on the other, each carrying a revolver. At first, these ten persons do not dare to use their revolvers. The five people with sticks can laugh at them with impunity. Suddenly a young fellow turns up and rushes on the five of them with a loud cry. Only now does the group of ten draw its revolvers and shoot down its five defenceless opponents. In this analogy the young chap who runs out shouting is fascism, and the ten armed individuals are the bourgeoisie and their legal state-power. The five people with sticks represent the organised working class. In short, the emergence of fascism never alters the real balance of class-forces between the bourgeoisie and the proletariat. If the proletariat were really stronger than the bourgeoisie, it would win, with or without fascism. However, if the capitalist class is objectively the stronger force, then the emergence of fascism can bring about the collapse of the workers' movement.

In Central and Southern Italy Mussolini protected the landowners from an agrarian revolution and they became his closest friends after 1921. The mass of the small peasantry fell back into submission, as before, once the peasant-leagues had been demolished. They kept quiet and obeyed, but they were not active Fascists. To the petty bourgeoisie of Central and Southern Italy, moreover, fascism remained something quite external. In Northern Italy, on the other hand, in the modern, advanced parts of the country, fascism became, after 1921, a real mass-movement. It is true that the large mass of organised industrial workers remained true to their earlier convictions. But here, in the North, apart from the capitalists who financed him, apart from the students, unemployed veterans and adventurers who flocked to his storm-troops,

Mussolini gradually won the active support of the urban middle-class. In the parliamentary elections of May 1921 he won an astonishing proportion of votes, chiefly in Milan, Pavia, Bologna, and Ferrara. He entered parliament at the head of 33 deputies.

It has often been argued that the modern middle-classes have a profound, fanatical hatred of the working class, that given the slightest chance they would take to arms and slaughter the proletariat. The middle-class (*Mittelstand*) lives in fear of its own proletarianisation, and out of the sense of anguish created by this prospect it loathes the workers and attempts to trample them under foot. This is a strange theory. Is it conceivable that the small artisans and traders should harbour such murderous hatred against workers who are often their best customers, and, in the working-class districts at least, the only people from whom they make any sort of living? Is it likely that the white-collar employees should harbour secret desires of betraying their blue-collar colleagues in the company? Is it likely that the students at school and university would actually be waiting for the chance to shoot their thoroughly oppressed comrades from the masses? One has only to recall the quite banal truth that in today's conditions there are innumerable and imperceptible gradations between the lower middle-class (*dem kleinen Mittelstand*) and the proletariat, that often in the same family one brother is a bricklayer, the second a small clerk, the third a master-craftsman, while one of them has a son who, through the collective efforts of the entire family, actually attends high school. This notion of the inveterate hatred of the middle-class against workers as the underlying *leitmotiv* of fascism is one of the clichéd illusions of a self-styled 'sociology'. There are many cases where the middle-strata have sided politically *with* the workers, and many others where they have opposed them as a hostile force. But in all cases the decisive factor has been the political situation of the moment, and certainly not the 'tactics' of the parties concerned. The general dogma clarifies absolutely nothing.

In periods of deep social crisis the middle-strata (*die Mittelschichten*) will side with the workers, *if* the party of socialism resolutely shows the road to salvation and to the construction of a new society. If, however, the socialist movement itself vacillates and lacks certainty, and shrinks from the tasks of revolution and social reconstruction, it is bound to lose the support of the middle-classes. In 1919 the Italian middle-classes (*Mittelschichten*) were as ready to participate in a socialist revolution as the German middle-classes (*Mittelklassen*) were after 9 November. When, in both situations, the socialists showed themselves incapable of carrying through their tasks, the middle-strata once more swung away from them. To this we should add a series of special factors. As I said earlier, in the years 1919–20 the Socialists in Italy had won a majority in many municipalities. There they and their local supporters came to occupy the leading positions. This was perfectly correct, and the new Socialist councillors worked at least as well as the earlier bourgeois ones had. However, if, at a time such as this, the masses are expecting a revolution from the Socialists and this does not come, if the misery of the unemployed and the hardships of the middle-class find no relief at all, and, on the contrary, one sees the Socialist councillors peacefully holding office in comparatively well-paid posts, then disappointment, disillusionment, and, finally, hatred are inevitable. These moods were of crucial importance in Germany as well, in the years leading up to the National Socialist capture of power.

The socialist functionaries who sat in paid positions on the town-councils, in the trade-unions and so on, were, in their overwhelming majority, incorruptible types who fulfilled their duties to the working class and the public at large with a true sense of loyalty. This was so both in Italy and in Germany. But in times of crisis much more was expected from them than this routine performance of duties. The middle-classes and many workers became progressively more enraged at the new socialist bureaucracy that had created comfortable positions for itself by using the class-movement of the poorest groups.

To all of this we must add certain tactical mistakes that were made in the organisation of strikes, especially in sectors of vital importance to everyday life. When transport-services or gas and water-services shut down, this creates numerous inconveniences for the bulk of the population, including other workers and the middle-class. Now if the strikers could show people that their cause is a justified one, that they have to go on strike to defend basic living conditions for themselves and their children, then the majority of people would understand the reasons for the strike and put up with the hardships caused by it. However, in the sort of situations that Germany and Italy lived through in the years 1919 and 1920, the activity of the working class would dissolve only too easily into minor struggles over wages, instead of the important political movements. The masses will support strikes as links in the chain of a major revolutionary offensive, but when the political movement is itself crumbling, isolated wage-struggles are not likely to elicit much support from the public, especially when those struggles proceed from the better-paid groups of workers and inflict severe hardship on the rest of the population.

In 1919–20 the Italian middle-classes were expecting a socialist revolution, but it never came. Consequently, the economic crisis only worsened and the mass of people sank deeper into poverty. Yet, at this precise moment, the Socialist leaders occupied well-paid positions, and the transport-workers and workers of other public services were paralysing the life of the cities to push their wage-levels higher. The middle-class now lost the sense of feeling that it must fight side-by-side with the workers against the capitalists and profiteers. On the contrary, it came to see in the organised working class a self-seeking oligarchy that looked only to itself and its leadership, and was bent on extorting higher and higher wages, that too at the cost of the public at large, of the taxpayers and above all of the middle-class itself. This is why the Italian intelligentsia, commercial businesses, government-employees and artisans slowly came around to believing that the socialist organisations were the real traitors to the people. That is how there emerged a general rage against the 'big-shots' (*die 'Bonzen'*), as they would come to be called in Germany, and against the 'strike-specialists'. This is when the middle-strata developed a positive feeling of pleasure in strike-breaking and the will to wreak vengeance on the Red Flag. A section of the middle-class joined Mussolini's stormtroopers and the rest helped the Fascists by voting for them.

Margherita Sarfatti writes, in her malicious but psychologically interesting book on Mussolini,

> Then began a strike of workers in the water-supply department, the railways came to a standstill, the electricity went off, public transport, the pride of punctual Milan, became a pure disaster, and the unplanned creation of municipalities with the enormous number of bureaucrats they brought into being, weighed down on the tax-payers. Once dustmen started drawing ministerial salaries, the normally clean streets became perpetually dirty, and in winter one could hardly walk through them due to the snow, so that Milan started cursing. On these unswept streets, on this snow, Karl Marx was destined to die in Italy.

It is far from obvious that Marx ever supported the idea of garbage piling up on the roads, and under the then-Socialist municipal administration even the brave Milan street-sweepers would not exactly have received 'ministerial salaries'. But this passage does reflect, in a superbly clear form, the general mood of the Milanese middle-classes during the rise of fascism: Marxism = strikes and filth, fascism = a return to order and cleanliness! Here is Sarfatti's eulogy of the strike-breakers:

> In August a new general strike that spread across the entire country assumed the fancy name of a 'legal strike'. Fascism sprang on this strike and castrated it. Engineers, people from all professions and future ministers took the place of the skilled employees on strike and brought the factories and means of transport back into motion. At that time one saw students courageously performing factory-labour for 10 to 12 hours, or running trains through the rebellious parts of the city and working as conductors with unusual politeness.

At the Third Congress of the Fascist Party of Italy, the leadership released the results of a survey it had conducted among some 151,000 party-members regarding their particular occupation. The result is deeply significant, and worth considering, even if objections are possible to some of the numbers claimed. The statistics comprised:

Merchants, traders, shopkeepers	14,000
Factory-owners	4,000
Landowners	18,000
Students and teachers	21,000
Members of the liberal professions	10,000
Civil servants	7,000
White-collar workers	15,000
Industrial workers and sailors	25,000
Agricultural workers	37,000
	151,000

The very large number of agricultural workers who figure in this list consisted for the most part of 'members' who had joined under compulsion – in places where the Fascists had destroyed the existing organisations of agricultural workers and incorporated their former membership into their own organisations. Such forced membership would also, to some extent, apply to the category of 'industrial workers'. Moreover, the statistics make no distinction between employed and unemployed. Again, under the category 'merchants/ traders' (*Kaufmann*) almost anything can pass, from large entrepreneurs down to unemployed commercial agents. Under 'factory-owners' a certain number of independent master-craftsmen are included. Surprising, but thoroughly consistent with the history of fascism, is *the extraordinarily large number of students and intellectuals in the party*. A specifically petty-bourgeois tendency of fascism (*kleinbürgerliche Tendenz des Faschismus*) does *not* emerge from these figures. Rather, towards the close of 1921, Mussolini became the leader of a typically bourgeois party (*eine typisch-bürgerliche Partei*), with a particularly strong dash of intellectuals and academics, and a certain following (*gewissen Anhang*) among workers.

In the years from 1919 to 1922 the programme of Fascism underwent an extraordinarily rapid and fundamental transformation. To Mussolini, the tactics of seizing power were everything. Questions of programme were, compared to this, quite secondary. In 1919, at the inception of the Fascist movement, when all of Italy had moved far to the Left and the capitalists were not particularly bothered about Mussolini, he had drafted a left-radical programme. He intended to win working-class votes through a kind of nationalistic socialism. At that time, among other things, he supported a people's government (*eine Volksherrschaft*), based on a general and equal franchise, with the right to vote for both women and men; the proclamation of a Republic in Italy; the dissolution of all industrial and financial joint-stock companies; the restructuring of production on corporatist lines with direct profit-sharing by all the workers of the enterprise; and several other nice things. But when the big industrialists and large landowners began to put their sympathies and their bank-accounts at the Fascists' disposal, Mussolini's programme changed rapidly. In November 1921, at the above-mentioned third congress of his party, he assured them that while he was of course opposed to liberalism in the political sense, he was unconditionally in favour of economic liberalism: 'If possible, I would even be inclined to hand the railways and post and telegraph back to private enterprise in order to relieve the state of economic functions that are really quite uneconomical'. In this way fascism finally returned to an unconditional defence of private capitalism.

Mussolini gave whole-hearted support to the landowners of Southern Italy in their struggle to forestall an agrarian revolution, yet he was never quite disposed to restoring to these semi-feudal bosses the decisive influence they had wielded in the so-called 'liberal' period of Italian history. Fascism was and remained the party of the advanced North. Mussolini once compared his own work with that of the Turkish leader, Kemal Atatürk, who, from

Ankara, sought to create a new bourgeois state in opposition to the feudal Constantinople of the Sultanate. Precisely in this sense, Mussolini projected the reassuring image of himself as leader of Milan, Italy's Ankara, waging a struggle against Rome, the Italian Constantinople. Indeed, Italian fascism always fought on two fronts. This naturally does not refer to the quite fictitious 'two fronts' of the petty bourgeoisie which, supposedly, struggles simultaneously against capitalism and the proletariat. As manifold and variable as Mussolini's successive programmes were, none of them show any specific interest in the petty bourgeoisie (*das Kleinbürgertum*), and the fascist form of activity in Italy was quite unlike a petty-bourgeois one.

In 1921–2, through its daily assaults and violence, fascism defeated the organised socialist working class. Yet at the same time, it broke the dominance of the backward feudal cliques of Central and Southern Italy. To the landowners and the local power-élites of the South, it was at that time a question of choosing the lesser evil – not unreasonably, they perceived the agrarian revolution from the Left as the greater evil, and therefore went over to fascism. But at the very same time they were aware that with the victory of the Fascists their former dominance was doomed. Of course, they retained their landed estates and other possessions, but they could no longer hope to exert *political* influence with the help of the 'liberal' politicians. Mussolini was the leader of the modern Italian North, with its bourgeoisie and its intelligentsia. That is the secret of his comparatively lasting success. Mussolini has now (1933) been in power in Italy for 12 years, and for the moment the end of fascism in Italy is not yet a real prospect. Had Mussolini really been a leader of the petty bourgeoisie, he would not have lasted even twelve months.

In 1922 fascism emerged as the great 'united front' of all the active bourgeois and anti-socialist forces in the country. Behind Mussolini stood the capitalist class, the middle-classes and the intellectuals, landowners (who had mixed feelings), a major part of the unemployed, who would find a source of income and something to do in the storm-troops, and even individual groups of workers (*einzelne Arbeitergruppen*). The Socialist and Communist organisations were demolished completely, and the old bourgeois parties seized by a rapid process of dissolution. The state-bureaucracy had got so used to seeing Mussolini as the true leader of the nation that neither the army nor the police ever seriously contemplated a struggle against the Fascists. Even the King of Italy slowly came around to seeing that the liberal-feudal period was over, and quickly made his peace with the *Duce*. Under these conditions, it was a pure formality when Mussolini chased the last helpless 'liberal' ministers from parliament and put himself in their place.

In Italy the industrial proletariat is only a minority of the population. A victory of the Socialists thus depended crucially, after 1919, on a democratic coalition of the workers with the peasants and the middle-strata. In 1919 and 1920 hopeful beginnings were made in the direction of such a coalition. However, this coalition was shattered before it could be consolidated. Within the vacillating mass of the petty bourgeoisie, the Fascists forcibly suppressed the rural half, and won over, to their side, the urban half. Both these processes, the destruction of the left-wing organisations in the countryside as well as the renewed division between the urban middle-class and the proletariat, were only possible due to the serious mistakes committed by the Italian Socialists. Once these processes were accomplished, however, the bulk of the propertied class was again unified, this time under the new banner of Fascism. The working class now faced a completely new situation. Prior to 1914 the modern bourgeoisie had never really exercised power in Italy. In this sense it still had a historical task to make up for.

So the celebrated slogan about the trains now running on time has its deeper significance. Obviously, this is not to be taken in the sense of wondering whether the train-services really did improve under Mussolini, or really were that bad before his rise to power.

The basic fact is that there was a real problem for Italy. In England, America, France and Germany the railway-system is naturally the most modern in the world. But in semi-feudal countries, such as Russia and Italy were down to the War, this was far from self-evident. Here the task of adapting these countries to the latest bourgeois technology still had to be accomplished.

Fascism ended the exaction of tribute by the Mafia and Camorra. The public funds that were formerly intercepted by the local cliques were now entirely subordinated to the interests of modern capitalism. The state-capitalist concentration of the country in the so-called 'corporatist system' facilitated control of the country by the most efficient groups of capitalists. Heavy industry, chemicals, automobiles, aircraft, and shipping were all systematically developed. Where in all this is the 'petty-bourgeois' spirit that is supposed to form the essence of fascism? Here I am not concerned with taking up positions for or against, but with historical facts: it is a fact that the productive forces of the country *were* developed further by Italian fascism, at least down to the beginning of the great world-crisis. Because of this, Mussolini gained the prestige of a successful politician, and Fascism gained a mass-following in the propertied strata (*bürgerlichen Massen*). Mussolini himself had sufficient authority to be able to convert the stormtroopers into a sort of auxiliary police-force of the newly-consolidated bourgeois state, once their terrorist methods became superfluous.

Of course, Mussolini has not been able to solve the agrarian question in Italy. The expansion of capitalism *post* 1922 has in fact only increased the weight of the working class. In the next major crisis, the Italian capitalists will face renewed opposition from the mass of workers and poor peasants. At that stage it will no longer be possible to deflect the social revolution with the notion that the task of building a fully capitalist society must first be accomplished. In the 12 years of Mussolini's régime, Italy has roughly come up to the level of the countries north of the Alps. Consequently, no special path now remains open by which it can avoid the general European forms in which the class-struggle will be settled.

3. Germany

The decisive difference between Italy and Germany lies in the quite different occupational structures of their respective populations. It follows that in Germany fascism was forced to take a different tactical path to the seizure of power. It is not quite as easy to clarify the occupational co-ordinates of the voting patterns in Germany. The two sets of figures, those relating to occupations and those to votes cast, do not cover the same groupings. Many German citizens who can vote, for example, housewives, are not included in the occupational census. On the other hand, youth under the age of 20 have no voting rights, even when they have some form of employment. Nonetheless, it is necessary to form some idea of the class-composition of the German electorate, for only on this basis will it become possible to grasp the political movement of the masses after 1919 and the rise of National Socialism.

The occupational data relating to Germany for 1925 give a total economically active population of just under 36 million persons from a total overall population of over 62 million. In that year there were, in Germany, 5½ million 'self-employed' persons (*Selbständige*). This category includes both owners of enterprises, for example, industrialists, master-craftsmen, farmers, etc., as well as business-executives, directors, and top bureaucrats. The number of family-members helping out was roughly as large. On the other hand, the census showed 14½ million workers, just under 5½ million white-collar employees (*Angestellte*) and civil servants (*Beamte*), and roughly 5 million domestic employees and persons without any occupation. A tiny fraction of the so-called 'persons without occupation' are capitalist rentiers, but the vast majority are people who were once employed and were now drawing social-security benefits, old-age pensions, and so on. The unemployed are not classified separately in these figures, but counted under their original occupation. The point of all this is to establish, from these figures, the specific relation of forces between the propertied elements of the population and the proletariat. In making this calculation we also have to include family-members not classified as having any occupation. In the case of family-farms and small-scale enterprises, wives and older children almost regularly appear as 'family-members who help out' (co-workers). In the case of all households other than the 'self-employed', however, wives are only counted when they themselves practise some occupation of their own. Among the rural and middle-class households, roughly two-thirds appear in the statistics as 'self-employed' or as 'co-workers'. In proletarian households, this proportion is roughly half, in contrast. Applying these criteria, it turns out that in Germany in 1925 there were *c.* 17 million persons in households with property, substantial or otherwise (*des großen und des kleinen Bürgertums*), and 45 million persons in families of paid employees and proletarians in the broadest sense.

One can see that an impressive majority of the German population belonged to households dependent on wage-employment (*Arbeitnehmerschaft*). Even if the whole of the self-employed petty bourgeoisie and all peasant-households down to the smallest are included in the category of propertied classes, the latter would still account for barely one quarter of the total population. Marx's predictions about the future social evolution of the advanced industrial countries have been decisively confirmed. However, it is important to avoid a misunderstanding. Germany has an overwhelming majority of people in some form of paid employment, but not a majority of *industrial workers* in the strict sense of the word. As the figures cited earlier suggest, within the proletarian camp, over against the 14½ million workers, there are also 10½ million government-employees, office-workers, pensioners, house-maids, etc. Moreover, under those 14½ million workers we have to include 2½ million agricultural workers as well as apprentices in craft-enterprises. It is difficult to draw any very clear line between a 'craft-enterprise' based on manual labour and a 'factory', but, even so, the number of craft-apprentices would amount to at least one million. It follows that of the total of 25 million paid employees and proletarians in the broadest sense of the word, at most only 11 million were factory-workers in the true sense, whereas 14 million comprised other categories.

These figures can be presented more graphically in roughly the following way: in 1925, out of every hundred German citizens (family-members included, naturally), about 28 belonged to the propertied classes (in the broadest sense of the term) and 72 to paid employees and proletarians (also in the broadest sense). However, in the latter group, only 32 were factory-workers in the strict sense, whereas 40 were employed outside the factory sector. Doubtless this calculation is a precarious one, but its sole aim is to present a superficial overview of the actual relationships. During the Reichstag elections of the Weimar period, the 28% formed by owners of property were in the habit of voting almost exclusively for the bourgeois parties, and the 32% formed by the factory-workers would vote, in their vast majority, for the Social Democrats or the Communists. On the other hand, of the remaining 40% formed by the general mass of paid employees excluding the factory-workers, only a minority supported the Social Democrats, while the majority – white-collar workers, government-employees, agricultural workers, apprentices, etc. – supported the bourgeois parties. This explains the fact that after the Revolution of 1918 elections in Germany always yielded a bourgeois majority. However, in Germany the sheer weight of the vast mass of the population composed of the unemployed and of wage-earners is so compelling that no German government has been able to ignore it completely.

At the end of the War and beginning of the Republic, the war-weary masses of Germany were in a decidedly socialist and democratic frame of mind. Not only did the entire mass of Germany's wage-earning groups (*Arbeitnehmerschaft*) declare allegiance to the Republic, and want to have nothing to do with the domination of the nobility, the officer-corps and the big bourgeoisie, but large sections of the middle-class stood with the Revolution.

In the elections to the National Assembly in January 1919, the Republican camp consisted of the following parties: the SPD, the USPD, the Centre Party, dominated at that time by the Christian-Democratic trade-unions, and the German Democratic Party (DDP) that drew its support from white-collar workers, civil servants and sections of the middle-class. The landowners and capitalists were represented by the German National Party (DNP) and the German National People's Party (DNVP). 30 million votes were cast in the 1919 elections. Of these the Republican parties received 25½ million, and the parties of the Right 4½ million! Of the 30 million voters there would have been roughly 8 million property-owners and 22 million wage-earners in the broad sense. The result of this election shows that, at that time, the wage-earning population of Germany supported the Republic and democracy almost down to a man. Likewise, almost half the middle-class declared its support for the new political system. This popular mood was simultaneously the cause and the result of 9 November. If this mood had persisted, we should never have seen either fascism or the Hitler regime in Germany.

But this huge democratic-Republican majority soon crumbled, in part from the pressure of objective conditions, but also as a consequence of the profound mistakes of the Republican camp. Capitalism survived, unreplaced by a socialist form of society, and even any genuine democracy failed to materialise, in so far as the army, the administration, the judiciary and the educational system remained almost entirely in the hands of the old bureaucracy. The labour-movement was not united, rather, its individual tendencies stood on opposite sides in the civil war. The middle-strata, large sections of the white-collar and government-employees who had greeted the Republic in November with enthusiasm, would soon stand aloof from it in sheer disappointment. The leadership of the German Republic was accused of not fulfilling its promises. On the contrary, the general feeling was that the new constitution had only created hardship and poverty, inflation and civil war. On top of this, the Republic was loaded with responsibility for Germany's desperate position thanks to the Versailles Treaty. This is how the preconditions were established for the growth of an anti-republican, nationalistic mass-movement that regrouped the estate-owners, the capitalists and the middle-classes.

I noted earlier that the ruling classes of Imperial Germany had no desire to be especially popular. Of course, whenever the Reichstag elections came around, the Conservative Party drove the subaltern masses in the countryside to the poll-booths, and in the towns a certain percentage of the petty bourgeoisie voted Conservative. But no-one thought of creating a conservative or nationalist (for example, Pan-German) *mass*-movement in the big cities and industrial areas to compete with the Social Democrats. In the large urban centres one generally left bourgeois agitation to the Liberals and the Centre Party. Prior to 1914, the Conservatives never thought of trying to win a majority in the Reichstag on their own resources. They were quite content to shape Reichstag policies through a coalition with the Centre Party and the National Liberals. When a member of the clergy, Stöcker, sought to build a conservative, urban-based mass-party, his work was deliberately sabotaged, first by Bismarck and later by Wilhelm II. If the aristocracy were serious about winning votes among the urban masses, they would have to descend to the level of the masses, agitate in popular meetings and newspapers, and agree to their general demands. In the Imperial epoch all this seemed to be a pure waste of time, because the estate-owners already exercised power without recourse to demagogic manoeuvres.

But after 9 November the earlier forms of class-dominance fell to pieces, and the Red Flag flooded the bulwarks of traditional property and inherited authority. Now the aristocrats were compelled to go to the people to save whatever there was left to save. From the very first days of its existence, the DNVP [the leading party of the German conservatives] began to speak a totally new language. The old, reactionary slogans of 'monarchy', 'militarism', and 'defence of bourgeois and feudal property' were cleverly disguised in nationalist clichés and sentimental promises: 'Every true patriot chooses the black, white and red flag!', or, 'Germany's on fire! Vote Laverrenz' (so said the chief DNVP candidate in Berlin) – one heard this kind of stuff as early as 1919.

DNVP pamphlets promised a return to the 'Germany of Luther, Bismarck and Hindenburg'. Often they carried pictures of these and other 'heroes', and juxtaposed them with caricatures of Republican and socialist leaders. The capital of popular trust that the German Republic had started off with in January 1919 was largely used up barely a year later. The Reichstag elections of June 1920 showed a completely different picture: this time, of the total of 28 million votes cast, the pro-Weimar parties got only 18 million votes and the various anti-democratic, monarchist and nationalist parties of the Right 10 million. When one looks at the occupational breakdown to interpret this result, it shows that by the summer of 1920 the reactionary, right-wing movement had already won back the overwhelming mass of the propertied middle-class (*des besiztenden Mittelstandes*) and made a substantial dent in the wage-earners' front. The depressing process of absorption of ever-larger masses of people by the nationalist Right can be tracked from one election to the next. This development was not in the remotest sense the work of Adolf Hitler. Hitler and the Nazis only reaped what others had sown before them.

To take only one typical election in the period before the main expansion of the Nazis, viz. the elections to the post of *Reichspräsident* in March 1925: in these the parties of the Right put up a common candidate, the aristocrat Jarres. The latter possessed no special qualities that would in any sense have made him popular. He was nothing but a safe representative of the black-red-and-white nationalism. Yet he received 10½ million votes from a total of 27 million. Apart from Jarres, there were two other candidates representing forces opposed to the Republic. Held, on behalf of the federalist Bavarian People's Party (BVP), polled 1 million votes, and the National Socialists' rival-candidate, Ludendorff, just under 300,000. In 1932, the vast majority of those who voted for Jarres would go over to Hitler, even if, in the meantime, Ludendorff himself had abandoned the Nazis. The Nazis could *never* have made such substantial electoral gains *post* 1930 without the preparatory work the other parties of the Right had successfully pulled off in the years following 1919. The fundamental features of the nationalist and anti-republican ideology of the right-wing parties of Germany remained basically unchanged after 1919, even if they were inflected rather differently according to the economic conjuncture and the international situation.

The right-wing parties as a whole polled 12 million votes in the elections of March 1925, and parties that could in a broad sense be called 'Left' – the SPD, KPD, Centre Party, and DDP – 15 million. Of the 27 million voters who participated in the presidential elections, roughly 7 million may have been property-owners, and, of those, perhaps 6 million voted for the Right and 1 million for the Centre Party and DDP. In that case, of the general mass of wage-earners (defining this group, again, in the broadest possible way), 6 million would have voted for a Right opposed to democracy and 14 million for the Left. So one can see how substantially the percentage of the salaried or wage-earning population that was *opposed* to the Revolution had increased since 1920.

It is well known that in the second round of the presidential elections held in April 1925, all the right-wing groups united around Hindenburg, whose votes totalled over 14½ million, signifying a gain of 2½ million votes for the Right compared to the first round. Yet Hindenburg attracted many voters largely by the authority of his name, from sectors of the electorate that were otherwise indifferent, so one cannot form an accurate assessment of the strength of the German Right simply by using these figures. In fact, in *all* the elections that would take place in Germany down to 1933, the Social Democrats, together with the Communists and the Centre, obtained an absolute majority, even if the margin was a narrow one. This majority was composed, sociologically, of the greater part of the industrial working class, a significant share of other salaried or wage-earning groups, and sections of the Catholic peasantry and petty bourgeoisie. Despite all the mistakes of the pro-Weimar parties, despite their internal divisions and the catastrophic nature of the period, the pro-capitalist nationalist Right could still not win power by legal parliamentary means. To the very end what ruled that out was the sheer strength, in numbers, of the workers and other wage-earners who supported the Marxists and the Catholic Centre. To succeed, the counter-revolution was compelled to take recourse to extra-parliamentary methods. Ideological fascism had to be supplemented by the terrorist fascism of the storm-troops.

Stormtrooper-fascism in Germany developed out of the *Freikorps*, which had to be installed by the government of the German Republic as early as 1919, and much against its will. The ruling majority that supported the Republic had to defend itself, at that time, against the attacks of small, ultra-left groups of workers. However, the Republic was incapable of forming an army recruited from the more trustworthy democrats and socialists, but once again confided its fate to the Imperial officer-corps. Demobilised officers then collected together other similarly unemployed veteran-elements. It was these squads that suppressed the so-called Spartacist uprisings of 1919–20. In a formal sense, the officers were deployed to defend the Republic. However, most of them were in their heart of hearts supporters of the old régime. They fought the radical wing of the workers' movement and looked forward to the time when they could wreak vengeance on the authors of the November Revolution. In strictly objective terms, this triumphal march of the *Freikorps* disarmed the labour-movement and signified a re-arming of the counter-revolution. Those elements of the bourgeoisie who were opposed to the Republic and hostile to the workers' movement soon grasped the new elements in the situation and established contact with the *Freikorps*.

The *Freikorps* was not content with the services it rendered to the German Republic in 1919, but fought its own private war in the Baltic. There it struggled initially against Bolshevism, then against the Latvians and Estonians, formed an alliance with the Russian White Guards, and transformed the Baltic into the central theatre of the German counter-revolution. The Baltic adventure had roughly the same significance for German fascism as the Fiume episode had had for the Italian Fascists. When, under Entente pressure, the *Freikorps* was forced to evacuate the Baltic, it decided immediately on a *coup d'état* in Germany. The Kapp Putsch of 1920 was smashed by the resistance of the working class, but also floundered on the disunity that plagued the German counter-revolutionary forces. Elements closest to the *Freikorps* had rushed into battle before unifying completely with the major capitalist parties and movements. So from the very first days of the Kapp Putsch, the front of counter-revolutionaries splintered, and there was no means of patching it up. Only Bavaria showed a well-planned conspiracy and an effective collaboration between the illegal armed organisations and the perfectly legal bourgeois political parties. In Bavaria the conspirators seized power in 1920, and legalised their coup with the help of the bourgeois majority in the state-government (*Landtag*). When in the rest of the country Kapp's retreat was followed by a renewed consolidation of the Republican government, the Bavarian counter-revolution gave the appearance of once more adapting to the constitutional framework. From that time on, German fascism found its legal basis in Munich. All conspirators who could not stay in other parts of the country found a cordial reception in Bavaria, and it was in Munich that preparations could proceed, without hindrance, for further assaults on democracy in Germany.

The defeat of the Kapp Putsch did not bring about any real strengthening of the democratic Republic in Germany. When the government established the official *Reichswehr*, part of the *Freikorps* stayed outside the ranks of the regular army. On paper the *Freikorps* had been dissolved, in reality it continued to exist, in all possible disguises. Apart from this organisation, there was a whole mass of other organisations – 'leagues' and 'associations' – that recruited students and other activist elements of the German counter-revolution. Definite links persisted between the officers in the regular army and their comrades in the so-called 'Defence Associations'. The attacks on the Poles in Upper Silesia soon provided a further occasion for the mobilisation of the *Freikorps*. When in 1923 the government of big capital, headed by Cuno, initiated military operations against the French troops in occupation of the Ruhr, it formed a regular reserve-force called the 'Black Army', with the help of the *Freikorps*. Instead of the official policy of passive resistance, individual groups of *Freikorps*-elements started active resistance against the French. Other elements of the *Freikorps* made attempts to assassinate prominent leaders of the Weimar Republic. Erzberger and Rathenau became victims of this campaign of assassination. Over the same years, 1923–4, the *Freikorps* and various Army Leagues developed the habit of trying and executing real or imaginary traitors.

Down to the end of 1923 the German Republic lived in constant fear of a new counter-revolutionary coup by the *Freikorps*, the veterans' leagues and their supporters. Moreover, at that time there was a whole series of government-officials, especially in the army, who maintained close contact with the *Freikorps* and the counter-revolutionaries. The German democratic Republic was completely undermined and destroyed by the power of big capital, the large estate-owners and all the friends of the old régime in the army, judiciary and civil administration. However, the illusory appearance (*der Schein*) of a democratic and parliamentary Republic was always maintained, and so the German fascists could even play the convenient rôle of revolutionaries who were working for the day when the 'German people' would punish the 'November criminals'.

The *völkisch* [racist] movement arose after 1919 as a product of the active collaboration of the *Freikorps* with the student-youth. As early as 1919, *the vast majority of German students were already advocating the ideology which is today called National Socialist* – this at a time when, in most German universities, Adolf Hitler was a complete non-entity. The well-known leader of the Baltic expedition, Graf von der Goltz would later write an important essay on the 'patriotic leagues' in Germany, in which he discusses the possibility of seizing power on the basis of the *völkisch* action-groups, but does not deem it necessary to say even a single word about Hitler and the SA. That was in 1928. In the Reichstag elections of that year, the National Socialists polled a total of only 800,000 votes in the whole of Germany. They were an insignificant splinter-group in the country's massive Right. In 1928 it seemed much more likely that the *Stahlhelm* would unite all the German army-leagues and establish a *völkisch* state.

About the students, Goltz wrote at the time:

> When German youth came home from the trenches and the storms of steel, when they found that this homeland of theirs bore not the least resemblance to their ideals – ideals for which they had shed blood in other countries – when, with this terrible sense of deception, they joined the universities in Germany, there this whole war-generation of German students united with the sworn purpose of propagating in peace-time the very ideas and ideals that could not be realised in the war. From this awareness there arose the *Deutscher Hochschulring*, [a university-based association] which established local branches in all the universities. They accomplished their first serious action when they forcibly stopped the surrender of flags and standards won by Germany in her epoch of greatness, when they removed these from the arsenal and burnt them at the foot of the statue of the King of Prussia, singing of the God who detested slavery. But propaganda was not enough, they brought into being the working student who finances his own studies through the work he does, who has no pride of place, who stands shoulder to shoulder with workers, as he did in the trenches. The committees established by the new government to attract the support of the mass of students were soon captured by those students who carried the idea of freedom deep in their heart. The university-circles work for a unified German race that would draw together all the forces who, from a sense of their own common descent, history and culture, yearn for a German community of the German masses (*die deutsche Volksgemeinschaft aller Deutschen*) and thereby a re-establishment of the power of our people and our fatherland. It does not recognise the new boundaries and works jointly with German students in German Austria, Sudetenland and Danzig. It refuses to recognise distinctions among students, and repudiates only those who are enemies of the people.

On the programme common to all the German *völkisch* groups, army-leagues and former *Freikorps*, Goltz states the following:

> The enemies of the patriotic associations are twofold – the Social Democrats who are disposed to subversion and closely related to the Bolsheviks, and among whom, in times of crisis, precisely the radical elements gain the upper hand; and the materialistic, international, pacifist, destructive stock-exchange Speculators, who lack all ideals and have not the slightest feeling for the homeland, for indigenous values, blood-relationship, history, race, religion and the spiritual, psychological and moral uplift of the people. These two enemies are kindred souls, they almost always work together politically and in terms of party-politics. Both draw their spiritual and financial leadership from the Jews, a race whose sense of belonging stems purely from its rootlessness and its dispersion across the face of the earth, a history that spans two thousand years. Due to the massive immigration of the Eastern Jews since 1918, Jewry has become a danger to the state, as even the more intelligent and earlier Germanised 'conservative' Jews openly admit. It is quite deplorable that that other supranational power, Rome's Ultramontanism, collaborates with these subversive forces, even though they are its lethal enemies. But the supranational idea of stopping the national, racial and military rise of Greater Germany appears to be the stronger one. For this reason the dominant black-red-gold International is a threat to the future of the German people. From this flows the crucial task of insulating our people, especially the workers, from the influence of these circles. One day the time will come when the worker will see that it's not the German entrepreneur but the big capitalists of the Entente and imperialism who are his true exploiters and the ones really responsible for his miserable economic condition. The worker will then acknowledge us, his German comrades, bound to him by national and racial bonds, as his true friends and saviours.

All you need in this passage are the words 'Führer' and 'National Socialism' and you have here, already in 1928, the whole of Hitler's programme of 1933. Indeed, in his campaign against the German mother-tongue the *völkisch* Graf came to form a good intellectual companion of the Führer. A national mass-movement is inconceivable without an ideology peculiar to it. This is why the forces of the German counter-revolution, the capitalists and their lackeys, were compelled to forge an appropriate *Weltanschauung*, once they went to the masses after 1919. In bourgeois society the intellectuals have the specific function of elaborating the *Weltan-*

schauung necessary for the survival of capitalism, and the German academic intelligentsia has always devoted itself to this task with complete integrity. To this end they returned to the forms and conceptions of the prewar epoch, so far as these were usable under the new relationships.

German academics came of age, in the years after 1871, with a truly pious sense of devotion to Prussian militarism. The successive victories of the Prussian army in 1864, 1866, and 1870–1, were decisive blows that defeated German liberalism forever. Bismarck broke the backbone of the German bourgeoisie. Sections of this class now began to look on their liberal or democratic past with a sense of shame, and to look for a new way of life (*Lebensform*) that would blend service and obedience with an overbearing nationalism. One owed service as well as obedience to the authorities that ruled the nation. Thus even the relations of civilian life began to be reflected through the prism of 'superiors' and 'subordinates'. The men in uniform were the superiors (*der Vorgesetzte*) of anyone out of uniform, of all ordinary people. The government-official behind the counter was the superior of the public, the entrepreneur the superior of his workers and office-staff. The Prussian officer-corps became the model to which the younger elements of the propertied and educated bourgeoisie aspired. Whoever could not become an active officer would at least join the war-colleges or become a reserve-officer.

This readiness to render obedience to superiors, regardless of who they happened to be, found its complement in a crude nationalist arrogance, a hatred of everything that was not of German origin. For an arrogant and counterfeit aristocracy of this kind, hatred of the Jews is a perfectly apt pursuit. For in the Jew one comes to see the opposite of oneself, and the permanent delusion of Jewish 'inferiority' only reinforces the sense of one's own 'superiority'. In fact, the new German academic élites saw in 'the' Jew an image of all those qualities which they condemned. The Jew was perceived as a typical modern liberal, as the kind of person incapable of blind obedience, who would form his own ideas, who would not genuflect before authority, but use his capacities for rational thought. Antisemitism began to gain ground in the universities of Germany roughly after 1878, precisely in the years when the political defeat of German liberalism became obvious. Professor von Treitschke, based in Berlin, became the prophet of this racist-academic aristocracy.

For reasons cited earlier, in the Imperial epoch this academic antisemitism was as little capable of evolving into a political mass-movement as Stöcker's more petty-bourgeois and working-class tendency. Nevertheless, down to the War, racial antisemitism preserved its full vigour in the German universities and in German academic circles of Christian descent. Again, it was a Berlin professor, Gustav Röthe, who became the most celebrated representative of this type of thinking later in the reign of Wilhelm II. After 1919, as the German intelligentsia sought desperately to counterpose to democracy and socialism a new, national (*volkstümliche*) outlook, this prewar antisemitism gained a new lease of life. Now it was not enough just to be nationalist; rather, the youth of Germany had to develop populist-racist (*völkisch*) feelings, and endorse purity of race and rejection of the foreign Jewish element.

German heavy industry and big capital, which gained huge profits in the period of inflation, were from the start zealous promoters of *völkisch* ideas. They saw in them a means of eradicating the hateful trade-unions and, more widely, the influence of socialism over the masses. The inventory of *völkisch* ideas included the slogan of a 'true national community' (*Volksgemeinschaft*), to which, generously, workers too would be admitted, as long as they abjured the destructive and false theory of class-struggle. If the movement could gather momentum only because it supplemented its attacks on the 'Reds' with attacks on Jewish capital, so be it, at least the Christian and 'Germanic' heavy industrialists and bankers were not in the least bothered. On the contrary, *völkisch* and antisemitic slogans gave them a brilliant chance to replicate on German soil a manoeuvre notoriously characteristic of populist nationalisms worldwide – namely, instigating a movement that serves the interests of big capital but *appears* anti-capitalist at public meetings. The *völkisch* agitators found they could best take the wind out of the socialist sail with thunderous speeches against Jewish usurers' capital and calls for the destruction of 'interest-slavery'.

At first, in the period after 1919, the *völkisch* movement in Germany was not linked to any specific political party. On the contrary, it permeated *all* parties, organisations, legal and illegal associations of the bourgeois, anti-democratic Right. When the Kapp putschists and Baltic adventurers marched into Berlin in 1920, under the leadership of Captain Ehrhardt, they carried the *völkisch* swastika on their steel-helmets. Of the several million voters who supported the bourgeois Right in the various elections from 1919 to 1928, the majority were more-or-less infected by *völkisch* ideas. Above all, to the German intelligentsia of this period *völkisch* theory formed the gospel of the new Germany, the coming 'Third Reich'. Adolf Hitler himself was not the author of any of this, yet, due to a special configuration of circumstances, he could later exploit it to his and his party's advantage.

On 9 November 1918 the socialist labour-movement in Germany appeared to have all the trumps in its hand. But its influence declined rapidly after that. By 1920, due to the mistakes made and the disunity among workers, it was already a spent force, and the Centre Party had to take over leadership of the national government. The chancellors who came from this party, namely, Fehrenbach and Wirth, tried to save of German democracy whatever there was to be saved. Yet within two years their reserves were likewise spent. The government of the German Republic then fell into the hands of open representatives of big capital: Cuno's government of 1923 was, if you like, already the victory of legal fascism. The terrible crisis of 1923, which brought the German state and economy to the brink of collapse, found the German working class split and incapable of action. Towards the close of that year, it seemed as if the death-agony of German capitalism would be followed not by a socialist revolution, but, on the contrary, by a fascist dictatorship. In the country as a whole and in the individual states, the parliaments were reduced to defenceless empty forms. The executive lay in the hands of the army-generals. Attempted resistance by workers in Hamburg, Saxony and Thuringia rapidly fell to pieces. Yet in the spring of 1924 the military state of emergency (*Ausnahmezustand*) came to a bloodless and quiet end, and peace-time parliamentary democracy celebrated its return to life. Now started the longest spell of a firm, secure existence that the German Republic was ever destined to live through – the years from 1924 to 1929. But as the world-economic crisis swept across Germany in 1929, the evolution of German fascism resumed from roughly the point at which it had ceased at the end of 1923.

The astonishing revival of the constitutional Republic that set in after 1924 was not the work of the Democrats and Social Democrats; quite the contrary, the true Republican forces had been completely routed and reduced to impotence by the end of 1923. The shift was in fact a product of foreign intervention. World-capital, and chiefly the big American banks, were favourable to the idea of investing their surplus-billions in Germany. The so-called settlement of the reparations-issue that followed around this time formed the basis for this gigantic influx of capital. Now if the Americans were going to invest their money in Germany, they desired an undisturbed and peaceful democracy there. By the end of 1923 the leading German capitalists had come to realise that they would have to liquidate the adventure in the Ruhr. Passive resistance was therefore called off, and negotiations begun with world-capital. As a result, the prospect of an open fascist dictatorship in Germany was likewise called off, and the ruling powers, the big industrialists and bankers, the General Staff of the army and the top echelons of the bureaucracy, swung back to legality in a U-turn that was as sudden as it was elegant. Individual groups of nationalist conspirators and *Freikorps*-elements who did not grasp this turn fast enough were brought to heel with bullets. Hitler and the National Socialists in Munich were among the several forces stranded by this sudden swing back to democracy.

The origins of the Nazi Party back in 1920 are worth noting. As the name National Socialist 'Workers' Party' already shows, the original aim of the party was the creation of a new national workers' movement that could form an alternative pole of attraction – opposed to the Communists and Social Democrats. The famous programme of 24 February 1920 clearly contained many petty-bourgeois confusions, but side-by-side with these there were some distinctly socialist measures, for example, Point 13 relating to the nationalisation of all enterprises that lacked any significant private ownership. If Hitler had put Point 13 of the programme into actual practice on coming to power, then Germany really would have become a socialist state. That Hitler had not the remotest intention of carrying through his own party-programme is another matter. Moreover, serious propaganda for the programme as a whole would from the very start have put the Nazis into principled opposition to all the groupings of the *völkisch* counter-revolution. But Hitler and his cadre rapidly fell back into the usual rut of the *völkisch* movement. The party which they formed in Munich and the surrounding areas over the years 1920–3 was a typical *völkisch Freikorps*-party with its usual share of academics, dilettantes, adventurist officers and soldiers, its capitalist financiers and petty-bourgeois camp-followers. They had the necessary contacts in the army, and the SA was originally nothing more than the Munich branch of the Black Army. Thus, even in those years, Hitler's entire propaganda-campaign was pursued with the overt connivance of the counter-revolutionary elements in the Bavarian government.

The number of actual industrial workers who joined the Nazis in the first few years was negligible, percentage-wise no higher than the proportion of workers derailed into the other racist organisations in Germany. Nevertheless, the socialist elements of the Nazi programme were of extraordinary significance in the later years. While they obviously failed to do so in 1923, in the next major crisis to affect the country's economy and society the Nazis could successfully project themselves, to dispossessed masses, as the true socialists in Germany. The Nazis played a double rôle, one which none of the other *völkisch* organisations in Germany were able to play. When the *Stahlhelm* or Captain Ehrhardt assured the working class that the German worker was their fraternal comrade, this made scarcely any impression on the proletarian masses. The Nazis, in contrast, relying on their socialistic propaganda, made much more rapid headway in the impoverished and immiserised sectors of the population. But at the same time, the Nazi leadership would tell their financial backers among the big capitalists whatever the latter wished to hear. This dual character of the Nazi movement (*Dieser Doppelcharakter der Nazibewegung*) would speed up Hitler's seizure of power in precisely the way that afterwards it contributed to the disintegration of his party and political base.

Apart from their influence on workers, the radical and partly socialist elements of the Nazi programme had one further important result. The *Freikorps*-leaders and all the adventurist types who play a rôle in the German fascist counter-revolution are reliable auxiliaries of the capitalists and of the ruling powers more generally, in their struggle against Marxism and the trade-unions. However, they are not satisfied with merely refortifying the old order; rather, they themselves aspire to power. They do not eradicate the Marxists so that the General Staff of the regular army, the higher bureaucracy and its legal experts, the big landowners and the industrialists can rest in peace again. On the contrary, these adventurers and professional revolutionaries want power for themselves. They want to become generals themselves, or police-superintendents or all-powerful chiefs of some new organisation. Legal fascism (*Der legale Faschismus*) is of no use to them, because then the old power-holders remain in their respective positions. They need a violent revolution, or at least the appearance of one, because they personally cannot come to power by any other means. To give an ideological underpinning to their opposition to the established authorities, these fascist professional revolutionaries incline to the greatest possible radicalism in their formulations.

They profess National Socialism not because they actually want to bring about any such thing, but because this is the slogan under which they can successfully fight for their share of power and of worldly goods.

The socialist side of the Nazi programme played no significant rôle during the crisis of 1923. However, when the German big bourgeoisie made its sudden turn to legality towards the end of that year, some of the radical *Freikorps*-groups pushed on independently. In Northern Germany there was the action of the Black Army led by Major Buchrucker. In Munich the group of politicians led by Kahr immediately sought contacts with North German big capital and its new course. Independently, Hitler and the SA attempted to bring about the programme of 'national revolution' on their own and were easily suppressed by the Bavarian army.

In the years 1924–9 the German Republic appeared to be about as solid as the political systems of France or the USA: Germany basked in the radiant warmth of dollars, the Mark was stable, and foreign loans inundated the country. Suddenly, the big capitalists and the agrarians were supporters of democracy and of the rule of law, and consequently the leaders of the DNVP and DVP were likewise in favour of positive co-operation within the constitutional framework. The governments of the bourgeois bloc exercised power in the country in conditions defined by peace and legality, and the Social Democrats likewise formed a peaceful and legal opposition down to 1928. After that the Social Democrats re-entered the national government in coalition with the bourgeois parties in the centre (*den bürgerlichen Mittelparteien*). Because the leading layers of German capitalism now favoured legality, former *Freikorps*-elements were often quite badly handled, rather like poor relatives one is now ashamed of. The small Nazi Party no longer received funds from industrialists, and the judiciary began to convict in cases involving political executions (*die Fememörder*). At public hearings these heroes of the *völkisch* movement were tried in the same way as ordinary murderers, and the official prosecutors from the army could not recall ever having had anything to do with the *Freikorps*-people on trial. True, no death sentences were handed down for such assassinations – that was reserved for Hitler to do in 1934 (Heine and others) – but they received long sentences in jail (when they were caught) and were glad if they got out on general political amnesties.

In spite of everything, the stability of the German democratic Republic in the years 1924–9 was a pure illusion. The Weimar constitution remained firm as long as the loans came in from America. Once the flow of dollars ceased, it collapsed. In those years, the Social Democrats and centrist parties made no new moral gains. Compared to 1924, the percentage of Marxist votes in the national elections showed no perceptible increase. Within the bourgeois camp, the German Democratic Party (DDP) sank into pure insignificance, and within the Centre Party the truly democratic wing continuously lost ground. Apart from the Catholic bourgeoisie and landowners, even the influential Christian trade-union leaders developed an aversion to democracy: they collaborated with the DNVP within the various coalitions dominated by the bourgeois bloc, and were not averse to participating in experiments in fascism when the situation changed.

While democracy was losing its power of attraction over the workers organised behind the Centre Party, the millions of voters who generally supported the various right-wing parties retained their basic political and social conceptions. The great masses of the Protestant middle-class, the right-wing office-employees (*Angestellten*), civil servants and so on remained racist (*völkisch*) and antisemitic. They loathed the black-red-gold Republic and the Marxist 'big-shots' and longed for the time when the spirit of King Frederic and the black-white-red flag would once more rule Germany. The leaderships of the DNVP and DVP, with their Republican *Realpolitik*, were deluded about the real mood and feelings of their own electoral base. It is true that the average Protestant, including those who owned farms or worked in offices, voted for the DNVP, DVP or *Wirtschaftspartei* [Economic Party] over the years from 1924 to the Depression; but only as long as their material circumstances were tolerable and as long as these various parties appeared to guarantee the continued possibility of earning an income. But as soon as a new crisis emerged, the groundswell of *völkisch* anti-Republican sentiment re-exploded among sections of the electorate who voted for the Right. And of course, the leading German capitalists were at best 'Republicans by convenience'. Whenever it seemed necessary, they were always ready to re-extend support to dictatorship and fascism. As the storm of the Great Depression (1929–30) broke over Germany, the six peaceful years of the constitutional Republic were suddenly wiped out, and Germany reverted to the situation that had prevailed at the end of 1923.

In these six years, the German labour-movement had stagnated both in numbers and in terms of actual energy. True, the Social Democrats would increase their support at the Communists' expense, but only because the economic situation had visibly improved. The actual course of development appeared to contradict the gloomy forecasts of the Communists. The legal methods pursued by Social Democracy thus appeared perfectly justified. On this basis, the SPD could win votes in the national elections and retain its dominance in the individual states and districts. The unions made important practical gains for the organised workers. But even given all this, the socialist movement became the prisoner of Republican legality, and knew no other solution once a new revolutionary situation re-emerged after 1929. Over those very same years the KPD for its part wound up in total dependence on Stalin's Russian diplomacy. The independent life of the party was stifled from the top. One could attract a few million votes in Germany with empty, radical slogan-mongering and by exploiting the authority of the Russian Revolution. But as far as any real, proletarian-revolutionary action was concerned, the official KPD was totally useless.

The various *völkisch* groupings, the *Stahlhelm*, the Pan-German League, the leagues of officers and students, and all the other bigger and smaller organisations of the Right, did their best to survive the (for them) bleak years of the mid-1920s and to keep their message alive. However, they were all more-or-less dependent on the much bigger DNVP and were in some sense co-responsible for that party's legal opportunism. When the turning-point of 1924 came, it became clear, to everyone's surprise, how much the authority and control of these older organisations over the *völkisch* masses had actually declined. An independent German-*völkisch* political party that was founded in North Germany in these years went into dissolution almost immediately. On the other hand, Hitler succeeded in keeping the National Socialist Party alive, even if on a minuscule scale. Ever since November 1923, the National Socialists had broken their links with the army, the big bourgeoisie and the ruling bureaucracy. Therefore it was now free – undeterred by any obstacles – to launch the sharpest attacks on the existing régime and on all parties connected to it in any way, from the DNVP itself down to the Social Democrats. Of course, as long as the economic situation showed some stability, the Nazis made no significant electoral gains. Thus, in the Reichstag elections of 1928 Hitler obtained only 800,000 votes. But the mere existence of his party had the same impact on the millions of *völkisch* voters behind the DNVP that the tiny Spartacus League had had on the millions who supported the USPD in 1919 and 1920.

Starting in 1929, the economic crisis would create in Germany all the objective conditions (*alle objektiven Möglichkeiten*) for a decisive upsurge of revolutionary socialism. Although neither the SPD nor the KPD were capable of turning the situation to their own advantage, the capitalists were profoundly uneasy as they confronted an army of millions of unemployed and the growing impoverishment of the middle-class. To continue to rely on the methods of democracy in such times was too dangerous for the capitalist class. In short, it took a decisive turn in support of dictatorship. The coalition between Social Democracy and the bourgeois centre fell to pieces, and in 1930 the new national Chancellor Brüning formed the first of several régimes that were now strictly authoritarian dictatorships. In the national elections of that year, the Nazis' share of the vote increased, at one go, from 800,000 (in 1928) to 6.4 million.

In fact, the voting patterns describe the rise of the fascist mass-movement in Germany better than any words could. A comparison of the four Reichstag elections of 1928, 1930, July 1932 and March 1933 leads to the following conclusions. The total number of votes cast (in millions) during those four elections were: 30.7, 34.9, 37, and finally 39.3. As you can see, in these five years (1928–33) and under the pressure of the crisis, the politicisation of the German masses showed an extraordinary advance. The total number of voters increased by roughly 8½ million. The new voters comprised both apathetic layers who had been drawn into the political vortex, and youth who had come of voting age. The table below summarises the results, grouping the SPD, KPD and smaller socialist splinters under 'Marxist', and the Centre Party and the German Democratic Party under 'Democrats':

(millions of votes)	**1928**	**1930**	**Jul. 1932**	**Mar. 1933**
Marxists	12.6	13.2	13.3	12.0
Democrats	5.3	5.4	5.0	4.7
The Right, including Nazis	12.7	16.2	18.3	22.5
Nazis only	0.8	6.4	13.7	17.3

As the reader can see, the Marxists and the old Republican parties made no progress. The politicisation of newer layers was of no special use to them. What they may have gained in terms of new voters, they lost with the older ones. As against this, compare the expansion of the right-wing parties. In a political landslide without precedent, the total number of votes cast in favour of parties of the Right that were opposed to democracy almost doubled over five years. They alone were the beneficiaries of the huge influx of new masses into the electorate. Apart from which, they captured a significant share of the votes that had traditionally gone to the Left and centrist parties. Excluding the Nazis, the Right-parties obtained the followings totals: 11.9 million, 9.8 million, 4.4 million, and 5.2 million. It follows that in this period of five years, almost 7 million long-standing supporters of the *völkisch* Right cast their votes for Hitler. The curve of Nazi expansion is perceptible in the figures given in the last row above. The 16½ million *new* votes that the Nazis won over these five years might be broken up roughly as follows: 7 million traditional right-wing voters, 8½ million completely new voters, 1 million former Left-voters. In reality, the number of former Left-voters who went over to Hitler was almost certainly higher than that, since a corresponding number of new voters would have supported the Left.

In the last relatively free national elections to be held in Germany, on 5 March 1933, the Nazis won a total of 17.3 million votes, the other right-wing parties (including the Bavarian People's Party (BVP), counted here, as always, with the Right) 5.2 million. The Marxists won 12 million votes, the Centre and the Democrats 4.7 million. It may be hazardous to try and correlate these figures with the break-up by occupational groups that I cited earlier, viz., the distinction between self-employed + family-members (28%), industrial workers (32%), other wage-earners/employees (40%). Because industrial workers in the strict sense formed barely a third of the total number of voters, it follows that, despite all the unfavourable factors of these years, *almost the entire factory-based working class, including the greater part of the unemployed, remained true to their earlier convictions*. The following table is purely tentative, and may well contain major errors as far as details go. But taken as a whole, it gives a useful picture of the situation:

(Voting for, in millions)	Marxists	Parties of the Right	Centre Party & Democrats
Workers	10.0	1.0	2.0
Property-owners	0	10.0	1.0
Other wage-earners	2.0	11.5	1.7

In particular, the older factory-workers remained true to their class-consciousness at a time when the terror of the Brownshirts swept through Germany. The same is true of the vast majority of the unemployed. Moreover, not many of the workers organised in the Christian trade-unions fell for the bombastic propaganda of Nazism. On the other hand, the overwhelming majority of white-collar workers, of government-employees, and of jobless middle-class elements (*Berufslosen*) swung over to the Nazis. The electoral results from Berlin show that the suggested correlation between voting patterns and social class must, broadly speaking, be correct. In the district of Wedding, a stronghold of the industrial working class and the unemployed, as late as March 1933 the Marxists could win as many as 147,000 votes, and the Nazis a mere 62,000. The DNVP and DVP together polled just 16,000 votes. In the district of Zehlendorf, where the propertied bourgeoisie predominated, the Nazis got 18,000 votes, the Marxists 11,000, and the DNVP and DVP together 12,000. In the district of Steglitz, a residential area typified by white-collar and government employees, the Nazis got 63,000, the Marxists 34,000, and the DNVP + DVP 31,000. *So even as late as March 1933 the vast majority of industrial workers stood behind the Marxist parties*, whereas a strong turnout for the Nazis and the Nationalists (DNVP) actually reflected the low proportion of working-class families in those districts. The Nazis obtained their best results in areas dominated, socially, by white-collar and government-employees (*die Angestellten und Beamten*). However, where the affluent bourgeois element was more conspicuous, the DNVP did better.

All of which shows that Marxist socialism failed to have any traction with the masses in Germany precisely at a time of the most frightful economic misery and of strong mass interest in politics. Neither the SPD nor the KPD had any programme for the revival of Germany that the masses could find credible. To the vast majority of the German people the Communists came across as unreliable phrase-mongerers, while the Social Democrats appeared as part-responsible for the Weimar Republic and its capitalist order. That the older generation of workers remained faithful to the Red Flag is hugely to their credit and inspires one with considerable hope for the future. But in 1933 this loyalty could not alter Germany's fate. The various strata of the wage-earning population whose class consciousness was less firmly established, less tried and tested – the younger elements, apathetic layers, white-collar workers, the lower civil servants, craft-apprentices, agricultural workers – *all* rushed to the Swastika.

In the years when the Nazis were weak and capital could dispense with them, the German industrialists cared little for them. But when Hitler suddenly came to control some 6 million votes, contacts between big capital and the Swastika were re-established at the level they had reached in 1923. Leading big industrialists and bankers funded the growing financial needs of the Brown House (the Nazi headquarters). This section of the German big bourgeoisie welcomed the coming National-Socialist dictatorship and was prepared to accept the possibility that the Nazis would absorb all the other parties of the German bourgeoisie. The socialistic phrase-mongering used by Nazi agitators at public meetings scarcely bothered the pro-Nazi capitalists. They knew this was only a theatre-show for fools. What mattered most was Hitler's drive to destroy Marxism and ward off a Bolshevik revolution in Germany. But another section of German capitalists, as well as the big landowners, remained more pensive. For all the trust one might place in Hitler himself, the day-to-day agitation of the

Nazis stirred up such strong anti-capitalist feelings that this section thought some bulwark was necessary against the left or radical wing of the Nazi Party. This explains why powerful figures in German economic life and their political friends were unwilling to join the Nazis, but on the contrary sought to keep the DNVP alive, side-by-side with Hitler's party.

That is why even after 1930, initially two forms of German fascism persisted: on the one hand, the Nazis themselves, with their peculiar, historically rooted, double character (*Doppelcharakter*) which simultaneously promised both a renewal of German capitalism and the creation of German socialism; on the other hand, the old German conservatives in the DNVP, who were having trouble keeping the remnants of a once-substantial party together and sought to prop themselves up with the *Stahlhelm*, which was itself in sharp decline. This second tendency wanted absolutely nothing to do with socialism, and stood unambiguously and unconditionally for bourgeois private property. Next to and apart from these, there was yet a third form of German fascism that possessed no significant following either among the masses or in the top layers of the bourgeoisie, but happened to be able to exercise power in Germany in 1930–2 by exploiting a favourable conjuncture. They were the so-called 'Popular Conservatives' (*die Volkskonservativen*), or the Brüning tendency. It is true that Chancellor Brüning himself came ultimately from the ranks of the Centre Party, but his politics had nothing in common with the traditions of the Centre Party. He borrowed his ideas about government from a group of former *deutschnationale* politicians who styled themselves 'Popular Conservatives'.

The Popular Conservatives were unquestioned opponents of the Republic's democracy. They wanted an authoritarian government that would serve the interests of capital and of the ruling powers. Brüning based his government on emergency-decrees that were issued by the *Reichspräsident*, which the Reichstag would subsequently *have* to ratify. Brüning and the Popular Conservatives sought to throw the whole burden of the crisis onto the shoulders of wage-earners and of the unemployed, with the help of so-called 'austerity'- measures from which the big capitalists and agrarians were totally exempt. Any resistance to this dictatorial régime was suppressed with military and police-force. However, the *Volkskonservativen* distinguished themselves from the Nazis and the DNVP by their desire to avoid any dramatic transformation in Germany and to preserve the traditional forms as far as that was possible. Perhaps even the existing trade-unions could have been allowed to survive in the new authoritarian political dispensation they envisaged, in a suitably shackled form. As I said earlier, a leading group of Christian trade-unionists had already distanced itself considerably from democracy and veered over to fascist theories. By relying specifically on these elements, Brüning forced the Centre Party and the Catholic unions to support him. At the same time, using pure blackmail-tactics, he forced the Social Democrats to go along with his emergency-decrees. He played on the threat of a Nazi government, suggesting it was inevitable if they did not support him as the lesser evil.

The Nazis and the German conservatives were, of course, basically in agreement with Brüning's nationalist positions and his economic methods. What they rejected was his policy of a slow, carefully executed absorption of the Centre Party and the Social Democrats. They yearned for an immediate and open establishment of the *völkisch* state and a total destruction of Marxism and the Catholic parties. That is why Brüning could not carry through the compromise with the Nazis which he himself strongly favoured. Hitler was given the invaluable chance of playing the opposition for two more years. Brüning's austerity-measures only made the economic position of Germany worse than it already was. The number of unemployed and of the impoverished middle-classes grew from one month to the next. Brüning's terrible policies could actually appear as the line of the German Republic, thanks to the concurrence of the Centre Party and of the Social Democrats. The last remnants of any sympathy the Weimar Republic may still have had among the broad mass of people evaporated in the two years of his régime. Yet the Nazis struck a real chord in the deep sense of despair among the people with their relentless attacks on Brüning's policies. At the same time, the big capitalists and great estate-owners also came around to rejecting Brüning's tactics. When it turned out that in fact the Chancellor had no support of any note in any section of the people, the *Reichspräsident* dismissed him. And with Brüning there ended the whole sordid episode of *Volkskonservatismus* that was such a disaster for the broad mass of wage-earners. After the two short intervals of the chancellorships of Papen and Schleicher, the two remaining factions of German fascism jointly took over power: Hitler became Chancellor of the Reich, and agreed to have the leaders of the DNVP and the *Stahlhelm* in his cabinet.

The massive expansion of the Nazis after 1929 ushered in the heyday of the *Sturmabteilung* (SA). The old *Freikorps*-leaders, demobilised officers and academics who thirsted for civil war witnessed an influx of hundreds of thousands into the storm-troops which they controlled. It was chiefly the unemployed of all categories that joined the SA. Precisely because the stormtroopers attracted those who had been thrown out of work and were feeling quite desperate by now, *the proletarian element was more strongly represented in the SA than in Hitler's general electoral base.* Following a model Mussolini had established, the SA started a pogrom-style guerrilla-war against the Marxists, under Brüning's chancellorship. In fact Brüning's government, externally at least, had many points of resemblance with the last liberal governments of Italy. Like them, it was suspended in a political void and had no support among the masses. Like them, it promised justice to all sections, but could not stop the police and the judiciary from aiding and abetting the fascists when they attacked the workers. Brüning himself and the other Popular Conservatives in the cabinet would never have sanctioned pogroms against the Left on their own initiative. But German capital and the bulk of the intelligentsia were jubilant when the SA took decisive action against the 'Marxist traitors', and this mood permeated the police, the judiciary and other organs of the state. Wherever individual Social-Democrat ministers still held office in the individual states, their potential influence was paralysed by the situation prevailing in the country as a whole. The workers defended themselves against the attacks of the stormtroopers as well as they possibly could. Even as late as 1933, they would certainly have defeated the SA, if the police had remained truly neutral. In fact, whenever the workers took to armed struggle against the stormtroopers, they regularly had to face police-squads that were heavily armed and specially trained for civil warfare. Moreover, it was common knowledge that behind the SA and the police there stood the army, as the final and strongest reserve-force of capitalism. From the very beginning this awareness paralysed the power of resistance of the German working class, and led to the tragic (though, in the given circumstances, perfectly explicable) destruction of its movement in the year 1933.

The SA perpetrated the worst acts of violence against organised labour. It embodied a form of fascist terror that specially targeted Marxists and Jews. Yet, at the same time, it constituted the most proletarian element within the Nazi movement. Within its ranks one saw a fusion of the older professional revolutionaries who had come straight out of the *Freikorps* and of those unemployed workers who had become embittered and demoralised and were thoroughly confused about Marxism. Admittedly, in 1929–30 the SA fought the battles German capitalism wanted fought, but it was never a merely pliant tool of the bourgeoisie. Even for Hitler it formed a permanent threat, once he professed his open support for capitalism and was keen on demonstrating that with acts that would please the employers and large landowners. Obviously as long as the 'national revolution' was still unfinished and they had to settle accounts with 'the system', the Nazi Party stormed ahead, unified and resolute. The problems only came later.

Is it possible to describe the National Socialists as a 'petty-bourgeois party'? It is perfectly true that in 1933, the German middle-classes were almost solidly pro-Hitler. And yet, *any bourgeois party that aspires to become a mass-movement must win over the middle-class*. That peasants and craftsmen, office-staff and small rentiers generally voted for Hitler is not enough to transform the Nazis into a petty-bourgeois movement. For this a further condition is required – that the party should basically represent the interests of the petty bourgeoisie vis-à-vis the other classes. Before seizing power, the Nazis made far-reaching promises to the middle-class groups, just as, in fact, they promised every section of the people whatever they wanted to hear. At the very least, a truly middle-class party (*eine echte Mittelstandspartei*) would have had to close down the department-stores and consumer-cooperatives, especially if it came to power in a revolutionary way. But this did not happen. A truly peasant-party would have had to create room for the resettlement of the impoverished rural households through a re-division of the large estates. But this too failed to occur. A party of rentiers and those with savings would have had to take up the question of revaluation once more. And this, too, is something Hitler had no plans for. Finally, Nazi labour-law nowhere shows any sort of discrimination in favour of white-collar as opposed to production-line workers.

Indeed, under the German Republic, a whole series of truly petty-bourgeois movements did emerge on the political scene: there was the Economic Party of the Middle-Class, the Revaluation Party, the various peasant-leagues, and so on. One has only to compare the type of activity of these truly petty-bourgeois parties with the Nazis to be struck by the difference immediately. It is not typical of the petty bourgeoisie to enter the political fray as an independent force, in open opposition both to capitalism and to the proletariat. Rather, the petty bourgeoisie tends either to attach itself to one of the two basic social forces or to vacillate between them according to the situation. But supposing the petty bourgeoisie really does summon up the courage to play an independent political rôle, then it drags the whole baggage of petty grievances that stem from this or that professional sector onto the battlefield and raises innumerable demands of a particularistic kind. The Nazis' tactics and forms of functioning were completely different. They have never described themselves as a middle-class party, although they lay considerable emphasis on winning over the peasantry and heap every conceivable flattery on this social layer (*Stand*), true representatives of 'blood and soil'. Indeed, they have always courted workers and youth with as much zeal. It is precisely the worker, the peasant and the academic that they project as the three pillars of their power over the masses. Moreover, the 'productive', 'creative' factory-owner and entrepreneur are certainly an intrinsic part of the economic structure of the Third Reich.

The leading idea of Nazi propaganda is national renewal, a restoration of the former (*pre*-1914) dominance of the German Reich. Viewed socially, it was the big bourgeoisie that formed the chief bearer of this nationalist conception of German power in the decades leading up to 1914. It was Krupp & Co., and not some middling firm of bakers, that made money out of the German Empire. Likewise, today, too, it is Krupp and his closest colleagues who stand behind Hitler. The *völkisch* movement was a legacy of bourgeois nationalism. Obviously, to capture an industrialised Germany, it had to win over large masses of wage-earners too. The army-officers and the intelligentsia formed the connecting link between capital and labour. The petty bourgeoisie were fellow-travellers, but they never determined either the character or the true destiny of the movement. Mussolini's fascism is, in a certain sense, the party of a capitalism still capable of expansion. That is why the Italian fascists could openly support private property. Mussolini's radical programme of 1919 was of purely episodic significance, without any consequence for the subsequent fate of the movement. The Nazis, by contrast, are the party of a moribund capitalism, and to gain a foothold in proletarian Germany they are compelled to hide their capitalist character from the masses. That is why, from the very start, Hitler's dictatorship was burdened with insoluble inner contradictions that did not exist for Mussolini.

PART TWO

The growth of fascism in India

Vivan Sundaram, *Figure from History*

A subaltern fascism?

Kannan Srinivasan

This is an examination of certain aspects of the history of the Hindu Mahasabha and the political career of its sometime leader, Vinayak Damodar Savarkar.[1] By the time he came to head the Mahasabha in 1937 it had been in existence for two decades, but his leadership transformed it into a significant political force with an agenda directly opposed to the Congress and the Muslim League and to the national movement for independence. A former revolutionary terrorist, Savarkar had been incarcerated in the Andamans Cellular Jail after being sentenced in December 1910 to transportation for life and forfeiture of property for masterminding the conspiracy to assassinate A.M.T Jackson ICS, Collector of Nasik in Bombay Presidency in December 1909 and conveying the revolver employed for that purpose. In prison he became persuaded that the enemy was not the British but the Muslims and accordingly won increasing privileges. Released from imprisonment to detention, he asked for and was paid a pension, and was permitted to conduct anti-Muslim propaganda. Released from detention by the provincial Congress Government, he headed the Mahasabha from 1937 to 1942, when it set out a programme to arm Hindus against Muslims by recruiting them to the Indian army, promoting military education, influencing the administration of the princely states including their armies, gaining access to weaponry from their state forces to harass Muslims, obtaining arms licenses from sympathetic Congress ministers, attempting to set up a munitions factory at Gwalior in the expectation of support of the Darbars and the Birla industrial group, and exploring contacts with European fascists. None of this was discouraged by the British, who at the very same time suppressed anti-Nazi propaganda by left and liberal organisations. Despite its earlier praise for Mussolini and Hitler the Mahasabha hailed the proclamation of the new state of Israel in 1948 and promised it support. I shall argue that the Mahasabha pioneered what might be termed a *subaltern fascism*.[2]

Savarkar's exemplary conduct in jail won him favour.[3] When World War One began, he protested his desire to serve the war effort and asked for amnesty:

> The siding of Turkey with Germany as against England, roused all my suspicions about Pan-Islamism and I scented in that move a future danger to India. I...feared that in this grim struggle between two mighty powers the Muslims in India might find their devil's opportunity to invite the Muslim hordes from the North to ravage India and to conquer it.

To combat this he proposed a new British union with her imperial subjects where, from Ireland to India,

> an empire would emerge from the process, which can no longer be the British Empire. Until it assumed any other suitable name, it might well be called "The Aryan Empire".[4]

Savarkar's petition of 30 March 1920 claims that since he was 'without danger to the State', he should be granted a reprieve; for, far from espousing

> the militant school of the Bukanin (sic) type...I do not contribute even to the peaceful and philosophical anarchism of a Kropotkin or a Tolstoy.[5]

Accordingly, he promised that his release would be

> a new birth and would touch my heart, sensitive and submissive to kindness, so deeply as to render me personally attached and politically useful in future.[6]

George Lloyd, Governor of Bombay, later Lord Lloyd, an influential British imperialist who later administered Egypt, and a supporter of fascist movements in his subsequent political career, was persuaded not by Savarkar's grand designs but by the use to which he could be put as a former revolutionary. Accordingly, the Government periodically reviewed his loyalty. Only its assurance ensured each improvement in his living conditions and successive reductions in his sentence.

> To disarm any suspicion that may yet linger in the Government Quarters, the petitioner begs to solemnly pledge his word of honour that he shall cease to take any part in politics whatever.[7]

Thus Savarkar is said to have renounced all

> methods of violence resorted to in days gone by and I feel myself duty bound to uphold law and a constitution to the best of my powers and am willing to make the reform a success in so far as I may be allowed to do so in future.[8]

A new politics

He was released on 4th January 1924. He then published the lessons of his experience in the Andamans, which were that through his struggles he had managed to overcome every humiliation inflicted by the Muslim staff and prisoners, and persuaded the prison management to appoint him to run the key operations of the prison and subordinate the Muslims to him, thus creating 'Hindu rule'.

> CHAPTER X Miniature Hindu Raj. When I stepped into the Andamans there was in it, in prison and outside, what one may rightly call, Pathan Raj. Dressed in brief authority, the Pathan dominated the scene. It was overthrown, as I have described in this story, by the time that my stay in the prison had come nearly to an end. The Pathan Raj was gone and Hindu Raj had taken its place...The capital of that Raj was the oil-depot of the prison and as I have already mentioned before, I was its foreman and therefore the monarch of that Raj...The oil-depot being the main source of income for the Silver Jail, the man in charge of it was a person of great importance... every one connected with the oil-depot from top to bottom was a Mussalman, and mostly a Pathan...The wiliest, the

> intensely selfish, the most cunning and the most wicked person in the prison was often chosen for the job. During my seven to eight years of prison-life, an array of such men had adorned the seat. Now, in my ninth year, the seat had come to me. All the Mussulman tindals, petty officers and warders who had still remained in that jail, were full of fear that I was appointed to that office. The demi-god presiding over the oil-depot could only be propitiated by offerings in gold and silver. If the prisoner desired not to be ground down in the oil-mill of that place, they had perforce to propitiate its deity...Every single tindal began to approach me from now onwards with bated breath and in whispering humbleness. [9]

Now this seems a singular preoccupation: the warders and supposedly favoured Muslim prisoners in that remote jail may indeed have been oppressors but they were also poor men facing unattractive conditions. To triumph over them may seem like a strange achievement to record. It is stranger still that it has been so widely commended, for this is legend even for many on the Left. Savarkar had written a history of 1857 where he had spoken favourably of *jihad* against the British, and Hindu-Muslim unity against a common oppressor. That very Government still ran India at the time *Mazi janmathep* was published in 1927. Thereafter, as leader of the Abhinav Bharat Society he had led a terrorist conspiracy. Earlier he had a grand world-view, visualising Indian independence in the context of anarchist struggles and of the *Risorgimento*. Now all this is reduced to tyranny over a Pathan watchman at an oil-mill in Port Blair!

I think we can see the same world-view in his subsequent career, as he came to see mastery over Muslims in India as the single important political question, one that justified perpetuating British rule and postponing Independence. Indeed Savarkar was so transformed by his incarceration that he renounced entirely his earlier, more secular nationalism where he had approvingly employed the term *jihad* to describe how Indian Muslims took up arms against the East India Company. By blending these two phases of Savarkar's evolution, his earlier nationalism and the later culture of hatred of Muslims, the Savarkar scholar Bakhle, among others, has obscured the extent of the change that took place in Savarkar's thinking whilst at Port Blair.[10] She speaks of Savarkar's arrest by the police of an 'independent India he had fought for all his life'.[11] Yet he fought for independent India until he was incarcerated, but not, as the record shows, thereafter.

Savarkar concerned himself now especially with what he claimed was the most ancient subordination of India, namely its invasion and subsequent rule by Muslim sovereigns. This demanded the abandoning of unmanly attributes and a return to ancient warrior virtues celebrated in the Vedas. It also demanded dealing with the threat of the Muslim presence in India as the perpetual enemy within, the *outsider inside*.[12] These ideas were promptly adopted in India: his Mahasabha colleague B.S. Moonje was to describe the so-called Muslim threat from the North as follows:

> [It is] on this sector [the middle sector of the N.W. Frontier, KS] that whatever skill and manliness which we may possess have to be concentrated...Here lie... the famous passes...which have provided safe passages to enemy forces in invading India throughout its long history.[13]

Anti-caste movement to build a Hindu community

Moonje echoed Savarkar in seeing the basis of Hindu weakness in the caste system. Accordingly, the solution was to attack the caste system in order to build a larger Hindu community to fight Islam:

> Hindus generally...are known throughout the world, as meek, mild and docile people who, in their conception of spirituality and refinement, would prefer, if the Afghans were to invade India, to conquer them by love.

Moonje cites a Rao Bahadur C.V. Vaidya in support of this argument to claim that

> The result of the Caste System is that, in India, about 10% of the population is fit and disposed to fight; while the remaining 90% by nature and heredity, is...therefore, ready to accept the rule of any Nation.[14]

The anti-caste movement was to become a part of the Mahasabha agenda. On 9th April 1932, whilst interned at Ratnagiri, Savarkar spoke at a Mahar meeting of the Patit Pawan Mandir:

> the image of Patit Pawan which is standing before you will not be polluted if you touch it...Your brethren are trying to enter the Temple at Nasik, and there they are getting *lathi* blows...Have a manly spirit. A boy of your caste will now recite the Gaitri Mantras in Sanscrit...[15]

Fascism and its choice of weapons

For Savarkar, Moonje and other Mahasabha leaders the corollary to this was control of the state with its monopoly over violence. This would have to be done by *collaborating* with the dominant power in India and abroad, in other words, with Great Britain, to secure the sort of alliance that would help them prevail over the enemy at home, the Muslims in India.

Now Christophe Jaffrelot has identified difficulties in describing the Mahasabha-Sangh as fascist in the true sense, and therefore prefers to call them anti-liberal, totalitarian, and a specifically Indian variant of fascism, inviting the view that this might in an important sense be distinct from 'true fascism'.[16] Jaffrelot says:

> ...elements suggest that the RSS should be regarded as 'an Indian version of fascism'. As far as the formative years of the RSS are concerned, this expression is especially relevant if it implies that while the RSS belongs, with European fascism, to a general category of anti-liberal movements, it also represents a specifically Indian phenomenon which is not simply a reproduction of European fascism. (p. 51)

One feature he finds significant is that the RSS is committed to a *long-term* and organic change in the institutions of society by patient transformation– a trajectory quite different from the manner in which fascists have come to power elsewhere, by means of a coup or through the ballot box. According to him,

> An important difference between this totalitarianism and fascism in its various forms or Nazism is that the Indian version chose to work patiently on society over a long period rather than seizing power and constraining society from 'above' ...The RSS, by contrast, is not a putschist organisation and Golwalkar considered that Hitler's capture of the state was a mistake...it is true that it concentrates on long-term programmes rather than on the immediate capture of the state.[17]

By contrast, I would argue that the RSS should actually be seen in the context of its alliance with the other constituents of the Sangh Parivar – the Hindu Mahasabha, the Bharatiya Janata Party, the Vishwa Hindu Parishad and the Bajrang Dal. Perhaps Jaffrelot has given the RSS an autonomy it does not deserve, considering it in isolation from the other components of the Sangh Parivar. We shall see that the Mahasabha attempted to gain power by arriving at an arrangement with the Raj, so the commitment of the Sangh to patient long-term methods does not exclude other strategies; indeed several were deployed simultaneously. The extreme reverence for the state typical of Savarkar's Mahasabha was part of its strategy for a succession to the Raj as well as a classically fascist trait. It wanted to cooperate with the Raj in order to succeed it in office, which signified a considerable respect for the British Indian state and the various institutions it controlled. This also explains why the use of terror by Muslim fundamentalist groups or by gangsters has little to do with fascism, since they do not concern themselves with the state.

Secondly, the Mahasabha and RSS used their connections with sympathetic Congressmen and with the Durbars of friendly Hindu Princely States to gain access to weaponry and to other means of violence, so that they were able to intimidate, harass, and kill Muslims at the time of Partition, to drive them out of India, in order to change the demography of many regions. Their *Kristallnacht* would set the tone for many Muslim communities all over India and would play a part in changing culture as surely as the message conveyed by Hindu calendar art in a police station anywhere in India. This violence was an important *political* aim. Since they took it seriously, we should do likewise.

I suggest we *not* treat with excessive reverence the idea of a single classical fascism, with all other movements described as no more than inspired by it. In a recent paper Paul Arpaia argues that fascism is a response to the threat of democracy but not a coherent philosophy.[18] I also suggest that in subject peoples such as those of India under colonialism, not only was there a response to the challenge of Western power and the modern world, one that re-imagined the past and current religion, for instance both Hinduism and Islam,[19] but also, crucially, the threat of democracy that was posed by the mass mobilisations against colonial rule; the prospect of mass Muslim enfranchisement in the Punjab and Bengal was one that the Hindu Mahasabha recoiled from, thus embarking on a singular path which, as Jaffrelot correctly says, was anti-liberal. But this by itself is an *inadequate* description, and Jaffrelot's discussion of stigmatisation and emulation of the other is tantamount to no more than Japan's emulation of the West after July 1853.[20] The striking feature of the Mahasabha-RSS response was to see the supposed threat from the Muslim world in pathological terms. Only that can explain the ferocity of the recent pogroms in Gujarat in 2002, or the earlier ones in Bombay in 1992–93.

This anti-democratic strategy led it naturally to explore both collaboration with the Raj and emulation of the European fascists. At first sight, it seems curious that an aspirational fascist party should have been willing to cede the monopoly of force to an overseas imperial power rather than challenging it. But this is because it set out to court the prevailing coercive power in order to ensure an *authoritarian succession*. Without even control of the State, the Mahasabha's identified path to power was built on the expectation of power-sharing in a junior capacity, with the goal being reward for its service.

To return to Savarkar, on his release from imprisonment he was supported at government expense by the payment of a pension that he periodically requested be increased. Savarkar's pension was periodically reviewed as is evident in this letter from the Collector of Ratnagiri to the Home Department, Bombay.

> On 3rd January 1933, I personally informed Savarkar that his conditions would continue...He considered that the Rs. 60/- allowance was insufficient since he could be earning at least Rs. 600/- per month, but he looked forward to taking up Government Service when his conditions would be withdrawn as that fact would be proof in itself that Government had gained faith having tried him in the fire.[21]

Savarkar's activities were monitored, and he showed no sign of nationalism or any anti-British activity. When the District Magistrate told Savarkar his detention was being extended, his reaction was to plead his loyalty. He then got an item put into a local paper saying that he should be let off because he was no threat.

> Savarkar has been strictly observing the conditions imposed upon him for the last 8 or 10 years...There is peace and order in Maharashtra. It is not full of revolutionaries like Bengal. Mr. Savarkar is also devoted to activities that are harmless, to the upliftment of the untouchables.[22]

Though detained, his campaign against Muslim interests was given free rein. Supporting the right of Hindus to take out processions in front of mosques and play loud music at the time of prayer, he went on to promote this elsewhere in the Bombay Presidency and then all over India.[23] For example, advising the Hindu Mahasabha in Gharaunda in Punjab which claimed to face 'a case of the same type instituted here by the Mohammedans', he claimed that the Court in Ratnagiri had held that

> music is stopped in some places either by compromise or by courtesy; neither of these can be established a customary right...The reasons alleged are plausible but they are not sufficient ground to interfere with the inherent right of the Defts to use a public highway so long as they do so peaceably...*nuisance such as above yields no cause of action*.[24]

Such activities contributed to anti-Muslim mobilisation in India. But they did not win elections at the outset for the Mahasabha as a political party. Those to the provincial assemblies in 1937 under the new Government of India Act did not show it to be a force of great consequence.

Collaboration

But the declaration of hostilities provided the Mahasabha an opportunity to declare loyalty to the Crown and attempt to gain access to arms.[25] Hindus, according to Savarkar as President of the Mahasabha, should employ the War as an opportunity to seek high office under the Crown:

> The Hindu members must stick to their positions on the Defence bodies and the Councils...to capture as much political and military power as could possibly be done.[26]

They expected to get posts on the Viceroy's Executive Council and the War Advisory Council.[27] The Hindus, the Mahasabha leader B.S. Moonje said, are aware of the fact that 'there is no other ally other than Britain for them'.[28]

As Moonje explained in his plan for the Hindu Military Academy at Nasik, security for India lay in the Royal Navy:

> India being within the British Empire, possessing a Navy which no nation in the world at present can dare challenge, we may dismiss the question of our Naval defence for the present.[29]

Moonje quoted approvingly Sir Denys Bray, who, on retiring from the Government of India as Foreign Secretary, said that India still needed 'the generous and adventurous youths of England in her service'.[30] In this very spirit, Savarkar thanked the Viceroy

> for the ship-yard, the Aeroplane factories, the increased output of up-to-date ammunitions, the increase in the recruitment in the Military, Naval and Aerial to which Indians are allowed without any distinction of religion or caste, etc. (sic).[31]

But participation in the War became increasingly unpopular and the Congress campaign gathered force. The Mahasabha Conference that took place in Madura (later Madurai) over Christmas 1940 apprehended that the Congress strategy was succeeding. So it decided to emulate it, announcing it would start a disobedience campaign, if by 31 March 1941 the British Government had not made a satisfactory response to the demand for Dominion Status for India within a year of the end of the War.[32] Intelligence reports recorded that from the very outset there was no seriousness in this threat:

> no decision has yet been taken in regard to the manner in which "direct action" is to be launched, if launched at all.[33]

Soon even sympathetic audiences did not take these claims of the Mahasabha seriously. Savarkar proposed at a public meeting that should Japan forestall England in promising independence to India, 'she was likely to succeed in capturing the imagination of the Indian people', but this'was greeted by the audience with derisive laughter.'[34]

The Mahasabha's strategy was to acquire influence in the British Government of India in the expectation that this could be consolidated in the future, for, as the Intelligence Bureau noted, 'what weighs with him (Savarkar) most at present is the importance of conserving Mahasabha influence in places of authority '.[35]

Finally, the Mahasabha backed out of the threat to launch any "movement".[36] The Committee meeting Savarkar chaired at Calcutta on 14 and 15 June1941, held a 'patently artificial discussion' on the Madura resolution and postponed direct action indefinitely.[37]

A reorganisation proposed by Ashutosh Lahiri, General Secretary, sought the "broad-basing" of the Mahasabha. A programme 'which is exclusively dependent on the will and requirements of our foreign masters' lacked credibility. But that failed. Savarkar's objective remained what it had always been, namely, 'the establishment of Hindu domination'. To this end, he worked toward 'the strengthening of the Mahasabha hold on positions of administrative authority as and when favourable opportunities present themselves.' The former armed revolutionary terrorist now abhorred all confrontation with the Empire. 'In private discussions, the President made it clear that neither armed revolution nor "direct action" of the Congress variety was possible or likely to yield the best results.'[38]

Hindu Mahasabha policies seemed 'brazenly opportunist' to the British Director of the Intelligence Bureau.[39]At the height of the "Quit India" movement, in Punjab, "The *Hindu Mahasabha* has, at least for the time being, retired from the political arena".[40] Government informers provided it with an account of Savarkar's speech at a closed door Mahasabha meeting where Savarkar spoke of the need for a 'Hindu Army':

> it is understood that he said that independence could only be attained by resorting to arms, and Hindus should, therefore, cooperate with the British. .. If the army were Indianised Government would grant more concessions to India. He concluded with an appeal to Hindus to join the army, secure Commissions in it and develop martial spirit.[41]

The Intelligence Bureau noted the same theme prevailed in another Mahasabha meeting presided over by Madan Mohan Malaviya, Congress and Mahasabha leader, at a closed door meeting on 1 July 1941. This was 'attended by a number of Hindu Mahasabha leaders including Dr Shyama Prasad Mookerjee, Dr B.S. Moonje and Sir J.P. Srivastava...decisions were in favour of wholesale militarization of Hindus by enlistment in the army'.[42]

These policies of collaboration bore no great dividend. The Mahasabha and RSS had no mass base at the time of the transfer of power, so the British did not see any reason to reward them for their support of the War. The real significance of this Mahasabha strategy is, I suggest, that it should be seen as a precursor of the more recent eagerness to serve Western interests in South Asia.

The Military School and access to weaponry

During Savarkar's Presidency, his associate B.S. Moonje, who had travelled to Italy to meet Mussolini, worked on the Mahasabha project of a military academy with considerable British official support.[43] The Home Department and Defence Department noted in September 1935 that the "Central Hindu Military Education Society", registered in Bombay Province, was intended for "Hindus" only, to provide for their "Military rejuvenation". Prominent Mahasabha members such as Sardar Chandroji Rao Angre (who effectively ran the Gwalior Darbar), M.S. Aney and Keshav Rao Hedgewar, were Members of this Society, and Dr. B.S. Moonje of Nagpur its General Secretary. Two prominent donors were the Maharaja of Gwalior who gave Rs. 100,000 as announced in the

Times of India of 28 March 1938, and Motilal Manekchand, also known as Pratap Seth, who gave the same amount, when the Society had set its target of raising Rs 300,000. Commander-in-Chief (Sir Philip) Chetwode sponsored it in November 1935.[44] So did the Viceroy Lord Willingdon in March 1936. Willingdon's successor (Lord) Linlithgow wrote on the 10th July 1936 to express his support for 'your public spirited enterprise'.

Moonje met the Defence Secretary Sir Richard Tottenham to ask for 'permission to start a miniature range for .22 rifles'.[45] Applying for a firearms licence from A. P. LeMesurier, District Magistrate of Nasik, Moonje pointed out:

> a provincial Rifle Association was established by me in Nagpur C.P. seven years ago. It has got 5 or 6 branches in the districts of the Province of C.P. and Berar. ...Licence under rule 32 of the Rules under the Arms Act for ordinary and miniature Rifles has been granted to the Association; so that the branches need not apply for separate Licences.[46]

Tottenham endorsed this and LeMesurier recommended accordingly to the Home Department of the Government. The Bhonsla Military School was licensed under rule 32 of the Indian Arms Rules 1924, 'for target practice valid for such area as Government may prescribe'.[47] A letter from "HR" of the Home Department, Government of Bombay, to G.A. Shillidy, Deputy Inspector General of Police CID at Poona, stated:

> I know little of the objects of the School except that it is said to be anti-Muhammadan rather than anti-Government.[48]

Dr. Kurtakoti Shankaracharya said, whilst opening the school on the 21 June 1937, that India

> was mainly for Hindus even if the people of other religions lived in India. Some would rather have any rule in India than that of the British but he was content to have the British until India could defend herself.[49]

The *Times of India* reported that Moonje said:

> Britain has defended India for the last 150 years, now it is India's duty to relieve Britain of the arduous work, and to help defend the Empire.[50]

Moonje wrote to Dr Jayakar that the Commander in Chief's permission to give training employing rifles with live ammunition was historic, for

> In the 150 years (sic) history of British India, this is the first instance where permission for Target practice by actual Rifles has been granted to an Indian School.[51]

Moonje's proposal for the Bhosala Military Academy was informed by his concern to create a fascist personality from the clay of Indian manhood. Addressing the question 'Why should we establish a military school?', he answered:

> This training is meant for qualifying and fitting our boys for *the game of killing masses of men*...The same thought is repeated...by Signor Mussolini, the Maker of the Modern Italy...Germany has gone into the matter most scientifically...Revenge is one of the fundamental manly qualities of a person...we Hindus were taught on the battlefield of Panipat on one side and Plassey on the other.[52] (italics mine)

The Congress Chief Minister of the Central Provinces and Berar in 1937 was the Mahasabha sympathiser N.B. Khare. As soon as he came to office he set about the creation of a precedent by licensing Hindu schools to train students in marksmanship. Years later he answered the question as to what were his most important policies as Prime Minister of CP and Berar:

> I...gave permission for military training; I initiated a policy of starting rifle clubs attached to colleges and high schools.[53]

Savarkar wrote Khare on 1 July 1938 to note how gratifying it was that

> your government has assured the people that high schools in your province and I think presumably the colleges too will have no difficulty in future (in securing) govt. permission to introduce military training and shooting with real and up-to-date Rifles.[54]

and urged that he further this policy by setting up a military college in CP Berar.

On 21 September 1938 Savarkar circulated a copy of Khare's arms licence which laid down the terms under which such a licence could be issued to schools and colleges 'even under the present Arms Act'. He urged that other Hindu schools and colleges apply to their provincial governments citing this case, claiming that it would be very easy for all students to join such a 'rifle class as it requires no hard conditions nor does demand much time'. Khare's grant of this license to the Craddock High School at Wardha not far from Gandhi's ashram and close to the provincial capital of Nagpur on 29 July 1938 stated:

> The Government of the Central Provinces and Berar has approved of the grant to the Head Master, Craddock High school, Wardha, of Licence in form under rule 32 of the Indian Arms Rules 1924 for starting a shooting club to give selected public not below the age of 14, and teachers of the Craddock High School, Wardha target practice on the following terms: The Grant of the Licence will cover the following arms ammunition – 6 Miniature rifles of 22 bore. Ammunition: – 1500 cartridges.[55]

On its own the military school does not appear very significant; yet it is a part of a larger strategy of cultivating the military and infiltrating it that has long been a priority of the Mahasabha and its related and successor organisations. Two related features are worth bearing in mind. First, even as the Mahasabha recruited for the war effort and sought to gain access to the means of violence, it was regarded as no real threat by the British, which is why the activities of its related organisations were also tolerated. Secondly, as India moved towards Independence and in the decades thereafter, senior army officers have entertained the possibility of a more political role.

Provinces, Darbars, state forces, the arms factory, and pogroms

The Darbars or courts of the Hindu Princely States[56] were an important Mahasabha-RSS concern, because they controlled State Forces or armies which were, of course, nothing in relation to the

Indian Army but an important weapon against local Muslim populations. Moreover, important personalities circulated between various Princely Courts and important Provinces, frequently in high office, and quite openly associated with Hindu paramilitary forces that organised mass killings. Yet this did not seem to the British to be an issue for concern, at least not sufficiently so to provoke action.[57] The Report of the Resident to the Gwalior Court noted:

> 86. Activities of the Rashtriya Swayam Sevak Sangh have been reported on a fairly wide scale...One Lieutenant Phadke, a retired military officer of the State is said to have been arranging for arms and giving training to volunteers...The Gwalior UTC is reported to have been provided with 80 rifles, and one Prabhu Dayal Lavania has been appointed its commander.[58]

In keeping with this tolerance of the Mahasabha, claims by Muslims of discrimination by Gwalior State were treated very lightly by the Resident and the Political Department when protests were held in Lucknow about this. Presumably such protests could not be held publicly in Gwalior itself.[59]

> A meeting of the UP Muslim League was held at Lucknow on the 15th of April to voice a protest against the alleged anti-Muslim policy of the Darbar.[60]

But these protests were ignored. E.W.R. Lumby, a Political Officer, wrote that 'the separate reports by the Resident on this question, which were recently submitted, indicate that the Muslim grievances have been grossly exaggerated'.[61]

The Political Department echoed the Resident's lack of concern about Muslim grievances. A note in the margin added:

> We had much experience in Bombay of this exaggerated talk of 'grievances'. They generally boiled down to very little. HH of Gwalior has often told me that less than 1 per cent of his Muslim subjects feel this way and I believe him.[62]

Yet M.A. Sreenivasan, the newly appointed Vice-President of the Council, recorded his early impression:

> The communal hatred and violence... spread to the State and its capital, fuelled by the Hindu Mahasabha and the Rashtriya Seva Sangh (sic), active and powerful orgnizations whose anti-Muslim and anti-Gandhi stand had won them considerable popularity and influence in the Maharashtra belt...hundreds of Muslims were stripped naked, identified, killed and thrown out of the trains that traversed Gwalior state. There were days when twenty or thirty Muslim bodies were collected by the State police alongside the railway line...It was no longer a secret in New Delhi and elsewhere that the Maharaja had a soft corner for the Hindu Mahasabha and the RSS.[63]

Moonje moved to Gwalior for a period at Independence to lobby for a state-supported munitions factory managed by the Birlas to manufacture arms for Hindus at war with Muslims. Writing to M. A. Sreenivasan, Moonje said:

> I hope you have not allowed to pass out of your mind what I have put before you in my personal interview as regards the manufacture of fire-arms by private and state agencies in your state. I have personally seen Mr. Mandelia's workshop. Besides he is himself personally willing to undertake the work. He only requires little encouragement and connivance if not actual authority from you. I have also written to Mr. G.D. Birla in the matter.[64]

On the same day he wrote to the Maharaja in similar terms, and followed all this up with another letter to Sreenivasan on 2 September 1947:

> you yourself will be thoroughly reconciled to the idea that Moslems engaged in Police and Military service are now a danger to the Hindus besides being fifth columnists.[65]

Given the dangers Moonje claimed existed, he saw this as an opportunity to

> bring to your notice that my friend, Mr. Ghanshyam Das Birla writes to me in his letter of 24th August from New Delhi. He says, "Thanks for your letter. We are going to build up a very big workshop in Gwalior, and if so desired by the Government, there will be no difficulty in producing arms. The matter depends entirely on Government". This clinches the matter. It is now for you to decide whether to give your encouragement to Mr. Mandelia to begin producing arms. In Nizam Hyderabad arms are being manufactured, why should Gwalior lag behind ...If you be favour-

> ably inclined to the proposal regarding the manufacture of Fire-arms I may meet you and Mr. Mandelia the Manager of the Birla Cotton Mills together for further discussions.[66]

Sreenivasan wrote back to him sharply about the Mahasabha agitations in Gwalior but added:

> I have already taken action in regard to the proposal to depute Mr Kavadey to work in the BSA [Birmingham Small Arms] Factory. You may rest assured I shall keep the subject prominently in my mind.[67]

Yet, since Sreenivasan recorded his sharp disapproval of the Mahasabha in Gwalior and attempted to check its influence, he may not have given this proposal any support. On 2 September 1947 Moonje repeated these claims in identical terms to the Maharaja as well.

At Accession (of the Princely States to the Union of India) and at Independence in 1947 the same N.B. Khare who had earlier been Premier of CP Berar was now Prime Minister of Alwar (and informally advisor to the ruler of Bharatpur as well). A large Muslim minority primarily of the Meo community lived in these two states. Khare organized a pogrom by these two state armies that is estimated to have led to the killing of 82,000 Muslims in the course of a few days, possibly with the complicity of the Home Minister in Delhi, Vallabhbhai Patel.[68]

> But Moonje was damn pleased with what I did to the Muslims of Alwar.... He called me to Nasik and embraced me...More than anything else, what I did in Alwar and the way I broke the back of Muslims there pleased Dr Moonje immensely. I was in Delhi as a member of the Constituent Assembly in 1947. Moonje was also in Delhi in December. So he gave me a good party, a huge party, an At Home. When I went there, Moonje caught hold of me and embraced me saying, "Doctor, All of us are very pleased with what you have done in Alwar, whatever we have done to each other let us forget."[69]

Moonje, evidently on cordial terms with Vallabhbhai Patel, wrote to him about riots in Ahmedabad, replying to Patel's letter of 9 July:

> This state of things clearly proves the necessity of taking a more realistic view of the situation and of making arrangements immediately to train Hindus in the art of stabbing as well.[70]

Patel became Home Minister in the Interim Government a few months later. Moonje reminded him that when they last met with G.D. Birla on 17 June, Patel had promised to visit his military school, the purpose of which he explained was to prepare for civil war: 'If we must go through Civil Wars, let us go through it and be done with it'.

Khare's actions in Central Provinces and Berar as a Mahasabha-sympathetic Congressman bear some similarity to those of another Mahasabha-friendly Premier, Pandit Gobind Ballabh Pant of the United Provinces, recorded in his Home Secretary Rajeshwar Dayal's memoir.[71] B.B.L Jaitley, a senior police officer, submitted documentary proof that the RSS leader Golwalkar had personally organised a large pogrom of Muslims in the western districts of UP:

> blueprints of great accuracy and professionalism of every town and village in that vast area, prominently marking out the Muslim localities and habitations. There were also detailed instructions regarding access to the various locations.

Both Jaitley and Dayal demanded that Golwalkar be immediately arrested. But Pant procrastinated, organised a long Cabinet meeting to discuss the matter, sent a questionnaire to Golwalkar, who was tipped off that he would be arrested and thereupon fled.[72]

Changing masters?

By 1943, the policy of support for the British which Savarkar canvassed was tempered by the thought that the Japanese might win the War. Accordingly, in Bengal, the Mahasabha leader Shyama Prasad Mookerjee wanted British permission for a 'Bengal National Army'.[73]

> [T]he Mahasabha Minister, S. P. Mookerjee, has been increasingly insistent in his demand for a Bengal National Army.

The Mahasabha further entertained the prospect of switching sides.[74] Accordingly, Mookerjee proposed that 'until one or the other of the opposing parties in the present war established unquestionable superiority' the Mahasabha must 'contrive to sit on the fence and watch the results'. They should prepare themselves in the meantime, he said, to 'take as much advantage of the last results, when the war ends'.

Mookerjee explained to Lord Linlithgow, Viceroy, that Indians might well welcome Japanese rule in India as they had welcomed the Battle of Plassey:[75]

> Indeed a blind pursuit of a repressive policy may well create an atmosphere in India which will make us look upon the enemy as a virtual liberator from the hands of the oppressors, a state of feeling with which Indians hailed your ancestors under different surroundings in this very country about 200 years ago, when they gradually changed from their role of traders to that of masters of Indian affairs.[76]

It would seem then that this threat might signify no more than the possibility of exchanging allegiance from one master to another. This view was still openly expressed by Mahasabha leaders well after the War had ended, on the very eve of Independence, when B.S. Moonje issued a press statement with the rhetorical flourish:

> How can we admire and pay respect to the Congress which instead of showing the imperial mentality, as the British were doing, to rule over India democratically with a firm hand in justice and fairness both to Hindus and Moslems... (sic).[77]

The Parivar, fascism and the Government of India

The Mahasabha's public praise for Mussolini and Hitler invited no displeasure from the British Government of India. This was in part due to the ambivalence that Britain herself maintained about fascism until well into the War, with important colonial civil servants sometimes expressing similar views. The less important reason was that the Mahasabha as a loyal ally was permitted a measure of indulgence not afforded the Congress or the Communists. Consequently, Savarkar's admiration for the Axis Powers was not seen as a threat to the Government of India. As intelligence recorded, he 'dwelt at length on Jawaharlal's activities which it is said alienated the sympathies of foreign nations like Italy, Germany and Japan'.[78]

He had already propounded in 1938 that what Hitler was then doing to the Jews had its justification in the simple fact that they were not part of the German nation, seeing there an analogy to the position of the Muslims in India.

> Several communities may live in one country for thousands of years but this does not help in forming a nation...In Germany the movement of the Germans is the national movement but that of the Jews is a communal one.[79]

He elaborated on this the following year at Poona in his lecture to some 400 students at the Law College on 31 July, well after *Kristallnacht*. According to one report of this, he said:

> Nationality did not depend so much on a common geographical area as on unity of thought, religion, language and culture. For this reason the Germans and Jews could not be regarded as one nation. In the same way India was a nation of Hindus as they were in the majority.[80]

The RSS's evident militarism made the Government consider banning it in 1942, but it decided against doing so.[81] In the course of discussions, the Deputy Commissioner, Buldana, had thus described its activities in his area:

> the Sangh does not want to come into conflict with Government...The Rashtriya Swayam Sewak Sangh has, however, no plan to either fight Government or even to oppose it.

Special Branch reports on the RSS and Hindu Mahasabha in 1942 had already noted that in January B.S. Moonje and other prominent leaders advised Hindus to defend India not just from from external aggression but also the 'internal rapacity of the Muslims'. One Dr. P.G. Sahasrabudhe had addressed the volunteers on three occasions, on one of which, on 21 May 1942, he drew attention to the value of propaganda,

> quoting Russia and Germany as examples, and again extolled the virtues of the Leader principle, citing Mussolini's success.[82]

The Fourth Security Conference held at Nagpur on 8–9 March 1943 reconsidered the question of a ban:

> Item: 7 – ...in its organisation and behaviour Fascist tendencies are obvious... So far the Sangh has not provoked authority, indeed the impression clings that it has been careful to avoid conflict...The organisation of the Sangh is based on Fascist principles, the elective and committee systems being absent...The leaders of the Sangh (sometimes called organizers) are entitled "Chalak" (the exact Hindi equivalent of the word Fuehrer).[83]

The Conference noted that the RSS derived some support in places from well-wishers in the Indian National Congress:

> the Sangh is in places supported by Congressmen and at many places, especially in Marathi-speaking districts, by more moderate and pro-Government elements, like Rao Bahadur Khare of Amraoti and Mr. Kane of Yeotmal.[84]

Yet, none of this seemed sufficient grounds for taking any action. In 1942 the Quit India movement had demonstrated an extraordinary level of mass mobilisation against British rule, much of it spontaneous or connected with underground organisations.[85] By contrast, the RSS, drilling ceaselessly, and the Mahasabha, constituted no threat to British rule in India but constituted a threat only to the Muslims.

Even though India was not free in 1939, Savarkar saw as a significant achievement of decades of struggle that some (Hindus) could now bear arms even under British rule.

> The progress I see after 30 or 36 years is not disappointing...We have achieved some rights. The rifle clubs have been opened in places like Poona where the recital of Vande Mataram song was penalised...There has been so much progress that real rifles are being carried on shoulders in places like Poona and Nasik.[86]

Indeed, the Hindu Right has always nourished ambitions of reaching out to the armed forces. Some Army commanders on their part have long considered freeing themselves from democratically elected governments and building relationships with Britain and the United States. In such scenarios there is no declared military political party, but only a formation that prizes itself on being anti-political.

Shortly before Independence, Viceroy Mountbatten's Chief of Staff cabled him that Major-General Cariappa, the senior Indian staff officer in the Army had come to see him to advocate that the Indian army might take over from the British:

> Cariappa came to see me yesterday and volunteered the amazing suggestion that Indian Army with either Nehru or Jinnah as Commander-in-Chief should take over power when we left in June 1948.[87]

Ismay recorded that he at once told him that his proposal

> was not only wholly impracticable but highly dangerous, that throughout history the rule of an Army had always proved tyrannical and incompetent and that Army must always be servants and not masters. I added that Indian Army by remaining united and refusing to take sides could wield a tremendous influence for good in disturbed days that lie ahead but that they must always be subservient to civil power. I concluded by begging him to put idea right out of his mind and never to mention it again even in [the] strictest secrecy.[88]

Anti-Fascist mobilisation in India

Yet it is significant that even as fascist militias were not discouraged by the British Government of India, it was accepted nevertheless that anti-fascism signified a threat to public order. Anti-fascist activity in India was discouraged even after the War began by a police force which was concerned that no insulting references to Adolf Hitler be made anywhere in the Indian press. On 9 October 1939, T.K. Menon wrote to the Deputy Commissioner of Police, Special Branch (C.I.D.), Head of Police Station Bombay, enclosing copies of a poster he had published in his capacity as

(Post this in all Public Places)

WANTED! Dead or Alive! WANTED!

REWARD Rs. 50,000

ADOLPH HITLER

for MURDER

***alias* Adolph Shucklgruber**
***alias* Der Fuehrer**
***alias* Adolph Shickgruber**

Description:

Born in Branau, Austria, April 20, 1889; height, 5 feet 9 inches; weight, 150 pounds; build, medium; hair, black; lock of hair falls over one side of forehead; comblike moustache—Charlie Chaplain style.

Habits:

Loves parades, goose-stepping, browls like a donkey while addressing lectures; plotting murder, arson, loot and kidnapping are his hobbies.

Claims to be German, which he speaks badly, but is really Austrian. Formerly wallpainter and brick layer.

Modestly refers to himself as "John the Baptist", "Teuton Messiah" and sometimes even as God.

Warning:

It is dangerous to mention "democracy", "pacifism" and "truth" in his presence.

Relatives:

Sister, Paula, also psychopathic, dubbed "Frau Wolf." Lives in Germany. Brother, Alois Hitler. Austrian Police record reveal several convictions, not for political activity. Now runs a bar in Berlin and is very jumpy when he hears "Heil Hitler".

Private Life:

While in Austria courted a Jewish girl, but she snubbed him, since then anti-semitic. Once tried to commit suicide due to dissention in his party. Was shot at by Frau Schleicher when General Schleicher was murdered, but escaped with a wound on the hand. A confirmed women-hater. Proclaims that women are meant only to cook food and produce cannon-fodder.

Record:

Responsible for the death of Erich Klausner, leader of Catholic Action in Germany, and Abelbert Probst, leader of Catholic Youth. Responsible for wholesale arrest of hundreds of thousands of Priests, Nuns, Pacifists, Scientists, Thinkers, and Artists of international repute. Closed all Catholic Schools and confiscated their money, and decreed that all Nuns should bear children.

Responsible for the death of innumerable Protestant Pastors. Pastor Niemoeller, leader of German Protestant Church, now in prison.

Responsible for the rape of Czechoslovakia, Austria, Saar, Rhineland, Memel, Danzig and Poland.

Responsible for the Arab-Jewish civil war in Palestine and illicit arms traffic. Also Responsible for I.R.A. outrages in England.

Responsible for the murder of Dr. Dolfuss, of Dr. Schuschnig and attempted kidnapping of Dr. Benes. Robbed Czechoslovakia, of £ 80,000,000 in gold, all foodstuffs, clothing, army and police equipments, and levied Rs. 28 million per year for "protection".

Responsible for the death of nearly 500,000 people since 1933. Arch enemy of coloured people and all religions.

Abolished Free Press, Free Speech, Trade Unions and crushed the middle classes.

Has connections and agents all over the world, including in India and the East.

Last seen in Saar, Rhineland, Austria, Memel and Prague. Heading for Rumania, Hungary, Baltic States, African Colonies, Italy and the East.

Now trying to establish contact with Communists, for destroying democracy and peace.

INDICTED BY WORLD OPINION FOR MURDER, ARSON, LOOT & KIDNAPPING WITH INTENT TO KILL

He is holding 65 million people in bondage in Germany and many millions in Austria, Memel and Czechoslovakia. Six hundred thousand Jews are held for ransom by him and he demands two and quarter billion dollars. Demands one billion dollars as ransom from Catholics.

Pay him no money! Have no traffic with him and report any of his agents who try to sell you goods or poisonous political creeds—"National Socialism", and "Anti-Semitism".

This information is correct

THE ANTI-NAZI LEAGUE OF INDIA,
MINTO HOUSE - - - - BOMBAY 8.

Branches throughout India, and allied Societies throughout the World including Germany.

Hon. Secretary of 'The Anti-Nazi League in India', which he proposed to distribute in different cities of India:

> WANTED Dead or Alive! WANTED! REWARD Rs. 50,000 ADOLPH HITLER for MURDER... THE ANTI-NAZI LEAGUE OF INDIA MINTO HOUSE, Bombay 8 (Branches throughout India, and allied Societies throughout the World including Germany).

In Government's eyes Menon had issued an illegal poster without seeking its prior permission, 'which signified gross insult to the German nation and its Leader'. The Commissioner of Police warned him that 'such offensive propaganda could do no good to anyone' and 'action could be taken under the law'. This was on 22 July 1939, in other words, before the outbreak of hostilities between England and Germany.[89] In the Home Department in New Delhi a senior official, identifiable only by the letter "G", wrote by hand instructions on 17 October 1939 and marked the file to the Viceroy through his Secretary.

> This poster is (1) in bad taste (2) an unauthorised news sheet and (3) may be misconstrued in India as an incitement to murder. C (Commissioner Police, KS) may be asked to advise Mr. Menon as at (2) and Chief Presidency Magistrate may be asked not to authorise it. We might also write to *Times of India*.[90]

So, too, the Home Department Bombay, which then wrote to Francis Low, editor of the *Times of India,*[91] that the printed poster proposed to be issued by the Anti-Nazi League of India was an unauthorised news-sheet, because the printer and the place of printing were not mentioned in the publication itself, notwithstanding Menon's admission, and moreover that the Government considered 'the poster to be in bad taste and one that may be misconstrued in this country as an incitement to murder'.

Low wrote back to N.P.A. Smith:

> If the *Times Press* has done wrong in publishing the poster, all we can do is to apologise for our mistake and promise not to do it again.[92]

Mr. Menon was called up on 19 October, and thereafter the CID (Special Branch) seized all 5,000 copies of the poster.[93] In February 1940, in response to the British Consul at Damascus' request for copies of those posters to aid the War effort, the Home Department pronounced mutton-headedly that 'when we suppressed publication here it doesn't seem proper to encourage publication elsewhere'.[94]

Yet, all the above is *especially* curious given that at 11.15 GMT on 3 September 1939 Neville Chamberlain, Prime Minister of Great Britain, had announced that "this country is at war with Germany", and the British Empire and Dominions also declared war the same day, the declaration made by Viceroy Linlithgow on behalf of India.

By contrast, Khwaja Ahmad Abbas in the *Bombay Chronicle* of June 1939 shows a far greater alertness than British officialdom in India to the international situation of the time.

> The basis for Fascist propaganda in India is provided by the prevailing anti-British temper of the Indian People...some of these very "mountebanks of Asia" are today among the foremost Nazi propagandists in India. Some of them, still exiles living in Europe and, not unnaturally, nursing feelings against the British, are being exploited by the Nazi and Fascist Governments. They seem to forget the words of Hitler: "I as a German prefer much more to see India under British Government than under any other...I must not connect the fate of the German people with these so-called 'oppressed nations' who are clearly of racial inferiority" (*Mein Kampf*, German edition, p. 747). And the credit for this goes to the Socialist Pandit Jawaharlal Nehru who, during his two recent terms of office as the President of the Congress, did more than any one else to give the Indian Nationalist movement its correct perspective as a part of the larger world movement...At over a thousand meetings...he [Nehru] repeatedly explained the International situation, dwelt on the danger of Fascism and showed why the Indian Nationalists should beware of letting their movement take a turn for totalitarianism...Hindu communalist organisation[s] have often expressed sympathy with Germany and Japan.

Finally, Abbas warned of the danger that the Palestine issue posed for the Indian understanding of European fascism:

> But the cleverest trump card played by the Nazis in India as in other Muslim countries is the Palestine issue. The Muslims of India naturally have strong sympathies for the Arabs and the Nazi agents have cleverly exploited this to create anti-Jewish sentiment which was hitherto not very prominent.

Notwithstanding the Mahasabha's endorsement of Hitler's actions against the Jews during the 1930s and the War, when the new State of Israel was established a letter was received from an Israeli lobbyist in Bombay soliciting information about the Hindu Mahasabha and the RSS. The letter was received with great enthusiasm,[95] and the reply was prompt:

> We look upon Israel as the citadel against the menace of Muslim aggressiveness and Hindu Mahasabha stands for creating an indissoluble tie between Israel and India. Our All India Working Committee is meeting on the 10th and 11th September next and we hope to have a resolution passed demanding immediate recognition of Israel by the Government of India.[96]

Final remarks

As it became clear that the Mahasabha, unlike the Congress and the Muslim League, would not determine future constitutional arrangements for India, it (the Sabha) came to focus on the Hindu lobby in the Congress and the Princely states to be able to gain access to weaponry and state forces, for pogroms in 1946–48 that would change demographies. After Independence, and for decades, they concentrated on building a mass base as a sense of crisis deepened throughout the country. The Mahasabha's successor party the BJP can now play the game of anti-politics allying with authoritarians such as Anna Hazare who claim to be above party politics, and portraying corruption as an inevitable outcome of liberal democracy.

At the same time, in the years after Independence they have gained a great measure of respectability by participating in the common culture of national security that embraces all the major parliamentary parties, who also accept a variety of coercive acts performed on Indians. The demonisation of different communities in turn, and the insidious culture of national security, have been adopted by *both* the Hindu Right and the Congress, sometimes with the tacit approval of the Communist parties. Just as Congress hoodlums conducted the massacre of Sikhs in Delhi, the army, police and paramilitary organisations have been responsible for atrocities in Punjab and Kashmir, even as the Sangh and the Communists supported them. The attribution of magical powers to communities in order to demonize them is in fact closely related to the worldwide secular religion of "national security", that demands the coercive extortion of information and massacres in the name of a collective, for both pathologies identify a threat from the outsider within. Today the views of the Mahasabha's successors on questions of security are often indistinguishable from those of the Indian National Congress and the Communist Party of India (Marxist).

Endnotes

1 The All India Hindu Mahasabha functioned as a lobby within the Indian National Congress, and subsequently became an independent political party that gave birth to the Jana Sangh, which later changed its name to the Bharatiya Janata Party. The Rashtriya Swayamsevak Sangh and the Vishwa Hindu Parishad are closly linked organisations that collectively are often termed the 'Sangh Parivar'.

2 I had originally termed it 'subordinate fascism' but Jairus Banaji suggested this felicitous phrase.

3 Lt-Col R.M. Dalziel IMS, Inspector General of Prisons, Bombay Presidency, wrote to the Home Secretary: 'Kindly say if twelve months remission recommended by me should be given. I saw the convict recently in jail; his conduct is good and demeanour correct', 3 January, 1923, Home Department Special Branch 60 D (d) 1921-3.

4 Vinayak Damodar Savarkar, *My Transportation for Life*, second English edition (Veer Savarkar Prakashan, 1984), tr. V. N. Naik, pp. 338–40; orig. *Mazhi*

Janmathep (1927).

5 Home Department Special file 60D (1919) p. 63: Letter from Vinayak Damodar Savarkar Convict No 32778, Cellular Jail, Port Blair, to the Chief Commissioner of th,e Andaman.s, 30 March 1920.

6 Ibid.

7 S11 Home Department 60 D (d) 1921–23 19 August 1921. Humble petition of Vinayak Damodar Savarkar, Convict No. 558, in Ratnagiri District prison addressed to 'His Excellency the Right Honourable the Governor of Bombay, in Council'. Savarkar's original sentence of transportation for life had been commuted and he was at this time in Ratnagiri Prison.

8 S-145 Home Department No. 724 for Secretary to the Government of Bombay, 4 January 1924, to Director of Information: Extract from the Secretary's internal note dated 3 January 1924, explaining that 'Savarkar has already indicated his acceptance of these terms. He has also, though it was explained to him that it was in no way made a condition of his release, submitted the following statement…'

9 Savarkar, *My Transportation for Life*, pp. 494–5. I am indebted to S.P. Shukla for drawing my attention to this passage.

10 Janaki Bakhle, 'Country First? Vinayak Damodar Savarkar (1883–1966) and the Writing of *Essentials of Hindutva*', *Public Culture*, 22/1 (2010) 149–86; and Bakhle, 'Savarkar 1883–1966, Sedition and Surveillance: the Rule of Law in a Colonial Situation', *Social History*, 35/1 (2010) pp. 51–75, 2010.

11 Bakhle, 'Country First?', p. 185.

12 The concern was no longer that ritual purity might be defiled by women at a time of 'uncleanness' or by the lower castes as in traditional Hinduism. Rather the concern was with *outsiders concealed within* who might betray the community of Hindus. This pathology is evident in the curious witch-hunt instigated by Savarkar when he wrote to Indra Prakash, the Secretary, on 9 October 1940 that 'It is reported from several reliable quarters that Moslems are still allowed to enter and even stay on the Mahasabha ground. … The unchecked presence of Moslems is bound to be standing menace...I had again issued instructions months ago to you as the Hon. Secretary in charge of the Delhi Hindu Mahasabha Head Office that no Moslem should be allowed on the Hindu Mahasabha grounds...But in spite of that the Moslems are allowed to enter the precincts. – You should immediately stop the practice and cease to tolerate it under any excuse whatsoever. Life, property and even the sanctity of the Hindu Mahasabha grounds stand in hourly danger if this practice is allowed to continue'. To this the reply was prompt, on 12 October: 'It is a great lie that Muslims are still allowed to enter or even stay in the Hindu Mahasabha Bhavan...I am very sorry that Mr. Padam Raj Jain who

thinks himself a respectable man should be instrumental in instigating such lies and worry you for nothing....I also add for your information that even one Muslim teacher who was on the staff of the School has been turned out by the School Board. Another Christian has also left the School'.

13 *Moonje Memorandum on Hindu Military Academy*, p. 45, from the Parthasarathi Gupta papers, National Archives of India, New Delhi; hereafter *Moonje Memorandum*.

14 *Moonje Memorandum*, pp. 50, 54.

15 Weekly Confidential, Ratnagiri, 17 April 1932; Home Special 800 (74) (21) 1932–4.

16 C. Jaffrelot, *Les nationalistes hindous: idéologies, implantation et mobilisation des années 1920 aux années 1990* (Paris, 1993); Jaffrelot, *The Hindu Nationalist Movement in India* (New York, 1995).

17 Jaffrelot, *op.cit.*, pp. 61–2.

18 I am grateful to Paul Arpaia for helping me make this argument. See Paul Arpaia, 'Converging and Diverging Parallels: The Case of the *Gerarca* Luigi Federzoni (1878-1967)', in Jan Nellis, ed., *Catholicism and Fascism(s) in Europe, 1918–1945* (forthcoming).

19 'Re-imagined' in the sense used by Eric Hobsbawm, *The Invention of Tradition* (Cambridge, 1983).

20 'Such a process implied a defensive stigmatization of these Others, but it also represented a strategic emulation. It redefined Hindu identity in opposition to these 'threatening Others' while – under the pretext of drawing inspiration from a so-called Vedic 'Golden Age' – assimilating those cultural features of the Others which were regarded as prestigious and efficacious in order to regain self-esteem and resist the Others more effectively', Jaffrelot, *The Hindu Nationalist Movement*, p. 6.

21 Home Special 800 (74) (21) 1932-4,Weekly Confidential – Ratnagiri District – 18 January.

22 Weekly Confidential, Ratnagiri District Home Department Special, Bombay Castle, 18 January 1933, 800 (74) (21) 1932-4.

23 Savarkar Micro film R No 22 34 Misc. Correspondence 1925-37 In the Court of the First Class Sub Judge Ratnagiri, Nehru Memorial Museum and Library.

24 Ibid.

25 Director, Intelligence Bureau, Government of India, New Delhi, Saturday 11

February 1939, No. 6; Saturday 30 December 1939, No. 48. All references to these reports (henceforth DIB) are from the files contained in the India Office Records, British Library.

26 *The Bombay Chronicle*, 28/8/1941.

27 Resolution of the Working Committee of the Hindu Mahasabha, passed on 21–22 September 1940 and forwarded to the Viceroy.

28 Letter from B.S. Moonje, Nasik 12/13 Sep 1941: L/P&J/8/683 Law and Order Hindu Mahasabha, IOR, BL.

29 *Moonje Memorandum*, p. 43.

30 Bray's farewell address in the Chelmsford Club, New Delhi, on 23rd Dec. 1929, quoted by Moonje.

31 Savarkar to Viceroy, 19 August 1940: L/P&J/8/683 Law and Order Hindu Mahasabha, IOR, BL.

32 DIB 4 January 1941 No. 1.

33 DIB 18 January 1941, No. 3. The RSS and the Mahasabha do not find mention among the political parties considered revolutionary or acting against the interests of the Crown, e.g., "Revolutionary activities in India" (L/P&J/12/389), nor in the Reports of the Director of the Intelligence Bureau of the Government of India. The limited references to the RSS and Hindu Mahasabha in the index of L/P&J/12, indicate low surveillance.

34 IOR, L/P&J/12/484 Secret DIB No. 10, Saturday 7 March 1942.

35 IOR, BL: L/P&J/12/485, Saturday 27 February 1943, No. 9.

36 DIB, Simla Saturday 7 June 1941, No. 22.

37 DIB 21st June 1941. No. 24.

38 DIB, New Delhi, Saturday 15 May 1943, No. 20.

39 IB Report, New Delhi, Saturday, 31 July 1943 No. 31.

40 IOR, BL/ P&J/ 5/ 245 Punjab Governor's Reports, 1942 'Confidential Report on the situation in the Punjab for the second half of September 1942…2. Political'.

41 Weekly Confidential Report, District Magistrate Poona, 24 May 1941.

42 DIB, Simla Saturday 5 July 1941 No. 26.

43 The following discussion on military education depends on archival material gathered by the late Parthasarathi Gupta, for which I am entirely indebted to

Narayani Gupta.

44 The Intelligence Bureau noted that 'Dr. Moonje's proposed Military School... has... recently received the blessing of the retiring Commander-in-Chief in India. The moral and financial value of an appreciation of this nature from such a distinguished soldier cannot be overlooked'. Bombay Presidency Weekly Letter No. 49, 7 December 1935, IOR, BL.

45 The meeting took place on the 5 April 1937.

46 Home Special 812A 1935 Secret D.O. Ho. S.D. – 3099 Home Department (Spl.), Poona, 15 July 1935

47 Home Department, c/o. (Mr. Elwin) 9756 W.I.B. u/o. 5/C.H/36 of April 12,1938. No. P.O.L. – 962 From A.P. LeMesurier, Esquire, I.C.S., District Magistrate, Nasik to The Secretary to Government, Home Department, Bombay Poona Nasik, 30 August 1937.

48 10 July 1935, DO No. SD 3099, replying to Shillidy of the 8 July.

49 Home Department Special 812 A 1935–1937: Opening ceremony of the Bhonsala Military School, Nasik, performed on 21/6/1937.

50 5 September 1937.

51 7 June 1937.

52 *Moonje Memorandum*, pp. 1, 13, 15, 18, 29.

53 N. B. Khare interview transcript, Nehru Memorial Museum and Library, pp. 18–19.

54 Savarkar Papers, Nehru Memorial Library, Microfilm First Instalment F No 2, March 1937 to May 1939.

55 Ibid.

56 The Mahasabha's tender feelings for the Hindu princely states were most pronounced in the case of the Kingdom of Nepal: 'The Pathans had, at the moment, only one place to call their own and that was Kabul. But they swear by it at all times, while they eat, drink and sleep. The Hindus have a place which is their own, but very few know of it, and know that the place goes by the name of Nepal' (Savarkar, *My Transportation for Life*, pp. 354–55).

57 IOR, BL, Fortnightly Report of the Gwalior Residency for the fortnight ending 20 November 1944 from A.A. Russell, Resident at Gwalior Camp Bharatpur, 4 December 1944 to LCL Griffin Esq. CIE ICS Secretary to his Excellency the Crown Representative, Political Department Delhi.

58 IOR, BL, Pol. 1030/44, A.A. Russell Resident to L.C.L. Griffin Secretary

to the Crown Representative, New Delhi Fortnightly Report of the Gwalior Residency 4 December 1944 No. 87.

59 IOR, BL, Collection 21 Gwalior L/P&S/13/1197 File 5 from H.M. Poulton, Resident at Gwalior, 3 May1944.

60 IOR, BL, F. 3-5 Pol. 1030 44, Poulton Resident 3 May 1944.

61 Political Department POL 1030/44 Under Secretary 25.5 Gwalior Residency Report for the second half of April 1944.

62 IOR, BL, 1030/44, Resident to Secretary to Crown Representative, New Delhi.

63 M.A. Sreenivasan, *Of the Raj, Maharajas and Me* (New Delhi, 1991) pp. 219–21.

64 21 August 1947, BS Moonje File No. 66.

65 Nehru Memorial Museum Library, BS Moonje Papers File No. 66.

66 Ibid.

67 24 August 1947, 73 B, File No. 66, B.S. Moonje Papers, Nehru Memorial Museum and Library.

68 Shail Mayaram, *Resisting Regimes: Myth, Memory and the Shaping of a Muslim Identity* (New York, 1997) pp. xiv, 298, and Ian Copland, 'The Further Shores of Partition: Ethnic Cleansing in Rajasthan, 1947', *Past & Present*, 160 (Aug. 1998), pp. 203–39.

69 Moonje transcript, Nehru Memorial Library, pp. 98–99.

70 Moonje Papers, Hindu Mahasabha Papers, Nehru Memorial Museum and Library, F No. 66, Nasik 12 July 1946.

71 Rajeshwar Dayal, *A Life of our Times* (New Delhi, 1998) pp. 93–94: 'the Deputy Inspector-General of Police of the Western Range, a very seasoned and capable officer, B.B.L. Jaitley, arrived at my house in great secrecy. He was accompanied by two of his officers who brought with them two large steel trunks securely locked. When the trunks were opened, they revealed incontrovertible evidence of a...conspiracy to create a communal holocaust throughout the western districts of the province. The trunks were crammed with blueprints of great accuracy and professionalism of every town and village in that vast area, prominently marking out the Muslim localities and habitations. There were also detailed instructions regarding access to the various locations, and other matters which amply revealed their...purport...I immediately took the police party to the Premier's house. There, in a closed room, Jaitley gave a full report of his discovery...Timely raids conducted on

the premises of the RSS (Rashtriya Swayam Sevak Sangh) had brought the massive conspiracy to light. The whole plot had been concerted under the direction and supervision of the Supremo of the organisation himself. Both Jaitley and I pressed for the immediate arrest of the prime accused, Shri Golwalkar, who was still in the area....Pantji could not but accept the evidence of his eyes and ears...But instead of agreeing to the immediate arrest of the ring leader...he asked for the matter to be placed for consideration by the Cabinet at its next meeting...At the Cabinet meeting there was the usual procrastination...The fact that the police had unearthed a conspiracy which would have set the whole province in flames hardly seemed to figure in the discussion. What ultimately emerged was that a letter should be issued to Golwalkar pointing out the contents and nature of the evidence which had been gathered and demanding an explanation thereof...Golwalkar, however had been tipped off and he was nowhere to be found'.

72 see Joya Chatterji, Bengal Divided: Hindu Communalism and Partition, 1932–1947 (Cambridge, 2002) pp. 232–40.

73 IOR:/L/PS/5/149 Bengal Governor's Reports 1942 'From J.A. Herbert to HE the Viceroy and Governor General of India, *Confidential* GOVERNMENT HOUSE', Calcutta 22 March 1942.

74 IOR: L/P&J/12/485, DIB Reports, 1943, IB Report No. 1 New Delhi, 2 January 1943.

75 There is a local Bengal historical context for such references to Plassey that I discovered from Chatterji, *Bengal Divided*, pp. 180–7.

76 R/3/1/15 Governor Bengal's correspondence with Viceroy 12 August 1942, Shyama Prasad Mookerjee.

77 8 August 1947, Moonje Correspondence All India Hindu Mahasabha Papers, Nehru Memorial Museum and Library.

78 Home Special 1938 60D(G), S-65: Extract from the weekly confidential report of the District Magistrate, Poona, dated 11 August 1936.

79 Extract from the weekly confidential report of the District Magistrate, Poona, dated 21 October 1938.

80 Extract from the *Bombay Province Weekly Letter*, No. 20, 30 Sept., 1939.

81 822-II Secret Rashtriya Swayam Sewak Sangh Organisation and Development in each District of CP and Berar and the end of the year 1942 (Nagpur, 1943); Buldana District D.O. 174 S dated Buldana, 28 November 1942.

82 Home Special 822-11. Numbered Copy No. 63 SECRET Government of the Central Provinces and Berar, Rashtriya Swayam Sewak Sangh Organisation and Development in each District of CP and Berar at the end of the year

1942, Nagpur, 1943, p. 83.

83 Ibid., p. 63.

84 Ibid., p. 65.

85 This is evident in official and secret correspondence, e.g., *Confidential* No. S.D. 3305 Home Department (Special) Bombay, 4 September 1942: '3. Political *Congress Agitation*.– General Review. Outbreaks of violence and all important illegal activities'.

86 Extract from the *Bombay Province Weekly Letter* No. 20, 30 Sept., 1939.

87 Lord Ismay, Chief of Staff to the Viceroy to Rear Admiral Viscount Mountbatten of Burma via India Office Telegram, Mountbatten Papers Official Correspondence Files, Armed Forces Indian, Volume One Part One, Private and Personal Secret 10 May 8.44 pm received 11 May 9 a.m., see N. Mansergh and P. Moon, *The Transfer of Power*, vols. X to XII, London, HMSO, 1981–83, p. 755.

88 Ibid.

89 830 (1) pp. 157-158: "Mr T.K. Menon Secretary of the Anti Nazi League of Bombay", Home Department (Political) Bombay initialed "MSQ", 17 June 1940.

90 830 (1)/123 Secret No. 7253 - F/2014 (b) Home Department (Special) Reg. No. SD 5990 from M.N. Desai for Deputy Commissioner Police, Special Branch, Head Police Office Bombay, 16 October 1939 to K. Johnston Assistant Director, Intelligence Bureau, Home Department, Government of India, New Delhi.

91 830 (1)/131 D.O.S.D. No. 4011 Home Department (Political) Bombay Castle, 18 October 1939.

92 S.D. 6031 (19.10.39) to N.P.A. Smith Esq., Home Secretary (War), Home Department Bombay.

93 To N.P.A. Smith of the Indian Police the Joint Secretary to the Government of Bombay referred to his Secret D.O. No. S.D. 4011, dated 18 October 1939, and the Secretary's note of 17.10.39, about anti-Nazi activities by T.K. Menon.

94 Home Department (Special) 5 February 1940, handwritten note on file 830 (1) 145, initialed 'G'.

95 F. W. Pollack wrote, 'The Foreign Office, Government of Israel, has requested me to give them a clear idea about the present strength of the All India Hindu Mahasabha and of the R.S.S.... Your letter will be treated as strictly

confidential and will be forwarded to Israel by special messenger'. Manuscripts NMMLC-179, *India and Israel* (A Monthly Publication) Bombay, 15 September 1949, c/o Western Printers & Publishers, 23 Hamam Street, Fort.

96 The General Secretary, All India Hindu Mahasabha.

Acknowledgements

This is the first publication in a long-term project. Jairus Banaji first suggested I look at the archives to develop a fresh understanding of the Hindu Right. I am indebted to him for discussions, as also to Irfan Ahmad, Paul Arpaia, Niloufer Bhagwat, Vishnu Bhagwat, Vidyadhar Date, Rohini Hensman, Madhav Rao Patwardhan, Robert Paxton, Shereen Ratnagar, S.P. Shukla and Shaik Ubaid. Generous financial assistance has been provided by the CSD Adenwalla Trust, Naira Ahmadullah, Cyrus Guzder, Athar Hussain, the Indian Muslim Council-USA, Manjeet Kripalani, Monash Asia Institute, Saeed Patel,Shaik Ubaid and Marika Vicziany. V. Balachandran helped me greatly with access to the Special Branch archives in Mumbai. Faisal Devji very graciously lent me his flat in London for a month's research on the India Office papers at the British Library. Narayani Gupta gave me access to the research material gathered by the late Parthasarathi Gupta on the Bhonsla Military Academy. N. Balakrishnan, Deputy Director of the Nehru Memorial Museum and Library, was of great help in using NMML papers. Mahesh Rangarajan lent me his own copies of expensive books I should otherwise have had to purchase. Jay Barksdale of the New York Public Library provided me access to research material and a place to sit and write at the marvellous Wertheim Study. Avinasi Ramesh was kind enough to help me organize the many kilos of papers, and put them into some coherent form. To the staff of the British Library, London, the New York Public Library, the Maharashtra Archives at the Elphinstone College Library Mumbai, and the Nehru Memorial Museum and Library, I am most grateful.

The fascism of the Sangh Parivar

Sumit Sarkar

Fascism in contemporary Indian as distinct from the European historical context had appeared till the other day a mere epithet, worn out by overmuch, indiscriminate use, signifying little more than particular blatant acts of authoritarian repression or reactionary violence. With the 6th of December and its aftermath, elements frighteningly evocative of its totality of horror stalk our streets, obtain connivance and implicit sustenance from within the highest corridors of power, emerge from everyday conversations with relatives, colleagues, friends of yesterday. Not that exact parallels can be found, in most part India 1992–93 remains very different from the Germany of 60 years back. Yet a closer look at the pattern of affinities and differences may help to highlight certain crucial features – most notably, the ways in which the implications of the current all-out offensive of the Sangh Parivar go far beyond even the obvious and terrifying fact that the subcontinent has just witnessed the most widespread round of communal violence since the Partition years. The drive for Hindu Rashtra has put in jeopardy the entire secular and democratic foundations of our republic. An old warning of Nehru sounds particularly appropriate today. Muslim communalism is in its nature as bad as Hindu communalism, and may even be stronger among Muslims than its counterpart within the majority community. 'But Muslim communalism cannot dominate Indian society and introduce fascism. That only Hindu communalism can.' (quoted in *Frontline*, January 1, 1993) Probing the fascist analogy, then, may contribute towards a greater understanding of the dangers that confront us today. Just occasionally, it may provide us also with what is most needed, and is in woefully short supply: resources of hope.

Fascism had come to power in Italy and Germany through a combination of street violence (carefully orchestrated from above but still undeniable with great mass support), deep infiltration into the police, bureaucracy and army, and the connivance of 'centrist' political leaders. Crude violations of laws and constitutional norms consequently had alternated in Fascist and Nazi behaviours with loud protestations of respect for legality. It is not always remembered, for instance, that Hitler had become chancellor on January 30, 1933 in an entirely constitutional manner, as leader of the largest party in the Reichstag, at the invitation of President Hindenburg. He repeatedly asserted his party's respect for legality throughout the next month – but meanwhile Goering Nazified the Berlin police, organised street encounters in which more than 50 anti-fascists were murdered, and set the scene for the notorious Reichstag fire, after which first the communists, and then all opposition political parties and trade unions were quickly destroyed.

There is much, surely that is ominously reminiscent here. A mosque is systematically reduced to rubble over five long hours, in total violation of a direct Supreme Court order and repeated assurances given by the leading opposition party and its allies, and the central government does not lift its little finger. Countrywide riots follow; marked by blatant police partiality, with the guardians of the law not unoften turning rioters themselves. And then come strange political and judicial manoeuvres that in effect have allowed the land-grabbing vandals to build a temporary 'temple' complete with *darshan*, where curfew exists for Muslims and not for Hindus, and which suddenly is not a 'disputed structure' unlike the 462-year-old monument it has displaced, but something worthy of protection. Meanwhile the BJP alternates between an occasional apology and much more frequent aggressive justification, and VHP leaders add the Delhi Jama Masjid to Varanasi and Mathura, and openly denounce the Indian Constitution as anti-Hindu.

Expanding Target-Area

It is this wider dimension, in which the obvious, classically communal Muslim target area steadily expands, and efforts intensify to terrorise wider and wider circles of potential dissent that perhaps requires a little additional emphasis. The Hitler analogy is, once again, appropriate: Jew and communist had quickly expanded to cover social-democrats, liberals, Catholics, everyone who dared to think with any independence – even, by June 1934, a number of Nazis, massacred in the 'night of the long knives'. The BJP turn towards open terror had begun with two incidents in Madhya Pradesh unconnected with the Ram Janmabhoomi movement – the murder of Shankar Guha Niyogi, labour leader of unusual initiative and originality, in autumn 1991, and the public humiliation recently of B. D. Sharma, distinguished progressive retired civil servant. (The Shiv Sena of Maharashtra had shown the way even earlier, of course, smashing through street terror the once formidable Red Flag Unions of Bombay in the 1970s). The beating-up of journalists on December 6 is thus not an aberration, but part of a broader emerging pattern. The forces of Hindutva have assiduously cultivated the press, with great success till recently, but fascists always like to combine persuasion with the occasional big stick.

Certain little-reported developments in Delhi acquire relevance here, indicating once again the typical combination of street violence with administrative collusion even in a city where the December riots were relatively localised and minor,[1] right next to a central government which is said to have banned the RSS, the VHP, and the Bajrang Dal. Peace activists trying to do things as innocuous as singing songs, distributing leaflets calling for harmony, and staging street plays have been repeatedly attacked: the police come a little later, ignore the RSS-Bajrang Dal elements supposedly under a ban, but arrest and harass anti-communal groups. Even a peace march led by men as distinguished as P. N. Haksar and Habib Tanvir was obstructed by the police, while a Delhi University student in an anti-communal group whose name begins with Ram was slapped by a policeman who had arrested him: a man with such a name, he was told, should not be doing such things.

The Bajrang Dal thugs often openly declare that anyone who criticises the destruction of Babri Masjid will have to go to Pakistan, while in the selectively curfew-bound Muslim pockets of Seelampur in east Delhi, the police had rounded up all Muslim men in some areas, beaten them up unless they agreed to say 'Jai Shri Ram', and even pulled out the beard of a Muslim gentleman.

Myths As Common Sense

What is making all this possible is evidently a wide, though very far from universal, degree of consent, where large numbers may keep away from communal riots, maybe, even sincerely condemn them, and yet be participants in a kind of communal consensus in which a whole series of assumptions and myths have turned into common sense. Far from being a spontaneous or 'natural' product of popular will expressing a legitimate 'Hindu hurt', however, as the organised forces of Hindutva sedulously propagate, this consent is something constructed and carefully nurtured, a product of more than 60 years of strenuous and patient effort. The RSS, founded way back in 1925, and spawning from 1950s a whole series of affiliates manned at crucial levels by its cadres (among which the Jan Sangh/BJP and the VHP have been the most important), concentrated for many years on unostentatious, slow, 'cultural' work. *Shakhas* combined physical training of young men with indoctrination through *bauddhik* sessions, a chain of schools was built up, ideas were disseminated through personal contact and conversation, and even a very popular Hindu comic series was brought out (the *Amar Chitra Katha* extolling Hindu mythical or historical figures). It was for long, almost, a Gramscian process of building up hegemony through molecular permeation. Then, in the early and middle 1980s, came the efforts of Indira and Rajiv to play the 'Hindu card', communalising the state apparatus on an unprecedented scale through the anti-Sikh pogrom of 1984 and the subsequent cover-up of the guilty, and further eroding the rule of law through rampant corruption. All this directly prepared the ground for the Ram Janmabhoomi blitzkrieg of the Sangh Parivar, now spearheaded by the VHP. It must not be forgotten that it was the Congress government that updated the Ramayana epic into a pseudo-nationalist TV serial, and allowed access in 1986 to the idols installed inside the Babri Masjid by stealth and administrative collusion in December 1949, under an earlier Congress regime. The Sangh Parivar's war of position now gave place to a spectacular war of movement, pressing into service the latest in advertising and audio-visual techniques on a scale and with resources never before seen on the subcontinent. Hitler, by the way, had also been a bit of a pioneer in these matters, fully realising the importance of spoken propaganda through the then relatively new techniques of the loudspeaker and the radio.[2]

Unlike Fascism, then, which came to power in Italy and Germany within a decade or less of its emergence as a political movement, Hindutva has had a long gestation period. This, no doubt, has given it added strength and stability, time to get internalised into common sense. But there is an element of hope here, too, for despite the tremendous effort spread across decades, the conquest of hearts and minds remains far from complete. It needs to be recalled that around four out of five Indians voted against the BJP even in 1991 (its all-India percentage was 21.9) – and if that had been a vote about Ram, the UP victory was at best some kind of a mandate for a Ram temple, not for the destruction of the Masjid. The real base of the Sangh Parivar remains the predominantly upper-caste trader-professional petty bourgeoisie of the cities and small towns in the Hindi heartland, with developing connections perhaps with upwardly-mobile landholding groups in the countryside. Extensions beyond this remain unstable, as the panic evoked by Mandal and the Bihar example seem to indicate – and the whole bloated structure of today's Hindutva requires for sustenance constant excitement, a high pitch of hysteria, the stimulus of communal violence. Hence perhaps the gamble of sacrificing the BJP ministries, which could have got discredited and shown up as little different, if not worse, from Congress regimes by any long period of normal governance.

An early perceptive analysis of Fascism had defined it as 'not only an instrument at the service of big business, but at the same time a mystical upheaval of the...petite bourgeoisie'.[3] That a 'mystical upheaval' has happened around the slogan of Ram is undeniable, and its lavish orchestration indicates an evident abundance of funds. But the specific linkages of Fascism with capitalist interests have remained a controversial issue even for Europe, and most historians have found it necessary to make distinctions between various kinds of capital as well as across countries. Relatively underdeveloped Italy, for instance, differed quite fundamentally from highly industrialised Germany. Controversies exist also as to whether capitalist interests were linked to Fascism by positive intention, as the term 'instrument' suggests, or more through accommodation to circumstances.[4] The Indian situation is significantly different above all because of the absence of any major threat to propertied interests from organised labour or apparently impending socialist revolution. The scale and nature of the economic crisis is also not quite comparable. In post-Depression Germany, Nazism arguably could have appeared to many business groups 'as the last available means of preserving the capitalist system',[5] while Fascism in Italy had had a developmental, if anti-popular, 'passive revolution' aspect that Gramsci realistically recognised even from within a Fascist prison. Neither feature is particularly noticeable so far in India, where Narasimha Rao has been carrying through wide-ranging changes in economic policy with a degree of determination and skill conspicuously absent in his handling of Ayodhya. The Jan Sangh and the BJP have been advocating such a repudiation of the Nehruvian legacy of self-reliance and planning for many years, but the forces of Hindutva, in whose propaganda and activity matters economic so far have occupied only a minor place, can claim little credit for actually bringing about the shift. The Indian business groups that support Manmohan Singh's New Economic Policy (not necessarily the entire class) might still prefer a tougher anti-labour line under a Hindu Right regime no longer dependent even marginally on Left votes in parliament. Conversely, however, if the fascistic thrust of Hindutva, even now, encounters determined resistance, the traditional centrist option might appear more reliable and attractive for bourgeois groups, precisely because there is much less 'need' for Fascism in the interests of capitalist survival and profit than in inter-War Italy and Germany.

Suicidal Wobbling

It is in this context that the wobbling – and worse – of the Congress, and particularly of the Prime Minister, before and after December 6 appears so disastrous, indeed suicidal, even from the point of view of narrow party interests. There did exist a possibility of retrieval just after the 6th. The much-quoted Vajpayee interview was an indication that the BJP for a few days had been forced into the defensive. But Narasimha Rao, to quote a rather apt comment by a journalist, then proceeded 'to snatch defeat from the jaws of victory'. Sporadic, largely unimplemented, obviously half-hearted measures of repression, not backed up by any political campaign by the Congress, have by now been succeeded by what appears to be yet another attempt to compete with the BJP for the 'Hindu card'. Principles apart, elementary *Realpolitik* suggests that the more determined and consistent always win that kind of game. The shift in the attitude of the major Delhi-based dailies from virtually total condemnation of the BJP just after December 6 to much more ambiguous alignments in recent days might in this context be a straw in the wind of a most dangerous kind.

That leaders who subjectively no doubt demarcate themselves from the BJP, their principal political rival, can still stoop to such levels of opportunism indicates the degree of spread of what I have tried to argue lies at the heart of our present tragedy: a communalised common sense produced through sustained effort. Analysis-cum-critique of the varied components of this common sense is clearly vital for any effective resistance to what, with many qualifications, may still be called the Indian variety of fascism.

Fascist ideology in Europe had combined already quite widespread, crudely nationalist, racist, and in Germany anti-Semitic prejudices with fragments from much more sophisticated philosophies. That it had owed something to a general turn-of-the-century move away from what were to be the sterile rigidities of Enlightenment rationalism is not a fact without some relevance today, for not dissimilar ideas have become current intellectual coin in the west, and by extension they have started to influence Indian academic life. The ideologists of the Sangh Parivar (a Girilal Jain or a Swapan Dasgupta apart) may themselves be still largely unaware of the varied possibilities of post-modernism: that certain current academic fashions can reduce the resistance of intellectuals to the ideas of Hindutva has already become evident. The 'critique of colonial discourse' inspired by Said's *Orientalism*, for instance, has stimulated forms of indigenism not too easy to distinguish from the standard Sangh Parivar argument, going back to Savarkar, that Hindutva is superior to Islam and Christianity (and, by extension, to creations of the modern west like science, democracy or Marxism) because of its allegedly unique indigenous roots. An uncritical cult of the 'popular' or 'subaltern', particularly when combined with the rejection of Enlightenment rationalism as irredeemably tainted in all its forms by colonial power-knowledge, can lead even radical historians down strange paths.[6] It is not unimportant, therefore, to recall that Giovanni Gentile had defined Fascism as a 'revolt against positivism', or that Mussolini in 1933 had condemned the 'movement of the 18th century visionaries and Encyclopaedists' along with 'teleological' conceptions of progress. Ominously relevant, too, is another peroration of the Italian dictator, in July 1934, where he called for an end to 'intellectualising and of those sterile intellectuals who are a threat to the nation'. Hitler at the Nuremberg Nazi Congress next year similarly exalted the 'heart', the 'faith', the 'inner voice' of the German *Volk* over 'hair-splitting intelligence'.[7]

'Enemy' Image

This, however, has been a bit of an aside: far more central to Hindutva as a mass phenomenon (or for that matter to Fascism) is the development of a powerful and extendable enemy image through appropriating stray elements from past prejudices, combining them with new ones skillfully dressed up as old verities, and broadcasting the resultant compound through the most up-to-date media techniques. The Muslim here becomes the near-exact equivalent of the Jew – or the Black (more generally, immigrants felt to be inferior for one or another reason) in contemporary White racism. The Muslim in India, like the Jew in Nazi propaganda, is unduly privileged – a charge even more absurd here than it was in Germany, where the Jews had been fairly prominent in intellectual, professional and business circles. In post-Independence India, Muslims in contrast are grossly under-represented at elite levels, however defined. The alleged privileges, in the second place, are the product of 'appeasement' of Muslims by 'pseudo-secularists', and so very quickly the communal target starts broadening itself, and Mulayam Singh Yadav, to take one example among many, becomes a 'mulla'. The stock examples of 'appeasement' in recent days have been the destruction of temples in Kashmir, allegedly never condemned by the 'pseudo-secularists', and Muslim personal law permitting polygamy. Desecration must be condemned, whether by Muslims or by Hindus, but it is a strange condemnation that uses it to justify or condone the wanton desecration of December 6. The destruction of numerous Muslim religious places in riots (at Bhagalpur, for instance) is of course never mentioned. The Kashmir temples issue, incidentally, became very prominent in conversation just after the destruction of the Babri Masjid, indicating a concerted whisper campaign as well as, possibly, an element of guilt suppressed through verbal excess. The oft-repeated argument that Muslims must repent or atone for their acts of past or present aggression has meanwhile acquired a strange flavour in the context of some current reports from Bombay. Muslims offering to rebuild destroyed temples have been spurned by the Shiv Sena, and in Dharavi a group of them who were actually rebuilding one have just been stabbed (*Pioneer*, 9 January 1993).

On the Muslim Personal Law issue, the Sangh Parivar once again takes full advantage of Rajiv Gandhi's misdeeds, when he tried to counterbalance the opening of the locks of Ayodhya by the Muslim Women's Bill. The Muslim fundamentalist side of the appeasement (from which the only real and direct sufferers were Muslim women) is always mentioned, never the simultaneous appeasement of Hindu communalism. The real importance of the question, however, is in the light it can throw on the presuppositions, reminiscent of racism, of the Hindutva ideology. The continuation of the legal right of polygamy among Muslims is constantly linked up to assertions that Muslims consequently breed faster: 'hum panch hamare pachis', as the Delhi VHP leader (currently BJP MP) B. L. Sharma elegantly described it in an interview he gave to a group of us in April 1991. The Report on the Status of Women in India (1975), however, had found the rate of polygamy actually higher among Hindus than Muslims (5.06 per cent as against 4.31 per cent). The Muslims, then, become dangerous simply by going through the basic biological processes of birth, procreation and even – death, for we were told during an investigation of the 1991 Nizamuddin riots in New Delhi that a dead Muslim always grabs a bit of land by burial, unlike the self-effacing cremated Hindu. Racist attitudes, finally, are neatly encapsulated in the very recent coinage of the formula 'Babar ki aulad'. Alleged descent from Babar is sufficient to damn, no overt misdeed is really required, just as once in fanatical Christian circles all Jews stood condemned because of what their ancestors had supposedly done at the time of the crucifixion of Christ.

Such is Hindutva ideology at its crudest, engaged in the direct justification of communal violence. The slightly 'softer' or more insidious levels should also be considered, for these can indicate almost as clearly the fascistic implications of Hindu Rashtra. Fascism has often tried to appropriate elements, or at least terms, from ideals considered laudable and progressive in the society it sought to conquer: thus the Nazis claimed to be not only 'nationalist' in post-Versailles Germany, but also, keeping in mind the very strong working class political presence in the Weimar Republic, 'socialist' and representative of 'labour'. The Sangh Parivar, similarly, tries to establish its claim to be truly and uniquely 'national' by a 'democratic' argument: Hindu interests should prevail always in India, and maybe, it should at some stage be declared a Hindu Rashtra, for Hindus after all are the majority, by Census reckoning 85 per cent of the population. But democracy logically must connote two other features in addition to rule of majority: protection of rights of minority ways of life and opinions, and, even more crucially, the legal possibility that the political minority of today can win electoral majority in the future and thus peacefully change the government. Otherwise it becomes difficult to deny the status of democracy to the one-party regimes of Hitler, Mussolini (or Stalin), for all of them did go in for occasional elections of a single-list, plebiscitary type, and won majorities which may not have been entirely rigged. Democratic theory, in other words, stands in total contradiction of any notion of *permanent* majorities – but such, by Sangh Parivar definition, would be the position of the party that claims to speak uniquely for all Hindus: the BJP. Inherent in that claim is a second assertion, equally reminiscent of Fascism: only s/he is a true Hindu who accepts the leadership of the RSS-BJP-VHP combine. Any dissent runs the risk of being branded as pseudo-secular appeasement. So had Hitler and the Nazis arrogated to themselves the right to speak for all 'pure' Germans, along with the power to decide who was racially pure.

What the triumph of Hindutva, 'hard' or 'soft', implies for Muslims and other minority groups is already obvious enough: a second-class citizenship at best, constant fear of riots amounting to genocide, a consequent strengthening of the most conservative and fundamentalist groups within such communities. The near-coincidence in time between the destruction of the Babri Masjid and the barbarous assault on Professor Mushirul Hasan does not appear accidental – and the police, interestingly, were strangely absent or inactive in both cases. The fallout of December 6 has already strengthened Muslim fundamentalist forces in Pakistan and Bangladesh. The Muslims in India, it needs to be added, are not an insignificant minority, but 120 million – the biggest in the world next to Indonesia. The sheer size and diversity of the Indian people make secularism, democracy and the preservation of national unity more closely inter-dependent than perhaps anywhere else in the world. The permanent and total alienation the BJP seems to be working for can lead to a Lebanon or Yugoslavia on a vastly enhanced scale. The Sangh Parivar certainly has peculiar ways of living up to its much-touted claim to be more 'national' than anyone else.

Scope For Common Action

One major distinction between the Hindutva of today and European Fascism, particularly the Nazi variety, lies in a very different relationship with established religious traditions. Nazis sought to ground identity on race, not religion, and called on youth to build a new civilisation which could at times sound openly anti-Christian. The Sangh Parivar, by very definition, has to preach total adherence and deference towards Hindu traditions even while fundamentally transforming them. That this has been a source of tremendous strength hardly needs to be stated; just possibly, it could also be transformed into a weakness given effective counter-strategies. For Hindutva is really homogenising and changing Hindu beliefs and practices on a truly colossal scale. The statement of a VHP leader, exulting over the destruction of Muslim houses near what had been the Babri Masjid, epitomises this transformation: this was necessary, he said, to make of that area a Vatican. But the vast and enormously variegated Hindu world has never had what the VHP is trying to make out of Ram and Ayodhya – a single supreme deity and pilgrimage centre, steam-rolling out of existence differences of region, sect, caste, gender, class. Even more basic is the effort to transform what millions of Hindus sincerely believe – with what degree of historical accuracy does not matter very much in this context – to be a supremely tolerant and Catholic religion into a terrifying instrument of vandalism, murder, and usurpation of political power. The traditions of catholicity in our country are deep and themselves extremely diverse. They range from syncretic, at times radically iconoclastic, Bhakti-Sufi 'sants' and 'pirs', for some of whom, in the words of a Baul song, the path seemed blocked by mandir and masjid, purohit and mulla – to the conservative, yet profoundly Catholic, Ramakrishna, in whose vision Hindu, Muslim and Christian differed as little as *jal* from *pani* and water. And our thoughts today inevitably go back, time and again, to another dark January 45 years ago, when a man died, a devout Hindu whose last words had also evoked Ram, murdered by a youth reared in the culture of the Sangh Parivar. An ocean separates the Ram of Mahatma Gandhi, conceived of as both Iswara and Allah, from the Ram in whose name the Babri Masjid has been destroyed.

Secularism Has Many Meanings

What is necessary today is the recognition that secularism can and indeed does have many meanings, that its wide and varied spectrum can extend from the devoutly religious to the freethinker-atheist, on a common minimum ground of total rejection of communal hatred and a theocratic state. This does not mean that non-religious secularists should engage in a breast-beating exercise for having been 'alienated' from the 'mainstream' and suddenly claim to be more 'truly' Hindu or Muslim than the VHP or the Muslim fundamentalist.[8] It involves, rather, an awareness that even profound differences need not rule out common action in defense of basic human values, that, as Trotsky had once said while pleading for a united front against Fascism, it is possible to 'march separately, but strike together'.[9]

That the Hindutva forces are afraid of such unity is indicated by their persistent efforts to brand secularism and indeed all anti-communal attitudes as necessarily somehow anti-Hindu. Simultaneously they try to conflate secularism uniquely with the policies of the 'Nehruvian' state, thus making it bear the burden of the many sins of opportunism, excessive and bureaucratic centralization, and repression of which that state has been often guilty. Here, once again, current intellectual tendencies have provided respectability to such critiques, for it is often assumed nowadays that secularism was a creation of the now much-abused Enlightenment rationalism and scepticism, brought into India in the baggage of colonial discourse, and subsequently embodied in the repressive nation-states that have emerged on the western pattern. Actually, even in Europe, the roots of secularism go back at least another 200 years, to the times of the religious wars ('communal riots', we might legitimately call them) sparked off by the Reformation. The first advocates of toleration based on separation of church from state were not rationalist freethinkers, but Anabaptists passionately devoted to their own brand of Christianity, who still believed that coercion, persecution and any kind of compulsory state religion was contrary to true faith.

In India, as in other countries with multiple religious traditions, the need and therefore the bases of co-existence are broader and deeper than the teachings of the vast majority of holy men of all creeds or the policies of many kings, among whom Akbar is only the best remembered. They have been grounded in the necessities of daily existence itself, which might occasionally produce conflict, but also tend towards the restoration of interdependence – if allowed to do so by organised communal forces, which means less and less often nowadays.[10] And if communalism shatters everyday existence, it simultaneously halts and turns back all efforts to improve the condition of living through striving to reduce exploitation and want. It does so in two fundamental ways: by shattering the unity and struggle of toilers and all the subordinate groups, and fostering, within the rigid community boundaries it erects, tendencies towards ruthless homogenisation. Such homogenisation invariably helps the groups and interests occupying positions of power – in the context of Hindu communalism, most obviously, the high caste elite. It is noteworthy how every move towards implementing even the fairly limited measures towards social justice promised by the Mandal recommendations are being met by a Hindutva offensive. The noticeable silences so far about specific socio-economic issues in the programmes and activities of Hindutva (no effort has been made to spell out the 'roti' concomitant of Ram, and that slogan itself seems forgotten) can be made into a space for effective secular intervention – provided, however, the habit of segregating the 'economic' and 'political' from the 'cultural' or 'ideological', fairly deep-rooted in Indian Left traditions, is abandoned. Anti-communal campaigns cannot be left to seminars or middle-class cultural programmes alone, important though these are, nor can everyday economic struggles afford to skirt questions of religion, communalism and ideology in the facile hope that material issues and 'real' class identities will automatically assert themselves.

Thinking back about the Fascist era in Europe may seem a grim and depressing exercise, now that chauvinist forces are rearing their heads virtually everywhere. But the memories of the 1930s and early 1940s are not just of Storm Troopers, Holocaust, concentration camps, and the not unrelated deformations that have culminated today in the shattering of the world's first socialist experiment. They include the experiences of united, and in their time victorious, anti-fascist struggle, popular fronts, a Barcelona very different from the one seen on TV last year [1992], the heroism of Stalingrad and not just Stalinist terror. The time may have come to draw sustenance once again from the slogan of the defenders of Republican Spain: Fascism shall not pass.

Endnotes

1 In terms, of course, of the high standards set in Kanpur, Bhopal, Surat, Bombay and a host of other towns in a country where 213 places were under curfew at one point after December 6, affecting 97 million people: *Cry The Beloved Country* (People's Union for Democratic Rights, Delhi, December 1992).

2 For a more detailed account of the evolution of the Sangh Parivar, see Tapan Basu, Pradip Dutta, Sumit Sarkar, Tanika Sarkar, and Sambuddha Sen, *Khaki Shorts and Saffron Flags: The Politics of the Hindu Right* (New Delhi 1993).

3 Daniel Guerin, *Fascism and Big Business* (orig. 1936; New York, 1973), p. 10.

4 Guerin, *op cit*.; Alan S. Milward, 'Fascism and the Economy', in Walter Laqueur, ed., *Fascism: A Reader's Guide* (Berkeley, California, 1976; Penguin Books, 1979).

5 Milward, *op.cit*., p. 414.

6 Thus Gautam Bhadra, in an interview given to a Bengali journal in early 1991, managed to find elements of laudable subaltern assertion of identity in the first *kar seva* movement and even in the speeches of Sadhvi Rithambara. Dipesh Chakrabarti, another member of the *Subaltern Studies* editorial team, in a more recent article has argued that we need to search for creative elements in everything condemned by the "His Master's Voice" of the post-Enlightenment West. This, for him, explicitly includes Marx just as much as Macaulay (*Naiya*, February 1991; *Baromas*, October 1992).

7 Zeev Sternhell, 'Fascist Ideology', in Laqueur, *op cit*., p. 334 (the quotation from Gentile); Guerin, *op cit*., pp. 65, 168–69, 171.

8 They are less alienated, surely, from Indian culture or elementary human values than those young men of Surat who, in the name of Hindutva, videotaped their gang-rape of Muslim women. The tape, I have been told, is being avidly watched at evening parties in some affluent Bombay homes.

9 Leon Trotsky, 'For a Workers' United Front against Fascism', (December 1931) in Trotsky, *The Struggle against Fascism in Germany* (Penguin Books, 1975) p. 106.

10 The *Frontline* of 15 January, 1993, pp. 60–81, carries some moving reports of the striving of ordinary people to restore the torn fabric of inter-community mutual dependence even after the post-December 6 riots.

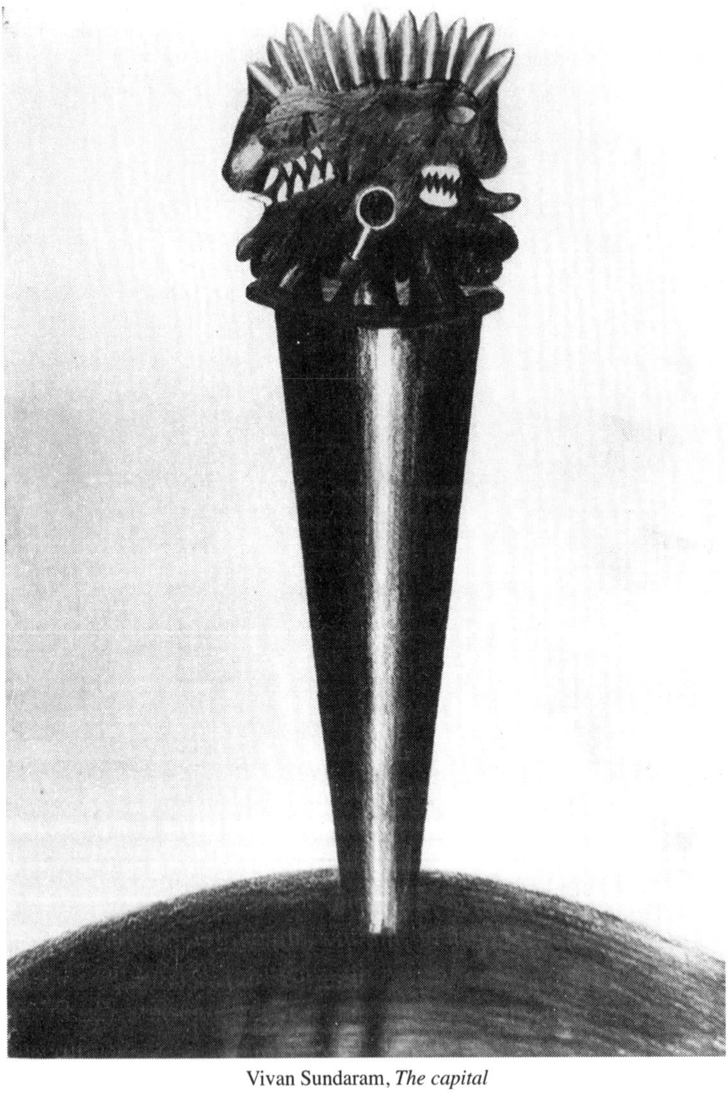

Vivan Sundaram, *The capital*

The law of killing
A brief history of Indian fascism[1]

Dilip Simeon

The permanent militarisation of society requires a permanent enemy.

Hoodbhoy & Nayyar

Politics is the plastic art of the state, just as painting is the plastic art of colour. This is why politics without the people or even against the people, is sheer nonsense. To form a People out of the masses, and state out of the People, this has always been the deepest sense of a true politics.

Joseph Goebbels in his novel *Michael* (1929)

The nation-state, incapable of providing a law for those who had lost the protection of a national government, transferred the whole matter to the police.

Hannah Arendt in 1948

Introduction

Is the term "fascism" relevant to India? The rhetorical use of the word has led to a semantic devaluation which is regrettable, because it can lead to a refusal to confront the reality of a fascist movement. In addition to this overused rhetoric, there is another problem, the reduction of politics to the platforms or doctrines of existent political parties. This essay is an effort to go beyond such rhetoric, to understand the origins, forms and activity of authoritarian politics in India, and to examine whether they approximate to the fascist phenomenon. Historically, fascism has three aspects to it, viz., ideas, movements and regimes. I use "fascism/fascist" to refer to right-wing populist dictatorships marked by ultra-nationalist ideologies, the abolition of the rule of law (or its subjugation to ideology and/or the will of a supreme leader), and the destruction of democratic institutions. I also use it to refer to movements that aspire to such regimes, and the ideologies that propel and accompany such movements. In some ways the movement and its ideas count for more than the regime, because fascist activity depends upon overt or covert official support for its successes, and its complete or partial control of organs of state power only accentuates tendencies that were already present beforehand. These tendencies – dynamism, the substitution of ideas by propaganda, the constant deployment of violence, the worship of power and a capacity for self-destruction – can lead the state itself towards disintegration. Which political interests benefit from this? Why does society allow this to happen? How are these matters related to Indian political reality? These are complex questions, admitting of no easy answers.

The notion that fascism may be properly recognised only when it seizes absolute power is dangerously misleading. This is because its hold on power arises primarily from intimidation and ideological influence, and is exhibited at the very first moment that organs of state tolerate or enable illegal and violent activities of fanatical cadre or crowds. Fascism invades the public sphere with controlled mobs. It represents an assault on politics, a replacement of democratic dialogue by violent intimidation, spectacular acclamation and automatic behaviour patterns. It is a cult of struggle, violence and war; a perversion of democracy towards 'directed' and theatrical activism in which charismatic leadership, perpetual motion and myth are essential ingredients.[2]

A further peculiarity is that fascist ideology is a mixture of archaic and modern elements – but nonetheless one that could arise only within mass democratic politics. This politics faces the question of legitimation in an age when the state is no longer grounded in the notion of divine right. Any state that appeals to this (divine) concept of sovereignty is faced with the problem of defining the agent who 'properly' represents divine law. Such an agent will automatically be above and beyond the control of the demos, or people, and hence such a polity will be something less than a democracy. In the absence of divine legitimation, conservative politics can take a populist turn which seemingly embraces democracy, but perverts it by means of a mythic ideal of the People, of the Nation, seen as a monolith with a unique world mission. Nationalism here takes on the aspect of prayer. The more it assumes such an aspect, the more it, too, moves away from democracy. Historically speaking, fascist leaders have tended to be those who are successful at deploying myths and sentiments as a means of defining the Nation. Such myths are generally militarist in nature and interpret history as a saga of victories and defeats. Nationalism, then, is the principal ideological ground of fascism. In an era of nation-states, fascism has emerged as an immanent tendency – not always successful – of so-called nation-building projects.

People and nation

The nationalist fascination with communal arithmetic was a dominant feature of politics in the twentieth century. The Great War of 1914-18 led to the dissolution of four major multi-national empires, the Ottoman, the Tsarist, the Hohenzollern, and the Hapsburg. The statesmen who re-drew the geo-political map of the world in 1919 sought to re-arrange their component parts according to the principle of self-determination that had acquired potency after the French Revolution had proclaimed the Rights of Man along with national sovereignty. Commenting on the links between 1789 and the ambivalent radicalism of the twentieth century, George Mosse wrote: 'The French Revolution...put its stamp upon a novel view of the sacred: it created a civil religion which modern nationalism made its own, and fascism, whatever its variety, was, above all, a nationalist movement.'[3] The ideal of the nation-state had a tortuous history through the nineteenth century, but, by its end, a powerful conviction held the world in its sway.

The nation-state denoted the disastrous marriage of territorial space and ethnic community.[4] It was inaugurated as a principle of international law by the geopolitical arrangements contrived by the Treaty of Versailles (1919), where Europe's statesmen were charged with the task of setting up a new international order that would enable a sovereign Poland to come into being, as well as stabilise the situation in the vast disintegrated territories of the Ottoman and Hapsburg empires. The ethnically scattered nature of the population of central, eastern and south-eastern Europe doomed the exercise from the start. It forced peoples such as the Slovaks, Croats and Slovenes into artificial states such as Czechoslovakia and Yugoslavia and bestowed the status of 'minority' upon others. This fabricated institution was the launch-pad for the invention of 'minorities' (which only came into existence because another, larger group was deemed to be the natural majority). An article written in 1923 by a member of the League of Nations Secretariat defined minorities as 'groups of persons who differ in race, religion or language from the majority of the inhabitants of the country.'[5] It also generated what was then called 'transfer of population' and nowadays, 'ethnic cleansing'. The first major instance of state-sponsored transfer was the mass expulsion via terror of Turkey's Armenian population in 1915, which resulted in up to one and a half million deaths. It took place at a time when the Ottoman Empire was in its death throes, and the ultra-nationalist Young Turk movement had begun to exercise its sway. The history of the Armenian genocide remains highly politicised and contested, although the massacres were made explicit in the text of the Treaty of Sevres (1920) between Turkey and the victorious Allied powers. [6]

With the advent of the nation-state, the state ceased to be an instrument of law and became instead an instrument of the Nation.[7] Certified by international law, the ideological arithmetic of the nation-state suffused the atmosphere of nationalist movements

– and as we know, nationalism covered a wide range of inclinations, from Nazism to anti-colonialism. Due to this, in Hannah Arendt's words, 'nationally frustrated population(s)' were 'firmly convinced' – as was everybody else – that 'true freedom, true emancipation and true popular sovereignty could be attained only with full national emancipation, that people without their own national government were deprived of human rights.' As a result, 'those peoples to whom states were not conceded, no matter whether they were official minorities or only nationalities, considered the Treaties an arbitrary game which handed out rule to some and servitude to others.'[8] She continues:

> The real significance of the Minority Treaties lies not in their practical application but in the fact that they were guaranteed by an international body, the League of Nations... The Minority Treaties said in plain language what until then had been only implied in the working system of nation-states, namely, that only nationals could be citizens, only people of the same national origin could enjoy the full protection of legal institutions, that persons of different nationality needed some law of exception until or unless they were completely assimilated...the transformation of the state from an instrument of the law into an instrument of the nation had been completed; the nation had conquered the state, national interest had priority over law long before Hitler could pronounce "right is what is good for the German people." Here again the language of the mob was only the language of public opinion cleansed of hypocrisy and restraint.[9]

The genocidal instinct towards imaginary alien elements/ internal enemies received political and legal impetus with the formalisation of the term *minorities* in modern nationalist discourse. There were many ideological ingredients to this exterminism, including Social-Darwinism and eugenics. But the articulation of national unity via the bestowal of an inferior status upon an entire community or communities was a central feature. The link between nationalism and war-mongering, evident in the emergence of nation-states, was vastly extended in the ultra-nationalist movements that emerged in Europe after the First World War, and that came to be known generically as fascist. It soon became apparent that these tendencies were nothing less than ideologically enforced projects that sought to criminalise the state, do away with the liberal-democratic concept of constitutional authority, nullify the neutrality of justice and abolish the rule of law. They were movements aiming at the all-round militarisation of civil society.

Antonio Gramsci used military metaphors in his analysis of fascism, terms such as 'wars of position', and 'strategic conjuncture.' These metaphors are as symptomatic of the ideological climate of modernity as they are analytically insightful.[10] Disdain for law and stable institutions are marked features of fascist movements, whose only 'law' is dynamism and the casting off of limits to human action, an almost worshipful celebration of the patriarchal will to power. Because of this, fascism cannot be reduced to utilitarian definitions, as an instrument of the bourgeoisie etc., rather, it is a powerful expression of the annihilationist drive endemic in capitalist modernity (there are others). More ominously, it is a populist movement, one that mobilizes the most base and destructive elements of the human spirit and mass psychology. In the words of the ex-Nazi Herman Rauschning, it is the revolution of nihilism.[11]

Historical events do not replicate themselves in pre-determined fashion, and in any case, fascism cannot be reduced to this or that event. The growth of fascism was a prolonged development with certain political and institutional features that underlay contextual differences. Nor was it always marked by seizures of power or the advent of war. Identifying it requires an eye to political tendencies. These tendencies are visible in colonial India and its successor states, although with distinctive features. The most distinctive common feature is that its successes depend more on ideological influence than organisational affiliation. In India this ideology is manifested in what we call communalism; and it includes the demonisation of entire communities that emerged in the West in the form of anti-Semitism.

Communal violence

The independence of India and Pakistan was preceded by much bloodshed. Every decade since the 1890s had witnessed communal violence, some of it spontaneous. By the 1940s the deliberate instigation of violence had begun. The Calcutta Killing of 1946, in which 5,000–10,000 people were killed, and some 15,000 wounded, was a turning-point. The violence was noted for savagery and mutilation, exhibiting the deep hatred known to accompany communal strife. Bengal was then governed by a Muslim League ministry led by Hussain Suhrawardy.[12] October 1946 saw massacres of Hindus in Noakhali district of East Bengal; this was followed by a pogrom of Muslims in Bihar, under a Congress ministry. The number of casualties in both instances ran into thousands, although precise figures are disputed. Thereafter the cycle of violence continued for over two years.[13]

The birth of Pakistan was seen as a victory for proponents of a Muslim Nation. It was accompanied by massacres all over north India and Bengal. Some fifteen million people were forced to migrate both ways, across a hurriedly drawn border. The genocidal 'cleansing' of Punjab's population along communal criteria led to a human catastrophe whose scars are yet to heal. Up to a million were killed in 1947.[14] After 1947 the killings continued, of Muslims in Hyderabad (India) in 1948 and of Hindus in East Pakistan in 1949 and 1950.

The Nizam of Hyderabad had resisted integration into the Indian Union, and his private militia, the Razakars, helped him maintain a 'standstill' status for a year, a period that also saw an unfolding communist insurgency. The Razakars' brutality earned them the fear and hatred of the peasant population, and also fuelled the agitations of Hindu communal organisations. In September 1948 the government initiated 'police action' via the Indian Army, which finally routed the Nizam's forces, but also unleashed communal warfare in a swathe of territory including but extending beyond areas affected by Razakar violence. In November 1948, the Nehru government deputed a respected Congressman, Pandit Sunderlal to lead an inquiry into these events. An undated letter from the Sunderlal Committee spoke of mass instances of loot, arson, desecration of mosques, forcible conversions and the seizure of houses and lands. It stated that 'communal frenzy did not exhaust itself in murder'; and that 'at some places even women and children were not spared'. It mentioned a 'well known Hindu communal organisation from Sholapur…as also some local and outside communists' as participating in the riots and in some cases leading the rioters. It also mentioned instances in which men belonging to the Army and police participated in and encouraged these crimes. It estimated the loss of life at between 27,000 and 40,000 Muslims 'who formed a hopeless minority in rural areas.'[15]

In East Pakistan, mass violence directed at caste Hindus as well as 'untouchables' continued through 1948 till 1950 and beyond. Jogendra Nath Mandal, Pakistan's first Law and Labour Minister, wrote that communal bias amongst officials and the police made Pakistan an 'accursed place' for Hindus. In his resignation letter to Prime Minister Liaqat Ali Khan (October 1950), Mandal spoke of nearly 10,000 deaths in Dacca and other districts.[16] In 1949, Sris Chandra Chattopadhya, a member of Pakistan's Constituent Assembly, protested against the Objectives Resolution, introduced by Prime Minister Liaqat Ali Khan, whereby sovereignty and authority were delegated to the State from 'God Almighty alone.'[17] The significance of this resolution may be gauged from the fact that its notion of sovereignty has been retained in the constitutions of Pakistan and Bangladesh. The targeting of Ahmadiyas for being 'non-Muslims' began in 1953.[18] This doctrinal assertion was inserted into the 1973 Constitution of Pakistan.

The above instances are meant to trace the trajectory of communal violence – they are by no means exhaustive. In recent times, major incidents have attracted world attention (there are thousands of smaller ones) – the pogrom against Sikhs in Delhi in 1984, against Muslims in Gujarat in 2002, and against Christians in Odisha in 2008. The Khalistani insurgency (of extremist Sikhs) during the 1980s resulted in the deaths of thousands of civilians in Punjab. The RSS-led campaign for the destruction of the Babri Mosque lasted eight years (1986–92) and resulted in four to five thousand deaths. The Kashmir insurgency cost tens of thousands of lives, mainly of Kashmiri Muslims. About 300,000 Kashmiri Hindu Pandits were forced to leave the Valley in the 1990s, and hundreds of them were killed by separatist and/or Islamist terror groups. (All figures are indicative rather than precise).

These traumatic events have left deep psychological scars, and contributed to the stabilisation of communal identity. Most of them have been accompanied by incidents of utmost brutality and assaults upon women and children. It is worth noting that concepts such as 'Hindu interest' or 'Muslim interest' remain fictions until they are goaded into existence by the reality of death and destruction. Fear is crucial to the fascist project, because only the dread of extinction can overcome class, caste and gender divisions in the daily lives of people of all communities. Hence fascists specialise in using hurt sentiment as a pretext for mob violence – sentiment and faith are beyond argument. The 'hurt' in this case is usually on account of perceived insults to tradition, religion, the nation or some other insignia of patriarchal honour. In India the targeting of artists, writers, women and young people over the content of artistic works, dress-codes and adherence to 'foreign' culture has been a marked phenomenon in recent years. Violent intimidation by both Hindu and Muslim communalists has been gently handled by the police, and has adversely affected women's safety, academic research and the creative arts.

Understanding Indian Communalism

Many scholars use prefixes such as *Hindu* and *Muslim* when speaking of communalism. Some speak only of majorities and minorities. I see it as a generic ideology, with different expressions. In colonial India, *communalism* referred to the idea that shared religious beliefs imply shared political interests. But Indians also possessed affiliations related to caste, region and language. Many such affiliations developed after the introduction of census operations by the colonial government. The latter half of the nineteenth century saw the emergence of caste-associations and coalitions and campaigns around language. Religion-based communalism emerged in an incipient contest with these, for it sought to establish an over-arching identity that would supersede caste and regional identities. It thus implied a goal, not a reality, and *communal* ideologies imagined an ideal religious unity. These had origins in what might be termed community protectionism, projects launched with the stated aim of educational advancement, preservation of a distinctive culture and access to administrative and political positions. These mild forms of communal mobilisation cannot be termed fascistic in inspiration or tendency. However they prepared the ground for the emergence of antagonistic discourses. When coupled with the mendacity of a colonial power in retreat, the extension of voting rights, mass populist campaigns and the climate engendered by communal riots, these relatively benign forms of thought and organisation could and did assume deadlier tendencies and structures.

The colonial conquest of India had taken an entire century, in the course of which the fragments of the moribund Mughal empire and various predatory polities were brought under a new dispensation. The complex social hierarchies in different areas, the long period of social pacification, the staggered pace of institutional change, and Britain's own historical transformation during this period, ensured that the reaction to colonisation was highly differentiated. Remnants of traditional ruling classes could oscillate between xenophobic resistance and collaboration, and the reaction of the plebeian classes could also change from passivity to rebellion. The scholars, teachers, priests and officials of the pre-colonial order retained their sources of livelihood; and their world outlook was not suddenly transported into so-called "modernity". As a colonial middle class slowly emerged out of elements of the traditional intelligentsia and other propertied strata, a chaotic upheaval of values and norms took place. Nostalgia for the passing of traditional monarchical power (after the Anglo-Maratha wars that ended in 1818, the Anglo-Sikh wars of the 1840s, and the failed revolt of 1857) took the form of revivalist doctrines that sought to explain defeat in terms of the estrangement from pure origins. However, the relationship between revivalist and reformist trends was complex. Often the two attitudes meshed together, for both sought to explain and overcome perceived decline. What is significant is that the perception of subjugated identity was forged – at least in part – in the language and mental universe of defeated aristocracies.[19]

In an important account of the Indian anti-imperialist movement, Bhagwan Josh characterises nationalism as 'a non-class ideology in the sense that it was not a direct rationalisation and articulation of the distinct economic interests of a class… it is indeterminate and open-ended in terms of what precise class interest it is to serve in the long run.' He adds, 'nationalism is not superior to "communalism" just because it claims to defend the interests of many communities, unlike the latter which defends the interests of only one community. The democratic impulse lies at the heart of nationalism while "communalism" is intrinsically authoritarian.'[20] However, the ambivalence Josh refers to is precisely what makes the distinction problematic when the colonised people are defined in religious terms. (Who does the defining? Why and how far does the definition carry conviction?) In this case, communal ideologies and nationalism get mixed together. Thus, in the last decade of colonial power, at a point when negotiations between the major national parties were becoming intractable, the Muslim League began using the concept of 'nation' to define its interest – if 'the Hindus' were a nation by themselves as Savarkar liked to say, so were 'the Muslims.' Henceforth the negotiations between the Congress and the League would have to be conducted along the lines of the formal symmetry that governed relations between equals, rather than a 'majority' talking to a 'minority' – this despite the fact that the Congress did not claim to be a representative body of 'the Hindus.' A verbal about-turn converted an inter-community discourse into an 'inter-national' one. The binary complex 'majority vs. minority' was inverted and replicated, by means of a semantic shift that inexorably moved onto a geo-political plane. The locus of conflicting communal power-relations moved out of the fragile Indian public sphere into the domain of international law. Because this law was rooted in the concept of the nation-state (itself defined as a living space for a homogenous 'national' community), it reproduced the formal language of majority and minority. The authoritarian trend in Indian politics emerged in the openings provided by this fluid connection of the 'nation' and the 'community'.

One of the earliest such ideological developments took place with the emergence of the idea of the Hindu nation. (*Nation* was still taken to mean an ethnically distinct people rather than a nation-state. As late as the 1940s it did not necessarily imply a delineation of sovereignty.) The reformist aspirations of the intelligentsia became increasingly political in the late nineteenth century. As the century progressed, outstanding literateurs took the distinctive step of naming India as naturally Hindu and Muslims as quintessentially alien.[21] Thus, Bharatendu Harishchandra (1850–1885), despite his attempts at forging Hindu-Muslim unity, could also write a poem welcoming the Prince of Wales in which British colonialism was depicted as an act of liberation for Hindus ground by centuries of Muslim oppression. Writers such as Vishnu Krishna Chiplunkar (1850–1882), Pratapnarayan Misra (1856–1894) and Swami Shraddhananda (1857–1926) narrated a history of Hindu society that sought to explain social evils such as *sati*, child-marriage and the caste system as survival mechanisms in a long night of Muslim rule. The word *Hindu* came to be used sometimes with a geographic, at other times with an agglomerative implication.

> 'Hindustan is ours because we are Hindus', and 'He who inhabits Hindustan is a Hindu' were two ways in which Hindu and India(n) were made synonymous. Moving one way, Harishchandra used the term Hin-

> du and insisted that it meant all Indians. Moving another way, Pratapnarayan argued that Hindus constituted the real India, and clearly stated that it was by virtue of their association with Hindus that non-Hindu inhabitants qualified as Indians. Whichever way one moved along this semantic circle – and the same person could move both ways – at its centre lay an implicit communal assumption.[22]

Gradually the pre-colonial state tradition was mythologised. The search for a counter-imperium led inexorably towards the contentions of an authoritarian mentality, as witnessed by the identification with Maratha, Sikh, or Sunni monarchs by sections of the intelligentsia with social roots in recently overturned state structures. These developments were not immediately political. They originated in the philosophical adjustment to the victorious colonial order on the part of the heterogenously constituted Indian intelligentsia. The *fatwas* of the Deoband ulema from the 1870s attempted to provide guidance to faithful Muslims in a context wherein the rule of the *sharia* could no longer be assured by the authority of a Sunni monarch. At a deeper level, the struggle over symbols during the formative years of the national movement carried a hegemonic aspiration. Such was the case, for example, with the competition for the appropriation of the popular symbol of 'Chhatrapati' Shivaji, characterised as a Sudra king by the oppressed-caste reformer Jyotiba Phule, and as *Go-Brahman Pratipalak* (Defender of Cows and Brahmins) by Bal Gangadhar Tilak.[23] It was also visible in the campaign for the propagation of the Devanagari script, which represented an aspiration for Hindi to emerge as the national language. About the latter, it has been pointed out that 'the struggle for Hindi, in a form from which its Urdu heritage was deodorised, became a means for the upper-caste groups, some of whom had substantial landed interest, to establish political identity.'[24]

The advent of the twentieth century saw major developments in national political consciousness and colonial policy. The government partitioned Bengal in 1905 – for administrative reasons with covert political ramifications. This step sparked off the Swadeshi agitation, the first mass campaign of modern Indian nationalism. A revolutionary terrorist movement emerged in Bengal, which had reverberations among émigré Indian patriots in Europe and North America. Élite landed interests set up the Muslim League in 1906, which was followed in 1909 by the grant of separate electorates for Muslims under the Morley-Minto reforms of 1909. During and immediately after the Great War of 1914–18 there took place an upsurge of mass nationalist consciousness (partly triggered by the Jallianwala Bagh massacre of 1919) that was reflected in campaigns such as the agitations of the Home Rule Leagues and the non-cooperation and Khilafat movements of 1919–1924. This period saw the setting up of the Hindu Mahasabha in 1915 and also the Lucknow Pact between the Congress and the Muslim League in 1916. In 1919 there emerged the agitation known as the Khilafat movement, which sought to protect the status of the Turkish Khalifa against British antagonism during the war. Gandhi's endorsement of the assertions of a narrow section of the Muslim clergy assumed that they represented something called the 'Indian Muslim'. It also gave the clergy leverage that temporarily boosted nationalist agitation but later produced baleful consequences. Composite nationalism began to develop communal schisms in the mid 1920s.[25]

The chief concern of communal historiography is conquest and subjugation. The ideal leaders for communalists are monarchs – this was adjusted to modernism by having permanent presidents. At the street-level, communal propaganda would evoke Hindu, Muslim or Sikh imperialism as mythic symbols of past greatness, a condition which the 'chosen' community could revive by ensuring the victory of this or that singular representative. Communalists always dreamt of the military subjugation of their so-called enemies. The enemy was not the British Empire, but another community. Communalism was and remains a battle over political language. It would be pointless to ask Hindus or Muslims to 'unite' if they were already unanimous. Rather, the slogans represented an attempt to *create* a communal interest. Indian communalism is not an arithmetical total of assorted fanaticisms, but a singular political style with different manifestations.

Inevitably, communalists spoke a language of inclusion and exclusion based upon religious criteria. Their style fitted well with an elite approach to the manipulation of crowds – the formula summed up in the words *affirmation*, *repetition* and *contagion*.[26] 'Fascism is not the product of an oppressive agenda put forward by a certain dominant group; rather, it is rooted in mass culture.'[27] Mass culture includes traditions of syncretism and co-existence, but it also carries patriarchal myths, cults of glory and martyrdom, and prejudice based on identity. That is why Indian communalists constantly fought for the 'purification' of what they termed tradition. Examining these contests can give us insights into the means whereby the class interests and prejudices of culturally-defined elites can be ideologically reproduced as new representations of 'the obvious', and can reduce social plurality to the binary dimensions of *Them* and *Us*.[28]

Communal politics in India developed before adult suffrage. In 1919 2.7% of the population had voting rights. This was extended to a mere 12% by the Government of India Act of 1935. In effect, this meant that until 1937 (when the first elections under the new regulations were held), less than 3% of the adult population had been permitted to act upon its political beliefs in a democratic voting process. A restricted electorate was the seed-bed of elitist and narrow-minded politics, and the British rulers used this to counter nationalist agitation. From the mid-1920s the government's stance towards communal riots was relatively permissive. It also used education, textbooks and news-films to portray India as hopelessly divided.

An example of the perverse political language of communalists is their reduction of democracy to a numbers game. In India it is a commonplace that 'democracy means the rule of the majority', and this definition was widespread in the political discourse of the national movement. The word *majority* remains empty until we know what we are counting, but the atmosphere of the times was heavily influenced by the ideal of ethnically homogenous nation-states. The patriotic Indian intelligentsia were sure they were counting religious communities. Once absorbed in the dominant discourse as part of common sense, the concepts of majority and minority displaced other significant elements in the definition of democratic governance – such as an independent judiciary, a free press, the rule of law and a self-correcting constitution. Thus whereas a liberal-democratic politics assigns the greatest importance to freedom of speech, belief and assembly; equality before the law, the right to combination and the peaceful resolution of conflicts; the ideology of nationalism tends to undermine these freedoms by downgrading them via a false counterposition of 'national interest' versus democratic rights. Democracy cannot be reduced to 'the rule of the majority' – a term that reeks of tyranny. But the pre-conception in all communal programmes is the assumption that religious arithmetic is the most significant factor in politics, and that democracy is about numbers, not liberty.

In this sense, Indian communalism was and remains a political philosophy of number. Its philosophical locus is the ideal of a nation-state with an ethnic community at its core. The minorities are *problems*, or *questions*, whose chief characteristic is that they are not naturally part of the nation. Hence they deserve constant surveillance and intimidation (in the eyes of the fascistic nationalists), or special protection (in the eyes of the moderate, or liberal nationalists). Either way, the ideology of the nation-state is a lens that casts a certain group or groups of its inhabitants as something other than ordinary citizens. We cannot assume that communal ideas denote a reality; but neither may we brush aside the fascist nature of these ideas merely because communalists have not (yet) overpowered the State. Fascism does not become fascism only when it attains total power. There is always a contestation underway, to which there is no foregone conclusion.

The national movement and private armies

The large-scale violence that marked the growth of communal politics was not a series of spontaneous outbursts. It required concerted action and in many cases was enabled and directed by well-armed militias. The existence of such groups in colonial India was no secret. An All India Congress Committee resolution in November 1947 warned that:

> The All India Congress Committee has noted with regret that there is a growing desire on the part of some organisations to build up private armies. Any such development is dangerous for the safety of the State and for the growth of corporate life in the nation. The State alone should have its defence forces or police or home guards or recognized armed volunteer force. The activities of the Muslim National Guards, the Rashtriya Swayamsevak Sangh and the Akali Volunteers and such other organisations, in so far as they represent an endeavour to bring into being private armies, must be regarded as a menace to the hard-won freedom of the country. The A. I. C. C. therefore appeals to all these organisations to discontinue such activities and the Central and Provincial Governments to take necessary steps in this behalf.[29]

Two months prior to this declaration, in September 1947, the Communist Party of India published a report entitled *Bleeding Punjab Warns*. This began as follows:

> What happened in the Punjab cannot be called a riot. It was a regular war of extermination of the minorities, of the Sikhs and Hindus in Western Punjab and of Muslims in East Punjab. It cannot be compared to Calcutta or Noakhali, Bihar, or even to Rawalpindi for in all these cases it was mobs of one community that took leading part in killing, looting and burning the minority in the area, their communal passions being roused to a pitch of frenzy and savagery…In the Punjab, however, in the recent biggest killing ever seen, it was the trained bands equipped with firearms and modern weapons that were the main killers, looters and rapers. These were the storm troops of various communal parties such as National Guards of the Muslim League in the Western Punjab, and the Shahidi Dal of the Akalis and the Rashtriya Swayamsevak Sangh of the Mahasabha in the Eastern Punjab. They were actively aided and often actually led by the police and the military in committing the worst atrocities.. in violence and in brutality, in the numbers killed (which Syt Shri Prakasha, India's Ambassador to Pakistan places at 1½ lakhs) in the use of plenty of modern deadly weapons, in the devastation spread

> over 14 districts of the Punjab and in the way in which the police, the military and the entire administration was geared not to stop the riots but to spread it – the Punjab tragedy is without parallel.[30]

The report describes numerous instances of atrocities carried out by the militias of various parties, as well as the extensive material support (including rifles, hand grenades, sten-guns, mortars and jeeps) given to them by the Hindu, Muslim and Sikh princely states of Punjab, including Patiala, Jhind, Nabha, Faridkot, Malerkotla, Bahawalpur and Kapurthala. It describes these states as 'the hotbeds…of cold deadly preparations for a war of extermination.' Whereas the Congress 'became more and more tongue-tied as it moved nearer and nearer acceptance of division,' it described the RSS as having taken over the towns, 'and roused the spirit of retaliation on the communal slogan of Akhand Hindustan by force'.[31] The report names 'financiers and blackmarketeers of the towns' as patrons of the RSS, and 'the most reactionary toady section of big landlords' as backing the Muslim League National Guards.

The Rashtriya Swayamsevak Sangh (RSS), or National Volunteers, was formed in 1925 by K.B. Hedgewar. It had 60,000 members by 1939, and colonial sources indicate the number had risen to 76,000 members in 1944 – and there are reports that the figure may have been closer to 100,000. Most of the membership was concentrated in the Central Provinces, Bombay and Punjab.[32] The ideological climate that nurtured these paramilitaries was Hindu religious revivalism with its profound unease at Gandhi's advocacy of non-violence and his assimilationist concept of Indian nationhood. The history of revivalism is a theme I will not explore here.[33] We may note that prominent nationalists such as Bal Gangadhar Tilak insisted that the controversy over means and ends was a tactical rather than doctrinal question. Many revivalists believed Gandhi's ideas and methods (which they saw as a manifestation of Christian rather than Hindu values) were bound to have a detrimental effect on the self-respect and capacity for resistance of Hindus. In 1922, for example, Dr Kurtakoti, the

Shankaracharya of Karvir Peeth, declared that Gandhi's ahimsa would encourage Muslim aggressiveness, and advocated a return to the militancy that he believed had been advocated by Tilak, Vivekananda and Aurobindo Ghose.[34]

The subtext of these ideas was the belief that it was India's Muslims rather than the British imperialists who were the 'enemy.' The revivalists were convinced that the foundation of the nation was the Hindu community, conceived as a monolith. These doctrines implied the need for the 'community' to develop military skills. Thus V.D. Savarkar, president of the Hindu Mahasabha from 1937 to 1943, launched a Hindu Militarisation movement, for which he coined the war-cry *Hinduise all politics and militarise Hindudom!*[35] In his presidential address of 1942, he asked members of the Mahasabha to join the armed forces as part of this movement, and further, to 'capture all centres of political power' such as legislatures, defence committees and ministries. Railing against the Muslim Leagues' new demand of 'self-determination' for Muslim majority provinces, he made clear that the threat of overwhelming force was what he had in mind to keep 'Hindusthan' united:

> The only organised body that had the courage to tell the Moslems that the consequences of their efforts to destroy Indian integrity would be in the long run as terrible had been the Hindu Mahasabha alone... Come out then to assert boldly and uncompromisingly on behalf of Hindudom – that just as in America, Germany, China and every other country not excluding Russia, so also in Hindusthan, *the Hindus by the fact that they form an overwhelming majority are the Nation and Moslems are but a community* because like all other communities they are unchallengeably in a *minority*. Therefore they must remain satisfied with whatever reasonable safeguards other minorities in India get and accept as reasonable in the light of the *world formula framed by the League of Nations*... no minority in India shall be allowed to demand to break up the very in tegrity of Hindusthan from Indus to the Seas as a condition of their participation in the Central Government or Provincial ones. No province whatsoever, by the fact that it is a province shall be allowed to claim to secede from the Central State of Hindusthan at its own sweet will...It will be well for the Moslems even in their own interest to bear faithful allegiance to the Indian nation on the same conditions offered to other

> minorities. But if the Moslems mistaking the pseudo-national yielding attitude of Congress for the attitude of Hindudom as such persist in their outrageous and treacherous demand for Pakistan or the principle of provincial self-determination then it is time, you Oh! Hindu Sanghatanists, that you must proclaim your formula from the very tops of the Himalayas. 'We don't want Hindu-Moslem unity at all on such conditions.'... Hindusthan shall and must remain an integral and powerful nation and a Central State from the Indus to the Seas, treating any movement on the part of any one to vivisect it, as treacherous and strongly suppress it just as any movement of Negrosthan would be promptly punished by the American nation!![36] (Emphases added)

Savarkar has been described as 'the first and most original prophet of extremism in India', who 'pioneered an extreme, uncompromising and rhetorical form of Hindu nationalism in Indian political discourse.'[37] It was his unwavering ideal to establish India as a Hindu Rashtra. In pursuit of this fantasy he formulated the strategy of seizing centralised power via ideological influence over the Congress, and control over crucial segments of state institutions. He evidently believed that such mechanisms could bend the Muslim League towards acceptance of the subordinate status of a minority, 'in the light of the world formula framed by the League of Nations.' In the face of the collapse of negotiations between the Congress and the League, he sought an explanation in the language of betrayal, and became a prime mover of the conspiracy to assassinate Gandhi.[38]

The development of radical conservative ideals among Muslim communalists is exemplified by Inayatullah Khan Mashriqi, educated at the University of Punjab and then at Cambridge. In 1924 Mashriqi wrote an interpretation of the Koran that argued for Islam as 'the most successful and universal principle of nation-building...the infallible and divine sociology.' After a trip to Cairo in 1926, he visited Germany and met Hitler, whom he took to be a kindred soul. (Mashriqi translated *Mein Kampf* into Urdu). He returned to India in 1931 and organised a militia he named the Khaksars (*khaksar* means humble), on an Islamic nationalist platform: 'In brief, the one aim of the Khaksar movement is to raise, once again after the lapse of thirteen centuries, soldiers for God and Islam... Our aim is to be once again Kings, Rulers, World Conquerers and Supreme Masters on Earth.' In 1940 the Khaksars were involved in a series of confrontations with the police in Lucknow and Lahore. After a spell in jail and a ban on military parading, he made peace with the authorities; and furthermore, shifted from an antagonistic to a deferential stance toward the Muslim League by the late 1940s.[39]

The following observations about the Khaksars depict the ideological climate of the period:

> Inayatullah Khan al-Mashriqi's real breakthrough occurred...after he had changed his primary role from intellectual writer to political activist. Directly inspired by world events, he began to emphasize a militant social Darwinist reading of his evolutionist theology. The paramilitary movement that he founded upon his retirement from government service in 1931 – the Khaksars – created a stir in late colonial politics and received widespread admiration in middle-class and petty bourgeois circles all over Muslim North India. Clad in khaki uniforms and following strict military discipline, Mashriqi's organisation appeared in many ways to be the Indian equivalent of Mussolini's *Fascisti* or the Nazi *Sturmabteilung*. The distinctive symbol by which they became famous was the spade, which the activists presented like a rifle in parades and used as a weapon in street fights with the police. The heyday of the movement was the years between 1935 and 1940, when they got involved in several carefully orchestrated stand-offs with government power. The essence of Khaksar political action was the creation of public spectacles in which both participants and bystanders could experience sensations of collective empowerment. On more concrete political questions they tended to remain vague.
>
> Mashriqi's social Darwinism, its political manifestation in a paramilitary volunteer movement and his pronounced leadership pretensions were hardly unique within the context of post-First World War India. This was a time of unprecedented political mass mobilization, of unbound promise as well as great uncertainty, when a whole generation of new political leaders was made. By the time of the Second World War paramilitary volunteer movements had proliferated to such an extent in India that there was hardly any political party or constituency without one. Despite some ideological differences, there were immediate similarities between the Khaksars and the extreme Hindu nationalists of the Rashtriya Swayamsevak Sangh (RSS), as well as with the Bengali

> radical Subhas Chandra Bose, who left the Indian National Congress to organize military resistance to the British during the Second World War. Within the context of Muslim politics, Mashriqi was arguably the most coherently social Darwinist voice, but his concern with militaristic self-strengthening and his rhetoric of Islamic glory continued a tradition that had become well established since the early 1910s. By the 1930s the ideological pull of fascism – and of "great dictators" more generally – was so strong that people like Hitler, Mussolini, Stalin and Pilsudski received more attention in Urdu glossy magazines than the British functionaries who actually wielded power over India. Various forms of scientism and historical evolutionism not only filled countless pages in the press, but also cropped up in various unexpected places in academic discourse. Arya Samaj Hindus and Tamil nationalist publicists (amongst others) resorted to ideas of ancient prehistoric origins and the dynamic battle of civilizations to buttress their identities. Mashriqi's ideological and organisational project developed in conscious reference to European models, particularly National Socialism in Germany.[40]

The Khaksars were but one of the latest paramilitary formations in a long history of armed groups maintained by political interests. The Muslim League had already established a National Guard that by the 1940s began adopting military trappings designed to project the Muslim League as an incipient state and 'the expression and guarantor of the cultural identity of the Indian Muslims.' The symbolism included flag-hoisting at the League's annual sessions as a means of affirming a claim on the loyalties of individual Muslims to the ideology of Pakistan.[41] The Muslim League National Guard (established in the mid 1930s), grew rapidly in Punjab during 1946, as did the RSS, and was involved in the organised violence that ravaged the province in 1947. In May that year, the colonial Governor of Punjab noted that 'all communities are said to be preparing for widespread rioting, and there is much talk about "volunteers" who constitute the "private armies" of the various communities.' An official report speaks of M.S. Golwalkar's extensive tour of Punjab in November 1946, during which he addressed large rallies holding the Congress responsible for the sufferings of Hindus in Bengal and elsewhere, and reportedly calling for 'the Muslims' to be fought 'without mercy'.[42]

The interaction between communal politics, class and bureaucratic interests, mob violence and human psychology was complex and dynamic. Thus, notwithstanding their militarist-fascist ideology, in Punjab Khaksar leaders and cadre were reported as doing their utmost to protect Hindus and Sikhs during the worst moments of rioting in Rawalpindi in March 1947.[43] In other places however, Khaksar cadre took part in the violence. Indeed, this was a moment when ideological moorings were melting away, and the events are a tragic object lesson in the nihilist character of fascism. Thus, while mainstream political parties were seemingly distinct from the communal militias, in actual fact the ideological osmosis between communal groups and moderate umbrella-type organisations ensured that the former would always exercise political leverage in the latter. The relationship between the major parties and various radical groups was complex, and altered dramatically as the withdrawal of colonial power approached.[44]

The activity of armed militias during this period shows the extent to which communal fantasies acquired substance during the violence. Slogans of 'Hindu Rashtra', 'Akhand Hindustan' and 'Khalistan' were raised, and Pakistan was visualised as the new Madina. Dhanwantri's Report mentions frantic efforts by the Sikhs in western Punjab to get the Akali leaders like Master Tara Singh to try and stop the violence against Muslims in East Punjab. 'But the Akali leadership was following a policy not based on the interests of the Sikh people but which expressed the expansionist aims of the Sikh princes. The Akali leaders ignored the entreaties of their own people...and kept on giving the boastful slogan of re-establishing the empire of Ranjit Singh.'[45] They issued leaflets in the name of the Government of Khalistan, one of which declared: 'Khalistan is the Empire of Khalsa as left by Maharaja Ranjit Singh, the Sher-i-Punjab. Every Khalsa must pledge himself to this and nothing else.'[46] Meanwhile, the RSS was denouncing Gandhi and Nehru, and there was talk of Nehru meeting the fate of the Burmese left-nationalist leader Aung San, who had just been assassinated in July 1947. The RSS-Mahasabha press called for their own leaders to be appointed to the positions of Governor and Premier of East Punjab.[47]

Notwithstanding the extremist slogans and military-style attacks on innocent people, what took place in 1947 was the inscription of an absolute line through the political map of India, made possible by the over-arching formal and legal authority of the British Empire. What the militias had accomplished, however, was the first large-scale act of ethnic cleansing. With lacs of people murdered for belonging to the 'wrong' community, the independence of India and Pakistan was marked by genocide. Aside from its various attributes, sovereignty is a form of annihilation.

The criminalisation of the polity

A significant aspect of the situation as reported by Dhanwantri and P. C. Joshi, both members of the Communist Party of India, the former a leading Punjab Communist, was the collapse of state institutions, primarily the police and military. Their report makes visible the impact of communal ideology on the ordinary personnel of these armed bodies of the state; and the gruesome consequences of the sudden realisation that their officers were no longer neutral. The state was now transforming itself into the instrument of the nation, which meant the community. The situation had begun deteriorating in March 1947, with the resignation of the Unionist-Congress-Akali coalition government, and the outbreak of mass rioting in Rawalpindi. As Governor Jenkins wrote to the viceroy in April 1947, 'We feel now that we are dealing with people who are out to destroy themselves and that in the absence of some reasonable agreement between them the average official will have to spend his life in a communal civil war. The Punjab is not in a constitutional situation but in a revolutionary situation.'[48] As the date of the Radcliffe Award (demarcating the boundary) came closer, uncertainty gripped the entire Punjabi population, not least the armed units of the colonial state. Policemen caught in areas expected to go 'the other way' were asked to disarm and proceed across the (as yet) imaginary lines demarcating Pakistan or Hindustan. With this implosion the chain of authority and legitimacy collapsed. Moreover, as new recruits were being absorbed into the police force to fill vacancies formed due to the migration of Muslims to Western Punjab, 'the RSS and the Akali bands are burrowing into these services. The RSS wants its own men to hold dominating positions in the east Punjab government.'[49]

The communal militias were now free to indulge their most bloody fantasies. The events are a case study in fascist violence. Children were butchered, women raped and dismembered, people were murdered in the most hateful ways possible by 'armed bands, fully drunk with liquor and with the lust for blood...roaming and falling on the poor victims actively assisted by the Hindu and Sikh police and units of the Boundary Force. Similar scenes were enacted in Lahore.'[50] Dhanwantri and Joshi give details of police and military involvement in massacres, manifesting the seamless connection between formal and informal armed formations during a time when state power melted away. The militias were aided by volunteers from the princely states as well as ex-servicemen. The deadliest danger to villagers was from attacks engineered by forces and militias from outside their villages. It states as 'a fact that everyone who was in Lahore and Amritsar during the months of April to August would testify that the biggest arson was committed during curfew hours with the police actively assisting or passively looking on. Respectable citizens or shop-keepers who came out to put out the fire were shot down by the police, not the gangs who went about committing arson.'[51] It speaks scathingly about Mountbatten's Boundary Force that was meant to keep the peace in August. 'Unchecked devastation' went on in 14 districts, in an area 'wholly under the Boundary Force'. On 13–14 August between 3000 and 4000 Hindu and Sikh refugees were shot down by men of the Baluchi regiment in the Lahore railway station, 'or they looked on while the Muslim National Guards massacred these refugees...In the same station the Dogra regiment also of the Boundary Force was shooting down Muslim refugees from

Amritsar who were arriving in Lahore thinking it would be safe.'[52] 'The fact is', said the Report, 'if the Boundary Force had not been sent to the Punjab at all, probably we would have had less people killed and less devastation. As it was it acted as the greatest single force that spread the destruction.'[53]

The Report went on to say 'the young TU movement lies shattered', for despite many workers refusing to submit to communal animus, they were selectively dismissed by factory owners. It reports railway officials trying to foment violence amongst railway workers. One communist worker named Siri Chand, a leader of the North Western Railway Workers Trade Union, worked tirelessly for peace and to shelter refugees during the riots in Lahore. Not only did the police refuse assistance, but he was arrested, and upon release, was shot dead outside the police station along with members of his family by two constables.[54]

The potential of criminal violence emanating from within the heart of the security apparatus of the state was visible long before 1947. Thus, in the Kanpur riots of 1931, it was reported that:

> Communal feelings infect police both in attitudes towards mobs and amongst each other. Police authorities often refused armed escorts for relief lorries but both Hindu and Muslim policemen gave such help on communal lines, even in defiance of orders. Shri Iqbal Krishna Kapoor told the Inquiry, "I am pretty sure that if the riots had continued for a couple of days more, the Hindu and Muslim policemen would have fallen out with each other even more seriously than the Hindu and Muslim population of the town".

This report also spoke of the terrible problems created by matters such as the disposal of dead bodies, many of which were being burnt 'at the spot'. It stated that the authorities not only ignored these problems, but created obstacles in the movement of relief lorries. One witness said that this was a departure from earlier riots, when there had been cooperation between volunteers and officials:

> The impression created...was that it was no business of the police to interfere, and they wanted the people to have it out amongst themselves...

> Fida Ahmed Khan Sherwani said, "My impression is that the riots started on the basis of strained communal feelings; but they soon developed into hooliganism and goonda rule, providing opportunities for loot by hooligans irrespective of their communities. I saw personally houses being looted together by Hindu and Muslim goondas, and they were not cutting each others' throats. Another fact which I noted was that the looting was done in broad daylight in a very leisurely and fearless manner owing to their consciousness that they were not going to be interfered with by the police"[55]

The persistence of paramilitaries has been the most widespread and the least commented upon feature of the Indian polity. It is not that the politically observant Indian literati are ignorant of the existence of such groups; rather, it is the partisan and selective character of their vision that indicates the strength of communal ideology: it is this ideology that sets into motion the violent activities of controlled mobs, the rampant propagation of hateful stereotypes and the deliberate violation of and contempt for law. All these phenomena are sometimes deplored, but they never cease, nor do governments take adequate measures to subdue them. The systematic nature of the massacre of thousands of Sikhs in Delhi in 1984 is well documented, as is the involvement in it of prominent Congress leaders.[56]

Thus, the activities of Maoists, Islamist jehadis and Khalistanis are cited as examples of terrorism, while the ideas and practices of the RSS and its various front organisations (Bajrang Dal, VHP, etc) and allies such as the Shiv Sena, are simply judged to be exaggerated expressions of patriotic fervour. The RSS played no role in the national movement, but came into its own in the 1940s, being especially active in the violence in Punjab, Delhi and later in Hyderabad. In a ban order imposed after Gandhi's assassination in January 1948, the government accused it of indulging in 'acts of violence involving arson, robbery, dacoity, and murder'; collecting illicit arms and ammunition; and 'circulating leaflets exhorting people to resort to terrorist methods, to collect firearms, to create disaffection against the government and suborn the police and military.' The order said 'the cult of violence sponsored...by the activities of (the RSS) has claimed many victims. The latest and most precious to fall was Gandhiji himself.'[57] Significantly, the links between the RSS and the Hindu Mahasabha were clearly mentioned in the Dhanwantri Report.

The RSS was banned again in 1975 and yet again in 1992 after the demolition of the Babri Mosque, a campaign led by the BJP leader L.K. Advani. Despite this, it remains entrenched in the Indian polity, and has not abandoned any of its ideas or altered its conduct. It remains a private army, continues to indoctrinate children and youth in "nationalist" ideas that demonise entire communities, and provides arms training to its cadre. Leaving aside the by now well-known murderous events that took place in Gujarat in 2002, the last major communal massacre (in Kandhamal, Odisha 2008) saw blatant displays of hate-speech and incitement to violence by the RSS front, the VHP. Its status as the patron of the 'mainstream' party, the BJP, remains unchallenged. Today the RSS has a network of fronts including trade-unions, schools, youth and women's organisations, military academies, and so-called 'religious charities'. It has adjusted itself to a prolonged battle for cultural and ideological hegemony. Its leadership renews itself via nomination by the preceding Supreme Leader. It has perfected the tactic of using the Constitution and state power to disguise itself (unlike the classic fascisms of the 1920s). Whenever it has access to state protection, it extends its influence in the bureaucracy, police and educational apparatus.

Then again, rural-based militias such as the Ranvir Sena and Salwa Judum are directly or (in the former case) indirectly supported by the state or 'mainstream' political parties.[58] Despite the occasional rebuke by the higher courts, local governments show no inclination towards curbing them. On the contrary, such formations have become stabilised in the Indian polity, demonstrating the truth of Gramsci's insight: 'A weakened state structure is like a flagging army; the commandos – i.e. the private armed organisations – enter the field and they have two tasks: to make use of illegal means, while the State appears to remain within legality, and thus to reorganize the State itself.[59] Gramsci cites the Italian Minister of War in 1932 as upholding an ideal vision of a militarised society: 'it is the merit of the Fascist regime to have extended to the entire Italian people so distinguished a disciplinary tradition.'[60] His discussion of Caesarism or Bonapartism focused on political regimes arising out of stalemates in the class struggle, or in situations of unstable equilibrium. He recognises coalition governments as expressions of such stalemates. He also discusses the post-war (1920s) situation in Italy, with its chaotic and disorganised political movements, lack of a coherent political will amongst opponents of the capitalist order, the existence of a large number of middle-class persons demobilised from the military, and the disintegration of the hegemonic apparatus of the State.

These comments are relevant to the current situation in India and South Asia. The state is not merely weakening, but over the decades has shown a tendency to become criminalised. This is not merely in an empirical sense, as with the criminal behaviour of individual officials, policemen or elected representatives, but goes further, into the violation of constitutional statutes such as Schedule 5 (protecting tribal lands); the officially-enabled seizure of agricultural lands for private enterprise; the establishment of and sustenance given to private militias; disregard of adverse comments against police and other officials implicated in communal violence; disregard of repeated recommendations on police reform by official inquiries, thus accelerating the decline of the criminal justice system and so on. The process of decline is coterminous with the stabilisation of private armies, the most prominent of which now commands a degree of influence in politics and the administration that is unprecedented in any but the most conflict-affected countries in the world.

The nation-state and the 'minority question' – the contrasting assessments of Ambedkar and the Communists

In September 1942, the Central Committee of the Communist Party of India (CPI) passed a resolution titled *On Pakistan and National Unity*. A Report by G. Adhikari under the same title (minus the first word) presented a detailed argument explicating the Resolution. The Resolution called for 'all-in national unity based on communal harmony', for which a united national front (UNF) was the need of the hour. It was evidently based on what Adhikari referred to as Stalin's 'pithy but pregnant definition of a Nation'. This was as follows: 'a nation is a historically evolved stable community of language, territory, economic life and psychological make-up manifested in a community of culture.' The Resolution insisted that 'in Free India, there will be perfect equality between nationalities and communities that live together in India.' It then asked for the national movement to recognise 'the following rights as part of its programme for national unity':

> 3 (a) Every section of the Indian people which has a contiguous territory as its homeland, common historical tradition, common language, culture, psychological make-up and common economic life would be recognised as a distinct nationality with the right to exist as an autonomous state within the free Indian union or federation and will have the right to secede from it if it may so desire. This means that the territories which are homelands of such and which today are split up by the artificial boundaries of the present British provinces and of the so-called "Indian States" would be re-united and restored to them in free India. Thus free India of tomorrow would be a federation or union of autonomous states of the various nationalities such as the Pathans, Western Punjabis (dominantly Muslims), Sikhs, Sindhis, Hindustanis, Rajasthanis, Gujeratis, Bengalis, Assamese, Beharis, Oriyas, Andhras, Tamils, Karnatakis, Maharashtrians, Keralas, etc.
>
> (b) If there are interspersed minorities in the new states thus formed their rights regarding their culture, language, education, etc., would be guaranteed by Statute and their infringement would be punishable by law…
>
> 4. Such a declaration of rights inasmuch as it conceded to every nationality as defined above, and therefore, to nationalities having Muslim

faith, the right of autonomous state existence and of secession, can form the basis for unity between the National Congress and the League. For this would give to the Muslims wherever they are in an overwhelming majority in a contiguous territory which is their homeland, the right to form their autonomous states and even to separate if they so desire. In the case of the Bengali Muslims of the Eastern and Northern Districts of Bengal where they form an overwhelming majority, they may form themselves into an autonomous region – the state of Bengal or may form a separate state. Such a declaration therefore concedes the just essence of the Pakistan demand and has nothing in common with the separatist theory of dividing India into two nations on the basis of religion.

5. But the recognition of the right of separation in this form need not necessarily lead to actual separation. On the other hand, by dispelling the mutual suspicions, it brings about unity of action today and lays the basis for a greater unity in the free India of tomorrow.[61]

A close reading of these documents raises many fundamental issues concerning socialism and nationalism in India. My concern here is to point to the CPI's erratic conflation of nation, nationality, sub-regional and religious identity; its refusal to theorise communal politics, and its resultant decision to support what it called the 'democratic core' or the 'just essence' of the Pakistan demand. It saw the Khilafat movement as a reflection of an 'upsurge of the Muslim nationalities in the East' (p. 21), although later in the text it referred to Pan-Islamism as a 'reactionary separatist theory', a 'weapon of disunity' that uttered slogans of 'extra-territorial loyalty' (p. 41). It characterised the emergence of linguistic or regional demands as an expression of 'multi-national consciousness' (p. 27), and compared the British colony in India to the multi-national Tsarist Empire. It supported 'the demand of every nationality for self-determination' (p. 27) and saw its acceptance as a basis for 'revolutionary Hindu Muslim unity' (p. 38).

The guarantee by the Congress of the right of self-determination of Muslim nationalities...should mean for the Muslim peoples not separation from the rest of India but a more glorious and more lasting unity within a free Indian Union, in which all – Muslim and non-Muslim alike – are equal partners. (p. 44)

It stated that in 1938 the CPI had not understood 'the real nature of the communal problem' (p. 29). Placing the word *communal* sometimes in quotation-marks and sometimes without, it stated that:

> To the ordinary patriot, this new aspect of the communal problem, as a problem of multi-national consciousness, has not yet become patent. We, the Communists, are able to see our way into the future by means of our theory and our ideology. By means of this, we are able to quickly see these elements in the present which are bound to develop in the future. (p. 27)

The CPI 'saw in the growth of the Muslim League not the growth of communalism, but the rise of anti-imperialist nationalist consciousness among the Muslim masses' (p. 29). It criticised the Muslim mass contact programme of the Congress 'which was rightly seen by the Muslim League as a move to destroy their organisation.' (p. 28). It supported the League's critique of the Nehru Report (on the future constitution) on the grounds that residual powers ought to vest with the states and not the centre in a future Indian constitution (p. 29).

> Their (the Muslim League's) conception of the federation for a free India was a federation of autonomous and sovereign states. Why? Because the Muslim League wanted autonomy for regions in which Muslim nationalities like Sindhis, Pathans, Punjabis, Eastern Bengal Muslims lived. It was a just democratic demand. This really is the crux and kernel of all the so-called "communal" demands raised by the Muslim League right from its inception up to the present time when they have finally been crystallised into the demand for Pakistan'. (p. 29)

The document referred to communal riots as being 'engineered by goondas in the pay of dark forces of reaction' (p. 22). The only references to fascism are with reference to the ongoing world war, wherein the USSR was on the Allied side – it is noteworthy that the period September 1942 to February 1943 was the darkest hour for the Red Army (the battle of Stalingrad was finally won by the USSR at the cost of millions of lives in February 1943). The CPI report talks of 'saving India from fascism', but only in the sense of warding off an Axis victory in the world war.

The Adhikari Report of the CPI is a dense, awkwardly written and highly confusing document. The reader can only guess at the impact it made on the Communist cadre. The only dim awareness of the implications of mixing up regional and cultural distinctions with religious ones occurs in a paragraph referring to the Muslim masses' fear of oppression and exploitation by 'Hindu India'. Attempting to explain this, it says, 'uneven bourgeois development creates conditions wherein one dominant nationality may be in a position to stifle the growth of less developed and weaker nationalities in a free India. We saw tiny germs of this even during the Congress Ministries...such a fear is an understandable fear' (p. 38). This implies, without stating as much, that Hindus were a 'dominant nationality'. Indeed, if people united by language and culture could still be distinguished as Muslim Punjabis and Muslim Bengalis, the same could be said of Hindu Punjabis and Hindu Bengalis. The existence of what the document called 'interspersed minorities' was, predictably, to be guaranteed by statute.

Finally, a year after independence, a 'Communist Party Publication' printed in Bombay and titled *Who Rules Pakistan?* had this to say:

> The year of freedom that has passed thus reveals that the people of Pakistan, whose religious feelings were exploited by the vested interests to reach to posts of power, are being cheated, betrayed and sold in economic and political bondage to the imperialists...The fake freedom and fake leadership have been unmasked in the last one year...the people of Pakistan, like the people of India, have yet to liberate themselves and save their country from being sold to foreign exploiters.. the Communist Party of Pakistan...carries on this fight for uniting the people in a common Democratic Front.[62]

In 1940, B.R. Ambedkar, later to become India's first Law minister and chairman of the drafting committee of its constitution, wrote a seminal book on the issue of Pakistan, then on its way to emerging as the dominant theme of the last decade of colonial rule in India.[63] The book was a fair-minded appraisal of the arguments of the Congress and Muslim League, and soon became a major point of reference, not least because it could not be assimilated to any partisan standpoint in the prevailing political firmament. I cite it at length here because it throws light upon the political perceptions of the time. Avoiding the axiomatic definitions preferred by the CPI, Ambedkar drew upon the French social and theological theorist Ernst Renan's 1882 lecture *What is a Nation?* to focus upon the subjective essence of nationalism. His observations draw our attention to the ideological content of nationalist mobilisation. He spoke of 'the mysterious working of the psychology of national feeling', referred to nationalism as a 'passion', and stated that 'the Muslims have developed a "will to live as a nation".' He described the 'Hindu' view on the undesirability of partition and the history of medieval invasions of India, and criticized both Hindu and Muslim nationalism, whilst taking care to present their arguments faithfully (pp. 18–19). He used official statistics and reports on demographic, financial and political matters, including what he termed a prolonged communal civil war that spanned the period from 1920 to 1935.

Ambedkar made a distinction between nationality and nationalism, and argued

> it is true that there cannot be nationalism without the feeling of nationality being in existence. But, it is important to bear in mind that the converse is not always true. The feeling of nationality may be present and yet the feeling of nationalism may be quite absent. That is to say, nationality does not in all cases produce nationalism. For nationality to flame into nationalism two conditions must exist. First, there must arise the "will to live as a nation". Nationalism is the dynamic expression of that desire. Secondly, there must be a territory which nationalism could occupy and make it a state (p. 19).

He also took the position that such recognition did not necessarily imply partition:

> there may be nations conscious of themselves without being charged with nationalism. On the basis of this reasoning, it may be argued that the Musalmans may hold that they are a nation but they need not on that account demand a separate national existence; why can they not be content with the position which the French occupy in Canada and the Eng-

> lish occupy in South Africa? Such a position is quite a sound position. It must, however, be remembered that such a position can only be taken by way of pleading with the Muslims not to insist on partition. It is no argument against their claim for partition, if they insist upon it (p. 18).

Ambedkar stated his antagonism not only to a communalised Hindu polity, but to Hinduism:

> If Hindu Raj does become a fact, it will, no doubt, be the greatest calamity for this country. No matter what the Hindus say, Hinduism is a menace to liberty, equality and fraternity. On that account it is incompatible with democracy. Hindu Raj must be prevented at any cost. But is Pakistan the true remedy against it? (p. 144)

He dwelt on the social ills of Indian Islam, and on the political life of Indian Muslims:

> Muslims have no interest in politics as such. Their predominant interest is religion...With the Muslims, election is a mere matter of money and is very seldom a matter of social programme of general improvement. Muslim politics takes no note of purely secular categories of life, namely, the differences between rich and poor, capital and labour, landlord and tenant, priest and layman, reason and superstition. Muslim politics is essentially clerical (p. 118).

Commenting on the Muslim League's demands in 1938, he said: 'The Muslims are now speaking the language of Hitler and claiming a place in the sun as Hitler has been doing for Germany' (p.132). He asked 'if the Musalmans are the only sufferers from the evils that admittedly result from the undemocratic character of Hindu society. Are not the millions of Shudras and non-Brahmins or millions of the Untouchables, suffering the worst consequences of the undemocratic character of Hindu society?' (143). He went further:

> Must there be Pakistan because the Musalmans are a nation? It is a pity that Mr. Jinnah should have become a votary and champion of Muslim Nationalism at a time when the whole world is decrying against the evils of nationalism and is seeking refuge in some kind of international organisation. Mr. Jinnah is so obsessed with his new-found faith in Muslim Nationalism that he is not prepared to see that there is a distinc-

> tion between a society, parts of which are disintegrated, and a society parts of which have become only loose, which no sane man can ignore (p. 141).

The book contains complex arguments that may be read as supporting one or other view. Aside from the use of agglomerative stereotypes such as the 'Muslim case', the 'Hindu case', 'subject race' and 'ruling race' etc., Ambedkar's analysis is striking for his own substantive views with regard to the solutions he envisaged. The last section summed up his stance on the way forward – he recommended a community-based referendum in the provinces directly affected by the demand: 'It must be left to be decided by the people who are living in those areas and who will have to bear the consequences of so violent, so revolutionary and so fundamental a change in the political and economic system' (p. 164).

Ambedkar did not believe partition to be a necessary or desirable solution to the communal problem and disliked the idea of communal parties. However, he was pessimistic about the capacity of the leaders involved to find a way out, or of the main protagonists in the drama to suddenly become amenable to reasoned argument. Hence his observations and suggestions carry an impression of pragmatism and realism. An assessment of this important work is outside the scope of this essay. The passages I cite here are not meant to provide such an assessment or to summarise its argument, but to focus on the concept of the nation-state found within it and the kind of demographic discourse it generated. (We should remember that this discourse was not his alone, but the common sense of the times, aside from being inscribed in international law). The ones most relevant to our discussion relate to the best way of dealing with what he termed 'the communal problem' and sometimes 'the minority problem':

> The best solution of the communal problem is not to have two communities facing each other, one a majority and the other a minority, welded in the steel-frame of a single government. How far does Pakistan approximate to the solution of the Communal Question? The answer to this question is quite obvious. If the scheme of Pakistan is to follow the

> present boundaries of the Provinces in the North-West and in Bengal, certainly it does not eradicate the evils which lie at the heart of the Communal Question. It retains the very elements which give rise to it, namely, the pitting of a minority against a majority. The rule of the Hindu minorities by the Muslim majorities and the rule of the Muslim Minorities by the Hindu majorities are the crying evils of the present situation. This very evil will reproduce itself in Pakistan, if the provinces marked out for it are incorporated into it as they are, i.e., with boundaries drawn as at present. Besides this, the evil which gives rise to the Communal Question in its larger intent, will not only remain as it is but will assume a new malignity. Under the existing system, the power centered in the Communal Provinces to do mischief to their hostages is limited by the power which the Central Government has over the Provincial Governments. At present, the hostages are at least within the pale of a Central Government which is Hindu in its composition and which has power to interfere for their protection. But, when Pakistan becomes a Muslim State with full sovereignty over internal and external affairs, it would be free from the control of the Central Government. The Hindu minorities will have no recourse to an outside authority with overriding powers, to interfere on their behalf and curb this power of mischief, as under the scheme, no such overriding authority is permitted to exist. So, the position of the Hindus in Pakistan may easily become similar to the position of the Armenians under the Turks or of the Jews in Tsarist Russia or in Nazi Germany. Such a scheme would be intolerable and the Hindus may well say that they cannot agree to Pakistan and leave their co-religionist as a helpless prey to the fanaticism of a Muslim National State (p. 52).

Discussing the pros and cons of the partition scheme, he said:

> If the evils flow from the scheme itself, i.e., if they are inherent in it, it is unnecessary for any Hindu to waste his time in considering it. He will be justified in summarily dismissing it. On the other hand, if the evils are the result of the boundaries, the question of Pakistan reduces itself to a mere question of changing the boundaries. A study of the question amply supports the view that the evils of Pakistan are not inherent in it. If any evil results follow from it they will have to be attributed to its boundaries. This becomes clear if one studies the distribution of population. The reasons why these evils will be reproduced within Western and Eastern Pakistan is because, with the present boundaries, they do not become single ethnic states. They remain mixed states, composed of a Muslim majority and a Hindu minority as before. *The evils are the evils which are inseparable from a mixed state. If Pakistan is made a single unified ethnic state, the evils will automatically vanish.* There will be no question of separate electorates within Pakistan, because in such a homogeneous Pakistan, there will be no majorities to rule and no

> minorities to be protected. Similarly, there will be no majority of one community to hold, in its possession, a minority of an opposing community. *The question, therefore, is one of demarcation of boundaries and reduces itself to this: Is it possible for the boundaries of Pakistan to be so fixed, that instead of producing a mixed state composed of majorities and minorities, with all the evils attendant upon it, Pakistan will be an ethnic state composed of one homogeneous community, namely Muslims?* The answer is that in a large part of the area affected by the project of the League, a homogeneous state can be created by shifting merely the boundaries, and in the rest, homogeneity can be produced by shifting only the population (p. 52) (Emphases added).

Ambedkar's solution to what he called 'the evils inseparable from a mixed state' was the transfer of minorities, which he deemed 'the only lasting remedy for communal peace':

> Some scoff at the idea of the shifting and exchange of population. But those who scoff can hardly be aware of the complications, which a minority problem gives rise to and the failures attendant upon almost all the efforts made to protect them. The constitutions of the post-war states, as well as of the older states in Europe which had a minority problem, proceeded on the assumption that constitutional safeguards for minorities should suffice for their protection and so the constitutions of most of the new states with majorities and minorities were studded with long lists of fundamental rights and safeguards to see that they were not violated by the majorities. What was the experience? Experience showed that safeguards did not save the minorities. *Experience showed that even a ruthless war on the minorities did not solve the problem. The states then agreed that the best way to solve it was for each to exchange its alien minorities within its border, for its own which was without its border, with a view to bring about homogeneous States. This is what happened in Turky, (sic) Greece and Bulgaria.* Those, who scoff at the idea of transfer of population, will do well to study the history of the minority problem, as it arose between Turky, (sic) Greece and Bulgaria. If they do, they will find that these countries found that *the only effective way of solving the minorities problem lay in exchange of population.* The task undertaken by the three countries was by no means a minor operation. It involved the transfer of some 20 million people from one habitat to another. But undaunted, the three shouldered the task and carried it to a successful end because they felt that the considerations of communal peace must outweigh every other consideration.. *That the transfer of minorities is the only lasting remedy for communal peace is beyond doubt. If that is so, there is no reason why the Hindus and the Muslims should keep on trading in safeguards* which have proved so

> unsafe. If small countries, with limited resources like Greece, Turkey and Bulgaria, were capable of such an undertaking, there is no reason to suppose that what they did cannot be accomplished by Indians. *After all, the population involved is inconsiderable and because some obstacles require to be removed, it would be the height of folly to give up so sure a way to communal peace* (p. 53) (Emphases added).

In answer to the hypothetical query "How will it affect the position of the forty-five million Muslims in Hindustan proper?", Ambedkar said:

> The answer given by the Muslims of Hindustan is equally clear. They say, "We are not weakened by the separation of Muslims into Pakistan and Hindustan. We are better protected by the existence of separate Islamic States on the Eastern and Western borders of Hindustan than we are by their submersion in Hindustan." Who can say that they are wrong ? *Has it not been shown that Germany as an outside state was better able to protect the Sudeten Germans in Czechoslovakia than the Sudetens were able to do themselves?* Be that as it may, the question does not concern the Hindus. The question that concerns the Hindus is: How far does the creation of Pakistan remove the communal question from Hindustan? That is a very legitimate question and must be considered. It must be admitted that by the creation of Pakistan, Hindustan is not freed of the communal question. While Pakistan can be made a homogeneous state by redrawing its boundaries, Hindustan must remain a composite state. The Musalmans are scattered all over Hindustan – though they are mostly congregated in towns – and no ingenuity in the matter of redrawing of boundaries can make it homogeneous. *The only way to make Hindustan homogeneous is to arrange for exchange of population.* Until that is done, it must be admitted that even with the creation of Pakistan, the problem of majority *vs.* minority will remain in Hindustan as before and will continue to produce disharmony in the body politic of Hindustan (p. 54) (Emphases added).

These well-reasoned arguments appear perfectly logical, but *only when seen against the template of an ethnically homogenous nation*. Ambedkar saw the nation-state in the form imagined in the Paris peace conference of 1919, a homogenous union of ethnicity and territory. One telling observation on this political phenomenon (made in a recent book review) is as follows:

> In 1918, the remnants of the multinational Habsburg and Ottoman empires were carved into sovereign nation-states, in accordance with the

> Wilsonian ideal of "national self-determination". As Hannah Arendt perceptively argued, the world stood convinced in 1918 that "true freedom, true emancipation, and true popular sovereignty could be attained only with full national emancipation, and that people without their own national government were deprived of human rights." The problem with this principle was that borders and nations were not neatly aligned in Eastern and Central Europe. Citizens of the Habsburg Empire's many linguistic, national and confessional groups were hopelessly intermingled. In many cases it was not even clear who belonged to what nation, because so many citizens of the empire were bilingual or indifferent to nationalism. Equally important, in spite of the rhetoric of national self-determination, the frontiers of the new successor states had been drawn with geopolitical imperatives in mind. Even though German speakers formed an absolute majority in the borderlands of Czechoslovakia (which would come to be known as the Sudetenland), and most wanted to join the Austrian rump state, the region was forcibly annexed to Czechoslovakia for the sake of the state's economic viability. A new so-called "minority problem" was born in interwar Eastern Europe.[64]

What is remarkable is that Ambedkar assessed the settlement between Greece and Turkey (made in Lausanne 1923) to be a success, and used it to argue that the 'transfer of minorities was the only lasting remedy for communal peace'. He also seemed to think that the scale of population involved in the Indian case was 'inconsiderable'. The Versailles Treaty had allocated parts of the defunct Ottoman Empire to Greece as a strategic measure. The Lausanne agreement followed the successful Turkish eviction (by the new Kemalist regime) of Greece from Anatolia in 1922. Even in the mid 1920s, it was apparent that Lausanne 'did little more than ratify a state of affairs that already existed. Of the 1.2 million ethnic Greeks affected by the convention, all but 190,000 had taken refuge in Greece before the fighting concluded. The number of Turks living in lands under Greek administration was only about 350,000. The physical removals, therefore, involved only about half a million people, a far cry from the numbers that would require to be moved after the Second World War.'[65] Lord Curzon, ex Viceroy of India, who was then Britain's Secretary for Foreign Affairs, is quoted as saying that the driving out of peoples was 'a thoroughly bad and vicious solution, for which the world will pay a heavy penalty for a hundred years to come.'[66]

The world war was in full spate whilst Ambedkar was writing his book on Pakistan, and the ideal of ethnic homogeneity was unraveling by the day, as he himself recognised. He must have known that the Sudetenland was seized by Germany in 1938, and the rest of Czechoslovakia annexed in 1939. Despite this, he was able without irony to cite Sudetenland as an example of the assured safety of a minority because of the proximity of a powerful neighbour with a shared ethnic demography. If Ambedkar indeed saw the transfer of Muslims en masse to Pakistan and of Hindus to India as a lasting solution to the communal question and moreover, considered the numbers involved to be slight, one can only remark upon the ideological impact that the nation-statist ideal had wrought upon the times.

The fascist mindset of communalists

The term 'reactionary', when used to refer to ultra-right-wing movements, gives the impression that fascism is somehow linked with an antipathy to modernity. This is a misconception. Just as there are socialist critiques of modernity tinted with nostalgia for the pre-capitalist past, there are conservative ideological currents that embrace modernity for its technicism, at the same time as they redefine the 'nation' and 'community' for completely novel political purposes. We need, therefore, to pay attention to radicalised conservatism and reactionary modernism.[67] Thus, V.D. Savarkar, who remains the foremost symbolic mascot of the Hindu nationalists, was by no means an opponent of modernity. In contrast to the rhetoric of his RSS acolytes (who continue to hark back to 'ancient Hindu values' and so on, and tend to blame modernity for all misfortunes), Savarkar defined progress 'in terms of European nationalism, constitutional practices, science, technology, theories of governance and the military and social revolution all this had brought about.'[68] He was also inspired by the Victorian English philosopher Herbert Spencer, the prime exponent of Social-Darwinism and the man who coined the phrase 'survival of the fittest'.[69] Social-Darwinism is an unpalatable world-view, but there was nothing 'traditional' about it – it was a very modern ideological ingredient of racist theories of imperialism as well as Nazism.

Savarkar's strategy for 'capturing centres of power' has effectively been adopted by the RSS/BJP. K.B. Hedgewar, the founder of the RSS, was another proponent of Hindu Nationalism, a doctrine which propagates sacralised geography and racialist nationhood. It sees Hindus as the national race and Muslims, Christians and communists as alien elements. Hedgewar's successor M.S. Golwalkar developed the ideal of *Hindu Rashtra,* in which the nation is venerated as an object of worship. Golwalkar was contemptuous of political activity, and although after the 1948 ban he went along with the decision of sections of the movement to join political life, he remained convinced of the need to attain his ideal via cultural hegemony.[70]

Both Hindu and Muslim communalists used the plight of Europe's Jews to make a point about unwanted minorities. Savarkar was quoted by the Nazi press in 1939 as arguing: 'A Nation is formed by a majority living therein. What did the Jews do in Germany? They being in minority were driven out from Germany'. In December 1939, he had said: 'Indian Muslims are on the whole more inclined to identify themselves and their interests with Muslims outside India than Hindus who live next door, like Jews in Germany.' He supported the Nazi annexation of Sudetenland, and in March 1939 announced the aspiration that 'Germany's crusade against the enemies of Aryan culture will bring all the Aryan nations of the world to their senses and awaken the Indian Hindus for the restoration of their lost glory.' And in 1939 Golwalkar was to declare his approval of Hitler's treatment of the Jews:

> German national pride has now become the topic of the day. To keep up the purity of the nation and its culture, Germany shocked the world by her purging the country of the semitic races – the Jews. National pride at its highest has been manifested here. Germany has also shown how well-nigh impossible it is for races and cultures, having differences…to

> be assimilated into one united whole, a good lesson for us in Hindustan to learn and profit by.[71]

Nazi propaganda was equally influential with Muslim communalists. Thus,

> During the Chamberlain regime there appeared irresponsible statements as these, reminiscent of German national socialist cries: "Pundit Jawaharlal Nehru's visits to England and other countries in Europe have been cleverly stage-managed by Leftist groups supported by prominent publicity through the Jewish press Reuter."; the Congress's "final objective, viz., establishment of Hindu supremacy under British protection in complicity with Bolshevik Russia and other communist agencies." In Sind, "the Hindus will have to be eradicated like the Jews in Germany if they did not behave properly."[72]

In 1950, Pakistan's first Law minister Jogindranath Mandal, an 'untouchable' leader who had joined the Muslim League, resigned his position. His letter to Prime Minister Liaqat Ali Khan (cited above, n.16) condemned the atrocities committed on Hindus in East Pakistan. Among his allegations was the complaint that Moulana Akram Khan, President of the Provincial Muslim League, had cited the holy Prophet asking for Jews to be driven away from Arabia. As we have seen, B.R. Ambedkar had precisely this in mind when he stated that 'the position of the Hindus in Pakistan may easily become similar to the position of the Armenians under the Turks or of the Jews in Tsarist Russia or in Nazi Germany.'

Indian public opinion is not particularly well-informed about the criminal nature of the Nazi regime, and Hitler has a large number of Indian admirers. Nor does it pay attention to the Nazi genocide of Romanis, though they are of Indian origin. As we can see, the communalists were attracted to Germany's method of dealing with 'minorities'. This easy combination of ignorance and aspiration is also partly due to the sanitisation of Nazism that flowed from Subhas Chandra Bose's alliance with the Axis powers in the Second World War.[73]

As I have argued above, Indian communalism cannot be simply contraposed with nationalism. In fact, the doctrine of a "natural" ethnic community forming the core of the nation-state lends itself to the hegemonic drives of communal ideologies. The ideologues of Hindutva have always seen it as equivalent to Indian nationalism. Nationalism has always been a deeply ambivalent ideology. Depending on the social forces which articulate it, it can be defensive or imperialist, tolerant or chauvinist, universalist or racist. It can contain all these elements because cultural and political homogeneity is a chimera. German nationalism was social-democratic up to 1848, Prussian-oriented and autocratic in the Bismarckian era, liberal-democratic after the Great War, and racist/expansionist under Nazism. The dominant stream in each phase expressed different social interests and popular moods.

Communalism is the Indian version of fascist populism and racist nationalism. *First*, it opposes to the time of the present its own ideal time, which is an amalgam of the past and the future, fused together in myths of communal potency. Muslim communalists spoke of 'Muslim sovereignty' as if the medieval Sultanate was the property of every Muslim. Sikh communalists harked back to the reign of Maharaja Ranjit Singh, misrepresenting it as the rule of 'the Khalsa'. And Hindutva communalists dreamt of a fantastic monolith, the 'majority community', which, as their political property, would enable them to bludgeon all enemies into submission. As Savarkar wrote in 1924, 'thirty crores of people, with India as their Fatherland and Holy-land, can dictate their terms to the whole world. A day will come when mankind will have to face the force.'[74] *Second*, communalism locates an internal enemy, deemed to be sapping the strength of the chosen, and makes it the target of mass hatred. The communal imagination sees enemies lurking everywhere, whose physical destruction is the only guarantee of "national" safety. Genocide is a logical conclusion for the communalist temperament, and the massacres in colonial and post-colonial India (and Pakistan) demonstrate that inclination. *Third*, communalism subverts humanistic rationality and replaces it with romantic, death-worshipping cults of unreason whose political functions are the creation of murder squads, the militarisation of civil society and the racist reduction of their hate objects into sub-humans. *Fourth*, communalism uses radical slogans to mobilise mass support; and uses democratic institutions to seize power (or fragments of it) and destroy democracy from a position of strength. An important consequence of the spread of communal ideas is the appearance of bias in the judiciary. As Franz Neumann observed in his classic study of Nazism, '(the counter-revolution) ... tried many forms and devices, but soon learned that it could come to power only with the help of the state machine and never against it... in the centre of the counter-revolution stood the judiciary'.[75] *Finally*, communalism energises the underworld with political tasks, links together hooligans and politicians, legitimises violence and institutionalises all these phenomena in stable organisations, creating the symbiosis between the state and the bestial personality which is the hallmark of fascism.

Ideology and annihilation

In her discussion of totalitarianism in power, Arendt discusses the existential predicament of human beings condemned to superfluity by ideologically driven authoritarian regimes:

> The atmosphere of madness and unreality, created by an apparent lack of purpose, is the real iron curtain which hides all forms of concentration camps from the eyes of the world. Seen from outside, they and the things that happen in them can be described only in images drawn from a life after death, that is, a life removed from earthly purposes. Concentration camps can be very aptly divided into three types corresponding to three basic Western conceptions of a life after death: Hades, Purgatory, and Hell. To Hades corresponds those relatively mild forms, once popular even in nontotalitarian countries, for getting undesirable elements of all sorts – refugees, stateless persons, the asocial, and the unemployed – out of the way; as DP camps, which are nothing other than camps for persons who have become superfluous and bothersome, they have survived the war. Purgatory is represented by the Soviet Union's labour camps, where neglect is combined with chaotic forced labour. Hell in the most literal sense was embodied by those types of camps perfected by the Nazis, in which the whole of life was thoroughly and systematically organized with a view to the greatest possible torment. All three types have one thing in common: the human masses sealed

> off in them are treated as if they no longer existed, as if what happened to them were no longer of interest to anybody, as if they were already dead and some evil spirit gone mad were amusing himself by stopping them for a while between life and death before admitting them to eternal peace.[76]

Arendt's observations show us a spectrum of annihilation contained within the phenomenon of 'concentration.' Annihilation does not always result in a sentence of death – rather, it refers to human beings 'treated as if they no longer existed', people who are undesirable and superfluous. Ghetto-fication is one end of the spectrum. For example, the relegation of so-called 'untouchables' in India to separate residential areas is a 'traditional' source of the politics of internment. Small and vast ghettos are to be found all over South Asia. They are occupied by refugees, troublesome 'minorities', etc. There are DP camps ('displaced persons' camps) all over the successor states of British India. There are also vast settlements of stateless persons, unwanted by any sovereign power. Further up the ladder of annihilation are the geographic zones of insurgency, whose defining feature is the suspension of law and constitutional protections (even if provisions for such protections exist on paper, which is not always the case). The exposure of these areas to perpetual violent conflict means that their populations exist on the border-line between superfluous life and sudden death.

Finally, there are the people caught up in the immediacy of so-called 'communal riots', the Indian euphemism for mass murder. The riot may last for days or longer, and are a display of genocidal intent. In recent years, such intent has also begun to be manifested in terror bombings of crowds, which target innocent civilians in a random manner. (The very category of innocence has been communalised). Such events cannot destroy an entire community – but the display of intent is sufficient to push the survivors into a condition of lifelong trauma, or towards the status of superfluity – or both. As for those who get murdered, all we may say is that they passed through the Hell of fascism on their way to extinction.

The conditions under which people condemned to physical sequestration on account of being declared a *problem* or the bearers of a *question* have been replicated in South Asia not once but regularly, from colonial times through all the events that marked independence and the decades that followed. Forced labour was known well enough in India's coal mines (during the second World War), tea gardens and elsewhere. This was not, however, the result of an ideological project. But the status of minority that was accorded to millions of Indians, Pakistanis, Bangladeshis, Sri Lankans, etc., was the first step that heralded an unfolding pattern. It is not my case that the label *minority* must inevitably lead to annihilation. But it cannot be denied that the so-called minorities must live with that ever-present danger. The arithmetical language by which the nation-state defines its own inhabitants ensures this.

Fascism in South Asia

Communal ideas have become normalised in South Asia. Memories of widespread and extreme violence before, during and after partition have contributed to this development.[77] The transfer of population and mass ethnic cleansing was a veritable marker of sovereignty for the two emergent nation-states. As one historian of partition comments:

> While some argue that the violence that erupted at the moment of Partition was popular and spontaneous and that it can't be considered as a general phenomenon due to the non-involvement of large-scale organisations, the nature and the extent of the violence clearly underline the organized and planned character of the attacks. Furthermore, it suggests the involvement of private armies such as the Muslim League National Guard, the Rashtriya Swayam Sevak Sangh (RSS) and the Akal Fauj. Although the State did not directly participate in the violence, the communalized role of the police, the complicity if not direct involvement of the political leaderships and the State's attitude of laissez-faire point to its responsibility. During its existence, between August 1 and 31, the 50,000 men Punjab Boundary Force was unable or unwilling to maintain peace and order. Violence was not just a marginal phenomenon, a sudden and spontaneous communal frenzy that accompanied Partition. It was on the contrary at the very heart of the event. Nor was it merely a

> consequence of Partition but rather the principal mechanism for creating the conditions for Partition. *Violence constituted the moral instrument through which the tension between the pre-Partition local character of identity and its postcolonial territorial and national redefinition was negotiated. Violence operated as the link between the community and its new national territory*. That is precisely what gave it its organized and genocidal dimension as it was meant for control of social space so as to cleanse these territories from the presence of other religious communities[78] (Emphasis added).

The project of ethnic cleansing is of course never done. Once the nation-state is constituted, inter-*nation* animus takes over. India and Pakistan remain *internal* to each others' ideological self-consciousness; it would not be off the mark to say that Partition disproved the Two Nation Theory. Thus, for Pakistan, the wickedness of Bharat and the Hindus is the necessary condition for its own existence; while for Hindutva fascists in India, the internal enemy are the 'minorities', primarily the Muslims, who are seen as Pakistani agents and an unclean element in the body politic. This attitude was widespread in the period immediately following independence, and has remained prevalent for decades thereafter.

It was commented upon by Jawaharlal Nehru, soon after the conservative Purushottamdas Tandon won the presidentship of the Congress in September 1950. Nehru deplored the fact that 'communalist and reactionary forces' had rejoiced at Tandon's victory. 'The spirit of communalism and revivalism has gradually invaded the Congress', he said. 'We have to treat our minorities in exactly the same way as we treat the majority.'[79] What is noticeable is his acknowledgement of the communal trend in the Congress, as well as the fact that the words *majority* and *minority* carried a symbolic charge, a habit that remains endemic in the discourse of the nation state.

For its part, because Pakistan was constituted as a Muslim majority nation[80] (despite Jinnah's declaration in August 1947 that religion would now lose its significance), a relentless and deadly pursuit of theological purification was set in motion within its polity, a process that continues to this day. The state's enforcement of religious doctrine is evident in Pakistan's blasphemy law and the persecution of Ahmadiyas. The pressure upon its minority Hindu population that its Law Minister J.N. Mandal drew attention to in 1950 led to a prolonged exodus to India and a transformation of communal demography in both Pakistan and Bangladesh. These facts lend credence to stereotypes about Muslim intolerance. They carry an ideological impact regardless of the fact that Pakistan and Bangladesh are independent and separate countries.

Communalist stereotypes are also strengthened by the persistence of the theatrical political stances adopted by conservative Indian Muslim leaders, some of whom continue to speak the language of hurt sentiment, and of a homogeneous community 'interest'. Demonstrations targeting religious groups such as the Ahmadiyas, or writers denounced as blasphemous, or academic research deemed to be offensive, have been accompanied by threats of violence. Across the subcontinent, the violent activities of terror groups with international Islamist links have fed the climate of hate and intolerance.

On the other hand, the dominant trend within the Indian establishment treats Islamists as anti-national but the RSS and its allies as extreme patriots. This benign approach persists despite the fact that the last instance of RSS-inspired mass 'rioting' took place as recently as 2008. Organisations and individuals associated with the RSS have been accused of involvement in the bombing of a train with Pakistani passengers in 2007, in which 68 people died. The central question remains their addiction to violence, but this is always downplayed in public discussion. Whereas Maoist violence is condemned by all, the lawlessness of the RSS obtains support or sympathetic forbearance. Numbers of senior policemen, retired and in service, have RSS leanings. In their communal form, therefore, extremist ideas have become respectable. People in high positions believe in collective guilt, mob violence and the efficacy of private armies.

What is also noticeable is the durable nature of the refusal to theorise communalism outside the minority/majority frame.

The addiction to arithmetical vocabulary is prevalent across the political spectrum, not least on the Indian Left, and this despite the desperate warning issued by Dhanwantri and Joshi in 1947, when Punjab's Communists spoke the language of humanity in the midst of a bloodbath. Of course, this is not a phenomenon limited to India and South Asia. The sacral language and idiom that informs nationalism (even in secular narratives) has not only breached, but shattered the internationalism and humanism of the Left. In India the retreat began with the CPI's conflation of religious and national identity, which further led to an advocacy of 'the rational essence of the Pakistan demand', as Adhikari put it in 1943.

The twentieth century has witnessed a prolonged and tactically sophisticated movement for the totalitarian transformation of South Asian politics. Opposing avatars of communalism run in tandem, and endless talk of minorities and majorities works like a magneto for generating animus, and undermining lawful governance and democratic institutions. This is why the partition of India and the history of Pakistan are a part of the same story. The ongoing criminalisation of politics and state institutions cannot be comprehended in nation-statist frames – this is akin to trying to understand communalism through a communal lens. It has to be taken as a whole, because the language of majority and minority has entered public consciousness *across* the international boundaries drawn by Radcliffe in 1947. What happens in India, Pakistan and Bangladesh affects public consciousness in all three nation-states, regardless of the formal boundaries of separation. The secession of East Pakistan in 1971 and the Kashmir conflict (as also the repercussions of the Babri Mosque demolition in 1992), exemplify the continuing relevance of 1947 to the political history of the sub-continent. The Kashmir conflict may be understood better when seen as a product of contending nation-statist projects. As a result, its population has been subjected to a combination of ethnic cleansing, on the one hand, and ruthless policing operations emanating from or enabled by state structures, on the other.

Two competing nationalist ideologies have been at work here (and of late a third nationalism has emerged), attempting to mould an ideal 'people' out of an ethnically mixed population. 'Politics is the plastic art of the state.'

South Asian fascism is more complex than the situation in pre-war Europe. This obliges us to rethink its elemental aspects. Here it is not a matter of a singular event such as a seizure of power by a fascist dictator, but a slow bleeding process that builds its strength incrementally and notches up victories in what Gramsci called a war of position. Here, fascism depends upon a battle of ideas, upon 'affirmation, repetition and contagion'. Here, it is not just mob violence but the climate of ideas that teaches us to expect such violence at all times, to justify it in a spirit of revenge, which provides energy to fascism. How far this ongoing decline has gone in the different successor states of British India is another debate.

Above all the de-facto preparation for civil war and the continued activity of militias and vigilante groups manifests a systematic attempt to militarise public space. War has now vacated the border – the place traditionally designated for it by the nation-state. It has spread inwards, into the entrails of the polity. There are conflict-zones within cities, areas referred to as 'Pakistan' and 'Bangladesh' merely on account of the identity of the people who live in them. There are lines of control in villages, marking the hostility between castes. Entire regions are affected by insurgency.[81] Armed groups (with overt or covert political links) operate in scores of urban and rural spaces. Some have embarked upon intermittent conflict with the state and obtain resources via taxes levied upon ordinary people, lower level state officials and corporate interests. Others operate with greater stealth, showing their fangs in occasional outbursts of communal and ethnic strife, as in the recent violence between Bodos and Bengali-speaking Muslims in Assam. Yet others enjoy varying degrees of state support or tolerance, depending on the interests and classes that willed them into existence. The largest private army, the RSS, aims at nothing less than the conquest of state power in the name of Hindu Rashtra.

Liberal democracy sits uneasily with nationalism. The communal project attempts to overthrow the very idea of democracy, and communal ideas are an effective means of introducing partisanship and bias into state institutions. In India the fascist thrust of communalism struck at the very moment of independence, creating millions of refugees and stateless people even as the people were declared sovereign. To cite Arendt again,

> The notion that statelessness is primarily a Jewish problem was a pretext used by all governments who tried to settle the problem by ignoring it. None of the statesmen was aware that Hitler's solution of the Jewish problem, first to reduce the German Jews to a nonrecognized minority in Germany, then to drive them as stateless people across the borders, and finally to gather them back from everywhere in order to ship them to extermination camps, was an eloquent demonstration to the rest of the world how really to "liquidate" all problems concerning minorities and stateless. After the war it turned out that the Jewish question, which was considered the only insoluble one, was indeed solved – namely, by means of a colonised and then conquered territory – but this solved neither the problems of the minorities not the stateless. On the contrary, like virtually all other events of the twentieth century, the solution of the Jewish question merely produced a new category of refugees, the Arabs, thereby increasing the number of the stateless by another 700,000 to 800,000 people. And what happened in Palestine within the smallest territory and in terms of hundreds of thousands was then repeated in India on a large scale involving many millions of people. Since the Peace Treaties of 1919 and 1920 the refugees and the stateless have attached themselves like a curse to all the newly established states on earth which were created in the image of the nation-state.
>
> For these new states this curse bears the germ of a deadly sickness. For the nation-state cannot exist once its principle of equality before the law has broken down. Without this legal equality, which originally was destined to replace the older laws and orders of the feudal society, the nation dissolves into an anarchic mass of over- and under-privileged individuals. The clearer the proof of their inability to treat stateless people as legal persons and the greater the extension of arbitrary rule by police decree, the more difficult it is for states to resist the temptation to deprive all citizens of legal status and rule them with an omnipotent police.[82]

Despite terrible conflicts the Indian constitution is by no means a dead letter – certainly not yet. But the rights promised by it to all

Indians are increasingly denied to millions of citizens. Democracy has sunk roots, but so have projects that seek to undermine it. Communal discourses aim at the conquest of the state by exclusivist ideas of the "Nation". The defining element of these projects is the dynamic of violence directed against the nation's enemies who, for the most part, are searched for *within* the country's borders. This dynamic functions as a self-fulfilling prophesy – the continual denial of constitutionally protected fundamental rights to vast numbers of citizens will ensure that people denied justice will view the state as inimical to their interests. Fascism is a machine for the endless production of enemies.

The argument presented here is intended to dispel apocalyptic theorisations of fascism, and point instead towards the dynamic interplay of ideas, movements, outbreaks of violence and state complicity. The attack on the Indian constitution by a section of the far left works only to assist a project that significant sections of the Indian establishment and communalists have already undertaken – with greater chances of success.[83] The defence of democracy in India implies a resistance to fascism and the ideas, interests and conditions that promote it. It implies a protection of human rights, civil liberties, freedom of speech and belief, trade-union rights and non-violent resolution of conflicts. It requires resistance to mob violence, vigilantism and the totalitarian idea of 'majority rule.' All this requires that we recognise the danger. Communalism was (and remains) a rope of infinite length, elastic over time, which connects elite interests with mass sentiment. The rope is handled by 'the masses', for many of whom the experience bestows a sense of potency, a fantasy of secure kinship and future power. But whereas affinity for one's culture and kin is the substance of everyday life, the tension running through this rope is marked by the noose at the end of it.

Endnotes

1 This essay is an extended version of an article entitled 'Armies of the Pure: the Question of Indian Fascism' that was published in *Revue des Livres*, Paris, September 2012. My master quotes are from Pervez Hoodbhoy and A. H. Nayyar, 'Rewritng the History of Pakistan', in Mohammad Asghar Khan, ed., *Islam, Politics and the State: the Pakistan Experience* (London, 1986); R. L. Rutsky, *High Technē: Art and Technology from the Machine Aesthetic to the Posthuman* (London, 1999) p. 68; and Hannah Arendt, *The Origins of Totalitarianism* (orig. 1948) (New York, 2004) p. 365. The phrase 'the law of killing' is from Arendt, *Origins*, p. 598.

2 For an elemental summary of fascism's essential features, see Noel O'Sullivan, *Fascism* (London, 1983).

3 George Mosse, 'Fascism and the French Revolution', *Journal of Contemporary History*, 24/1 (1989), pp. 5–26, at p. 5. He continues: 'The relationship between fascism and the Revolution involved a general reorientation of post-revolutionary European politics, a reorientation adopted at first by modern European nationalism, but subsequently by many other political movements as well. The basis of this reorientation was Rousseau's concept of the general will, that only when men act together as an assemble can the individual be a citizen. The general will became a secular religion under the Jacobin dictatorship – the people worshipping themselves – while the political leadership sought to guide and formalise this worship. Fascism saw the French Revolution as a whole through the eyes of the Jacobin dictatorship' (pp. 5–6).

4 I use the term *ethnic* in its twentieth century usage – 'often associated with race, nationality, or religion, by which the group identifies itself and others recognize it' (*The New Shorter Oxford English Dictionary*). This broad semantic range equips the word for many usages, which might change over time. President Wilson's Fourteen Points used *nation* and *nationality* interchangeably; and the term 'opportunity of autonomous development' to denote what later became famous as 'self-determination' (a political imperative influenced by the then insurgent Russian social-democracy). In 1929, Karl Kautsky suggested that *nation* be used to designate the population of a state. 'The further east we go the more numerous are the portions of the population that do not wish to belong to it, that constitute national communities of their own within it. They too are called "nations" or "nationalities." It would be advisable to use only the latter term for them'. Cited Horace B. Davies, *Towards a Marxist Theory of Nationalism* (New York, 1978) p. 6. The clear assumption here is that the nation is ethnically homogenous.

5 Helmer Rosting, 'Protection of Minorities by the League of Nations', *The American Journal of International Law*, 17/4 (1923), pp. 641–660.

6 http://www.armenian-genocide.org/Affirmation.236/current_category.49/affirmation_detail.html

7 Two excellent accounts of the minority question, separated by half a century, may be read in Arendt, *The Origins of Totalitarianism*, esp. the subsection called 'The "Nation of Minorities" and the Stateless People', pp. 344–368; and Mark Mazower, *Dark Continent: Europe's Twentieth Century* (London, 1999) Chapter 2, 'Empires, Nations, Minorities'.

8 Arendt, *Origins*, pp. 347, 345.

9 Arendt, *Origins*, pp. 350–351.

10 Antonio Gramsci, *Selections from the Prison Notebooks*, edited by Quintin Hoare & Geoffrey Nowell Smith (New York, 1975) pp. 210–240.

11 Hermann Rauschning, *The Revolution of Nihilism: Warning to the West* (New York, 1939).

12 See Claude Markovits, 'The Calcutta Riots of 1946', *Online Encyclopedia of Mass Violence*, November 2007, available at http://www.massviolence.org/The-Calcutta-Riots-of-1946

13 Gandhi was active in these places, attempting to quell the hatred, halt the deadly cycle of retribution, and calm traumatised spirits. For detailed accounts of his activity in this period, see Narayan Desai, *My Life is My Message* (New Delhi, 2009), vol. 4; *Svarpan (1940–1948)*, chapters 11, 12 & 14; and Dennis Dalton, 'Gandhi During Partition: A Case Study in the Nature of Satyagraha', in C.H. Philips and M.D. Wainwright, eds., *The Partition of India: Policies and Perspectives 1935–1947* (London, 1970).

14 Ishtiaq Ahmad, *The Punjab: Bloodied, Partitioned and Cleansed* (New Delhi, 2011), p. xli. A survey of Partition-related violence may be read in the *Online Encyclopedia of Mass Violence*, 'Thematic Chronology of Mass Violence in Pakistan, 1947–2007: Section 1, Partition Massacres, 1946-1947': http://www.massviolence.org/Thematic-Chronology-of-Mass-Violence-in-Pakistan-1947-2007?decoupe_recherche=noakhali

15 See 'From the Sundarlal Report': http://www.frontlineonnet.com/fl1805/18051140.htm

16 See http://en.wikisource.org/wiki/Resignation_letter_of_Jogendra_Nath_Mandal Mandal went on to say: 'Pakistan is no place for Hindus to live in and that their future is darkened by the ominous shadow of conversion or liquidation. The bulk of the upper class Hindus and politically conscious scheduled castes have left East Bengal. Those Hindus who will continue to stay accursed in Pakistan will, I am afraid, by gradual stages and in a planned manner be either converted to Islam or completely exterminated.'

About Bengali Muslims, Mandal said, 'They were promised autonomous and sovereign units of the independent State. What have they got instead? East Bengal has been transformed into a colony of the western belt of Pakistan, although it contained a population which is larger than that of all the units of Pakistan put together...'

17 See 'The Speech of Mr Sris Chandra Chattopadhya in Opposition to Objectives Resolution', Constitutent Assembly of Pakistan, 12 March 1949: <http://criticalppp.com/archives/5788>

18 For a brief history of the anti-Ahmadiya movement, see Nadeem Paracha, 'Tracing hate', <http://dawn.com/2012/12/13/tracing-hate/>. The official inquiry into the 1953 riots highlighted the erosion of criminal justice: 'If democracy means the subordination of law and order to political ends – then Allah knoweth best and we end the report.' See <http://www.thepersecution.org/dl/report_1953.pdf>

19 A more detailed account of revival and reform may be read in my essay 'Communalism in Modern India: A theoretical examination', *Mainstream*, 13 December, 1986; available at http://dilipsimeon.blogspot.in/2012/08/communalism-in-modern-india-theoretical.html

20 Bhagwan Josh, *Struggle for Hegemony in India: 1920–47. Vol. 2, 1934-41* (New Delhi, 1992) p. 61.

21 For different accounts of the emergence of Hindu nationalism, see esp. Sudhir Chandra, *The Oppressive Present: Literature and Social Consciousness in Colonial India* (Delhi, 1992); Vasudha Dalmia, *The Nationalization of Hindu Traditions: Bharatendu Harishchandra and Nineteenth-century Banaras* (New Delhi, 1997); Jyotirmaya Sharma, *Hindutva: Exploring the Idea of Hindu Nationalism* (Delhi, 2003); and Shabnam Tejani, *Indian Secularism: A Social and Intellectual History, 1890–1950* (Bloomington, 2008).

22 Chandra, *Oppressive Present*, p. 125.

23 Tilak is revered in modern Indian historiography as the founder of a populist nationalism. Nevertheless, he was an élitist who disapproved of the entry of oppressed castes into legislatures, bitterly attacked social reformers for their campaigns over the age of consent and the question of conjugal rights, and was one of the founders of the project of creating a Hindu political community. See Stanley Wolpert, *Tilak and Gokhale* (Berkeley & Los Angeles, 1962), esp. Chapter 3, 'Revival and Reform'.

24 Krishna Kumar, 'Quest for Self-Identity – Cultural Consciousness and Education in Hindi Region, 1880–1950', in *Economic & Political Weekly*, XXV/23, June 9, 1990, pp. 1247ff.

25 A critical assessment of the Khilafat movement can be found in Hamza Alavi, 'Ironies of History: Contradictions of the Khilafat Movement,' in Mushirul Hasan, ed., *Islam, Communities and the Nation: Muslim Identities in South Asia and Beyond* (New Delhi, 1998); also available here: http://hamzaalavi.com/?p=86. For further reading on nationalism see the bibliography provided by David Hardiman in *Gandhi in His Time and Ours* (Delhi, 2003), esp. Chapters 2 and 7, called 'An Incorporative Nationalism' and 'Fighting Religious Hatreds'. Also see Tejani, *Indian Secularism*.

26 O'Sullivan, *Fascism*, p. 118. O'Sullivan refers to Gustave le Bon's study, *The Crowd: A Study of the Popular Mind* (1896), where le Bon analyses the means by which a leader 'will imbue the mind of a crowd with ideas and beliefs.'

27 Saladdin Said Ahmed, 'Mass Mentality, Culture Industry, Fascism', *Kritike*, 2/1 (June 2008) pp. 79–94 at p. 82. See http://www.kritik'e.org/journal/issue_3/ahmed_june2008.pdf

28 This approach is developed in my essay 'Communalism in Modern India', available at http://dilipsimeon.blogspot.in/2012/08/communalism-in-modern-india-theoretical.html

29 AICC Resolution, 16/11/1947; *Collected Works of Mahatma Gandhi* (online) vol. 97, p. 480.

30 Dhanwantri and P.C.Joshi, *Bleeding Punjab Warns*, pp. 5–6, in the P.C.Joshi Archives, JNU, file CPI/108.

31 Dhanwantri and Joshi, *Bleeding Punjab*, pp. 8–10.

32 Walter Anderson and Shridhar Damle, *The Brotherhood in Saffron: the Rashtriya Swayamsevak Sangh and Hindu Revivalism* (New Delhi, 1987) pp. 38, 45, 65.

33 For a survey of Indian religious revivalism see my essay 'Communalism in Modern India', cited above (n.28).

34 Anderson and Damle, *Brotherhood in Saffron*, p. 20.

35 See the extracts from Savarkar's seminal text, 'Essentials of Hindutva' (1924), in W. Theodore de Bary, ed., *Sources of Indian Tradition* (Delhi, 1963). A pdf file of the entire text is available here : http://www.savarkar.org/content/pdfs/en/essentials_of_hindutva.v001.pdf

36 From Savarkar's Kanpur address in *Hindu Rashtra Darshan*, pp. 122–25; a collection of his presidential speeches that can be consulted here: http://liberalpartyofindia.org/communal/Hindu-Rashtra-Darshan.pdf

37 Sharma, *Hindutva*, p. 124.

38 The official report into the assassination makes clear Savarkar's central role in it. This crucial report can be accessed at http://archive.org/details/JeevanlalKapoorCommissionReport

39 W.C. Smith, *Modern Islam in India: A Social Analysis* (London, 1946) pp. 238–45.

40 Markus Daeschel, 'Scientism and its discontents: the Indo-Muslim "fascism" of Inayatullah Khan Al-Mashriqi', *Modern Intellectual History,* 3/3 (2006) pp. 443–72, at 450–452.

41 Ian Talbot, *Freedom's Cry: The Popular Dimension in the Pakistan Movement and Partition Experience in North-West India* (Karachi,1996) pp. 70–74, cited David Gilmartin, 'Partition, Pakistan, and South Asian History: In Search of a Narrative', *The Journal of Asian Studies*, 57/4 (1998), p. 1082.

42 Ahmad, *The Punjab: Bloodied, Partitioned and Cleansed*, pp. 130, 115, 128. The report about the RSS also remarked that the movement was 'not anti-government and its workers did not participate in the Congress civil disobedience movement of 1942' (p. 128).

43 Ahmad, *Punjab*, p. 216.

44 For more on the political background of these events, see David Gilmartin, *Empire and Islam: Punjab and the Making of Pakistan* (Berkeley, 1988); Ahmad, *Punjab*, Chapter 3; Ian Talbot, 'The Second World War and Local Indian Politics: 1939–1947', *The International History Review*, 6/ 4 (1984) pp. 592–610.

45 Dhanwantri and Joshi, *Bleeding Punjab*, pp. 12–13.

46 Dhanwantri and Joshi, *Bleeding Punjab*, p. 25.

47 Ibid.

48 Talbot, 'Second World War', p. 608.

49 Dhanwantri and Joshi, *Bleeding Punjab*, pp. 21–22.

50 Ibid., pp. 14–15.

51 Ibid., p. 9. Also, Ahmed, *Punjab*, p. 184.

52 Dhanwantri and Joshi, *Bleeding Punjab*, pp. 13–14.

53 Ibid., p. 13.

54 Ibid., p. 17.

55 Pandit Sunderlal's Report on the Kanpur Riots (1933), pp. 322, 327, 250–251.

56 See 'Who Are the Guilty', http://www.pudr.org/?q=content/who-are-guilty

57 D.R. Goyal, *Rashtriya Swayamsewak Sangh* (New Delhi, 1979) pp. 201–202. A brief account of Gandhi's last fast and the text of the Delhi Declaration of January 18, 1948, may be read here: http://dilipsimeon.blogspot.in/2012/03/another-time-another-mosque.html. Also see Gyanendra Pandey, *Remembering Partition* (Delhi, 2002) pp. 142–146.

58 For further reading on this theme, see Nandini Sundar, 'Public-Private Partnerships in the Industry of Insecurity', in Zeynep Gambetti and Marcia Godoy-Anativa, eds., *Rhetorics of Security* (forthcoming).

59 Antonio Gramsci, *Selections from the Prison Notebooks*, p. 232.

60 Gramsci, *Selections*, p. 218.

61 G. Adhikari, ed., *Pakistan and National Unity* (Bombay, 1943) p.15. The page references that follow in the text are to this publication. The full text of the Resolution may be read at <http://www.unz.org/Pub/LabourMonthly-1943mar-00093> An abridged version of the Report with the same title is available at <http://www.unz.org/Pub/LabourMonthly-1943mar-00087?View=PDF>

62 *Who Rules Pakistan?* (Communist Party Publication, Bombay, 1948), P.C. Joshi Archives, File CPI/147.

63 B. R. Ambedkar, *Pakistan, or the Partition of India* (Bombay, 1946). The first edition of the book appeared in 1940 as *Thoughts on Pakistan*. It was republished under a different title in 1946. A pdf copy of the book is available here: http://www.satnami.com/pakistan.pdf> Citations in this section refer to the 1946 edition of this book by Ambedkar.

64 Tara Zehra, 'A Brutal Peace', review of R.M. Douglas, *Orderly and Humane*. http://www.thenation.com/article/171484/brutal-peace-postwar-expulsions-germans#

65 R.M. Douglas, *Orderly and Humane: The Expulsion of the Germans after the Second World War* (Yale, 2012) pp. 71ff., where the author goes on to say, 'the Lausanne transfer was in many respect a fiasco'.

66 Ibid., p. 72.

67 A historical introduction to this theme may be read in Jeffrey Herf, *Reactionary Modernism: Technology, Culture and Politics in Weimar and the Third Reich* (Cambridge, 1984).

68 Jyotirmaya Sharma, *Hindutva: Exploring the Idea of Hindu Nationalism* (New Delhi, 2003) p. 136.

69 Ibid. Chapter 5 of Sharma's book deals with Savarkar's ideas.

70 Jyotirmaya Sharma, *Terrifying Vision: M.S. Golwalkar, the RSS and India* (New Delhi, 2007).

71 Marzia Casolari, 'Hindutva's Foreign Tie-up in the 1930s: Archival Evidence', *Economc and Political Weekly*, 35/4 (Jan. 22–28, 2000), pp. 218–28, at 223–224. Available online at http://www.sacw.net/DC/CommunalismCollection/ArticlesArchive/casolari.pdf

72 W.C. Smith, *Modern Islam in India*, p. 265.

73 See Romain Hayes, *Subhas Chandra Bose in Nazi Germany* (New York, 2011). More on the militarisation of Indian politics may be read here: http://dilipsimeon.blogspot.in/2012/06/hard-rain-falling-on-death-of-tp.html

74 William Theodore de Bary, ed., *Sources of Indian Tradition* (Delhi, 1963) p. 887.

75 Franz Neumann, *Behemoth: The Structure and Practice of National Socialism*, New York 1963, p. 27. A PDF may be read here http://www.unz.org/Pub/NeumannFranz-1942-00027

76 Arendt, *Origins*, p. 574.

77 See Pandey, *Remembering Partition*, and Vazira Fazila-Yacoobali Zamindar, *The Long Partition and the Making of Modern South Asia, Refugees, Boundaries, Histories* (New Delhi, 2008).

78 Lionel Baixas, 'Thematic Chronology of Mass Violence in Pakistan, 1947–2007', p. 2; available at <http://www.massviolence.org/Thematic-Chronology-of-Mass-Violence-in-Pakistan-1947-2007?decoupe_recherche=noakhali>

79 Nehru cited Ramchandra Guha, *India after Gandhi* (New Delhi, 2007) pp. 129–130. Also see Pandey, *Remembering Partition*, Chapter 7, 'Disciplining difference'.

80 See Venkat Dhulipala; 'Debating Pakistan in Late Colonial North India', *Indian Economic and Social History Review*, 48/3 (2011) pp. 377–405.

81 See Anuradha Chenoy and Kamal Mitra Chenoy, *Maoist and Other Armed Conflicts* (New Delhi, 2010).

82 Arendt, *Origins*, p. 368.

83 See Jairus Banaji, 'Fascism, Maoism and the Democratic Left' http://www.infochangeindia.org/governance/analysis/fascism-maoism-and-the-democratic-left.html

Further reading

W.C. Smith, *Modern Islam in India* (London, 1946)

Sudhir Chandra, *The Oppressive Present: Literature and Social Consciousness in Colonial India* (Delhi, 1992)

Harjot Oberoi, *The Construction of Religious Boundaries: Culture, Identity, and Diversity in the Sikh Tradition* (University of Chicago Press, 1994)

Vasudha Dalmia, *The Nationalization of Hindu Traditions: Bharatendu Harishchandra and Nineteenth-century Banaras* (New Delhi, 1997)

Jyotirmaya Sharma, *Hindutva: Exploring the Idea of Hindu Nationalism* (Delhi, 2003).

Bipan Chandra, *Communalism in Modern India* (Delhi, 1984) is a good short introduction to the history of communal politics.

For studies of the history of Partition, see

Ishtiaq Ahmad, *The Punjab: Bloodied, Partitioned and Cleansed* (Rupa & Co., 2011)

Urvashi Butalia, *The Other Side of Silence: Voices from the Partition of India* (New Delhi, 1998)

Gyanendra Pandey, *Remembering Partition: Violence, Nationalism and History in India* (Delhi, 2002)

Vazira Fazila-Yacoobali Zamindar, *The Long Partition and the Making of Modern South Asia: Refugees, Boundaries, Histories* (New Delhi, 2008)

Lionel Baixas, 'Thematic Chronology of Mass Violence in Pakistan, 1947–2007'. This paper may be read here: <http://www.mass-violence.org/Thematic-Chronology-of-Mass-Violence-in-Pakistan-1947-2007?decoupe_recherche=noakhali>

George Grosz, *The eclipse of the sun* (1926)

Trajectories of fascism
Extreme-right movements in India and elsewhere

Jairus Banaji

The term 'Theories of fascism' was trademark for the kind of discussion that went on in strictly Marxist circles, in Germany and elsewhere, in the sixties and early seventies. It was a major part of the revival of Left theory that characterised the radicalism of the sixties. In some ways the highpoint of this current of discussion came with the publication by Wolfgang Abendroth, in 1967, of a collection of Marxist texts that included essays by Otto Bauer, Arthur Rosenberg and August Thalheimer. These writings span the period from 1930 to 1938. Bauer, who was Austrian, identified the nationalism of the intelligentsia as a major cementing force in the ideology of fascism.[1] Rosenberg too assigned central importance to ideology and to the intelligenstia, seeing the latter as a key social base of the fascist movement, but unlike Bauer he saw the mass element in fascism as its distinctive feature. Thus, unlike almost all other left-wing writers of the period he underlines the mobilising force of anti-semitism, the power of this and other ideologies, especially nationalism, to feed into the construction of a fascist mass base.[2] The terrible fact that we have to face up to and learn from is that the great majority of the German people accepted the Nazi regime at least passively. I'll come back to this in a moment. The other important element in Rosenberg's analysis, which was by far the best to be developed by the Left in the 1930s, was the connivance or active complicity of the existing state authorities in condoning fascist violence, turning a blind eye to illegal activities such as conspiracies and political murders and repeated assaults on the Left. The police establishment and the judiciary played the main roles here in implicitly buttressing the fascist movements. In Italy the *squadristi* or fascist squads which first emerged in the rural areas of northern Italy and Tuscany to suppress sharecroppers and other workers could operate with total impunity *because* the government authorities stood by and simply allowed them to do so. In Germany the courts played an especially important role in being soft on right-wing violence. As Franz Neumann notes in his great book *Behemoth*, 'At the centre of the counterrevolution [he means against the Weimar Republic] stood the judiciary'. A third and final element that emerges from Rosenberg's analysis is what he calls the fascists' "peculiar tactic" of using stormtroopers. In fact, a plethora of paramilitary organisations emerged across the political spectrum and more even than the stormtroopers it was the paramilitarisation of wider nationalist circles in Germany and their use of targeted political assassinations that truly reflected the extra-parliamentary Right's resolute opposition to the new democracy.[3] Given that some 350 government politicians were assassinated by the nationalist terror groups, this backlash had the features of an armed insurrection against Weimar democracy but played out in slow motion and unevenly. I say 'wider nationalist circles' because on one estimate over 1 million German males belonged to the various paramilitary formations in the summer of 1919.[4] That is a staggering number. The culture of militarism that led into the war carried over into the Weimar Republic in the shape of this organised element, the so-called Volunteer Associations of which the most famous was the Freikorps. What I'm going to do in the main part of this lecture is return to some of these themes after suggesting a theoretical framework for dealing with them. We know that the violence of the Right often takes the form of pogroms but what *are* pogroms? Or to put this another way, how are pogroms intelligible in any theory that rejects positivism? In the final part of the lecture I'll look at the way fascism works in the context of Indian democracy, and then draw out the distinctiveness of India's fascist movement by comparing it with the German case.

Now the 'theories of fascism' strand of the literature on fascism had more or less run dry by the mid seventies, and the field was rapidly swamped by a burgeoning academic literature that became both more specialised and humongously massive in the scale on which books and articles began to appear. One offshoot of this explosion of the more purely academic work on fascism was that new themes were developed. Of these probably the most important was the literature on the Nazi genocide, supplemented by a whole lot of new research on the persecution of marginalised social groups such as women, youth and sexual minorities, and on the murderous policies of 'eugenic cleansing'.[5] This had such an impact on the field that it forced the more thinking elements of the Left to reconsider classic Marxist accounts of fascism, as Enzo Traverso did in his brilliant little book which was subtitled *Marxism After Auschwitz*. Did conventional Marxist explanations that prioritised the class base of fascism or the economic forces at work behind its emergence have any real sense of the kind of rupture that the concentration camps came to signify?

Let me start with one aspect of this broader issue. In his book *Une culpabilité ordinaire?* Edouard Husson writes, 'As for the so-called "ordinary Germans", it's plausible to argue that while not all of them participated in the massacres, all of them *have* to be held politically responsible for supporting the *Führer* who made the genocide possible – all, that is, except those who were politically opposed to Nazism'.[6] Husson is saying that the mass of ordinary Germans were responsible for the crimes of Nazism insofar as they bore political liability for installing the regime. The distinctions implied here are those that Karl Jaspers laid out in his famous lecture *Die Schuldfrage*.[7] Indeed, Jaspers argued that the notion of 'collective guilt' was only ever valid in the specific sense of political liability, but he also made it clear that he thought that 'those who went right on with their activities as if nothing had happened' were indeed morally guilty as well. He wrote, 'I, who cannot act otherwise than as an individual, am morally responsible for all my deeds, including the execution of political and military orders. It is never simply true that "orders are orders"'.[8] So how do we deal with this potentially huge mass of morally impervious individuals who, as Jaspers says, 'went right on with their activities as if nothing had happened'? They were not hard-core Nazis but they were crucial to the success of Nazism all the same.

To take this further, Sheehan writes that what the Nazis required of the bulk of the population was 'compliance, not conviction'.[9] In Germany in the thirties there was the overtly Nazi element, the direct perpetrators (both the Nazi leadership and Party organisations as well as 'large sections of the German non-Nazi élites in the army, industry and bureaucracy'),[10] and on the other side the bulk of the civilian population (ethnic Germans and Poles) who went along with the regime. The precise German term for the latter is *Mitläufer*. They were, it is said in the literature, morally indifferent to the fate of the regime's victims. But this characterisation, which comes from Ian Kershaw, doesn't seem even vaguely satisfying. Two holocaust historians Kulka and Rodrigue settle for the term 'passive complicity' as a stronger description of the role of the *Mitläufer*. Again, what does it mean to be passively complicit in the criminality of a regime, whether it's a fascist government or any other? What explanation or even sort of explanation is there for what Browning calls a 'widespread receptivity to mass murder' when speaking of Germans under Nazism?[11] No form of positivism is going to be able to match the kind of explanation we need. And that in part is why the horror of the holocaust confronts us as a sort of brute facticity, the sense of sheer intellectual defeat that Tim Mason expressed when he wrote

'I have always remained emotionally, and thus intellectually, paralysed in front of what the Nazis actually did and what their victims suffered. The enormity of these actions and these sufferings both demanded...description and analysis, and at the same time totally defied them. I could neither face the facts of genocide, nor walk away from them and study a less demanding subject'.[12]

So let's start with passive complicity. The only theoretical text I'm aware of that helps to make sense of this notion, to make it intelligible, is the massive enterprise Sartre undertook in the two volumes of his *Critique of Dialectical Reason*. The *Critique* was written at the end of the fifties, against the background of a savage war of repression in Algeria. Algeria figures in the *Critique* as Sartre's prime example of why exploitation has to be inseparable from oppression, as he puts it. Colonial regimes encapsulate a perpetual circularity between those moments, between practices of extermination, plunder and violence, and the inert functioning of the economic system itself with its seeming institutional autonomy and its institutionalised racism. The initial violence of the colonisers renews itself throughout the history of the regime and the struggle between classes under colonialism is neither purely comparable to the molecular order nor simply praxis through and through, but an interlacing of these moments or forms of intelligibility.[13]

However, the really interesting aspect of the way the French war in Algeria shaped the arguments of the *Critique* would almost certainly have remained permanently opaque to us if Simone de Beauvoir had not documented precisely how that background influenced both her and Sartre at the time. In *Force of Circumstance* she writes, 'I am an intellectual, I take words and the truth to be of value; every day I had to undergo an endlessly repeated onslaught of lies spewed from every mouth...What did appal me was to see the vast majority of the French people turn chauvinist and to realise the depth of their racist attitude. Bost and Jacques Lanzmann...told me how the police treated the neighbourhood Algerians; there were searches, raids, and manhunts every day; they beat them up, and overturned the vendors' carts in the open-air market. No one made any protest, far from it...'. 'It was even worse, because , whether I wanted to be or not, I was an accomplice of these people I couldn't bear to be in the same street with...'. [14] And later she writes, 'This hypocrisy, this indifference, this country, my own self, were no longer bearable to me. All those people in the streets, in open agreement or battered into a stupid submission – they were all murderers, all guilty. Myself as well.' And she adds at the end of a powerful passage 'Sartre protected himself by working furiously at his *Critique de la raison dialectique*'.[15]

What is striking here is her sense of sheer powerlessness in the face of the humongous propaganda that accompanies and justifies every war of repression (the French in Algeria, the US in Vietnam, the Indians in Kashmir and parts of the northeast). And de Beauvoir confesses to a sense of complicity in the crimes committed by the French in Algeria, by what her government was doing in the name (of course) of "all" French people, in 1957 and 1958. Now this sense of complicity resonates through large parts of the *Critique* as the powerlessness of a specific kind of human multiplicity that Sartre calls the 'series' or 'serialities'. Their impotence is experienced and lived in the face of the non-series, that is, the organised groups, especially those that make up the state, the state being for Sartre an ensemble of organised groups of the kind he calls institutions. So where do classes fit in this schema? Classes for Sartre are not unified subjects capable of some common class-wide action, as a certain voluntarism imagines, but 'shifting ensembles of groups and series',[16] hence simultaneously organised and unorganised, with a perpetual circularity between groups and series, that is, no guarantee that class-groups will not dissolve into seriality (into pure dispersion, the state of having no organised existence) or for that matter re-emerge from it in future.

The group for Sartre is the negation of seriality, it emerges as a transcendence of the state of pure impotence and dispersion that characterises the vast mass of any society. Overall it is seriality that defines the larger swathe of any class in the sense that even within the bourgeoisie it is only a minority that is sufficiently organised (formed into groups of one kind or another) to have the power to control and dominate the rest of society, that is, to dominate the serialities of its own and of other classes. The state of being part of a dispersed molecular mass defined by a reciprocity of solitudes, determined only by otherness, by what others are doing and feeling, unified solely from the outside, by some external object (unified with these people here by the bus we are waiting for; unified with this mass here that has come to Jantar Mantar to see Hazare fasting or descended on Ayodhya to demolish a mosque) is what Sartre means by seriality.

As for the relationship between groups and series, two are especially interesting. The essential point about the series is that it is inert, it can do nothing, engage in no action of its own, yet have many things done to it. It follows that the state 'can never be regarded as the product or expression of the totality of social individuals or even the majority of them, since this majority is serial anyway and could not express its needs and demands without liquidating itself as a series so as to become a large group'.[17] From this Sartre concludes that 'the idea of a diffuse popular sovereignty becoming embodied in a sovereign is a mystification. There is no such thing as diffuse sovereignty'. Serialities 'do not have the power or nature either to consent to or to resist the State'.[18] Our acceptance of the state's power is simply our interiorisation of the powerlessness to refuse it.[19] As a serialised mass the vast mass of any population has 'no means of either contesting or establishing legitimacy' for a given state.

A second more sinister relationship. Groups are constantly working series or working on them as the worked matter of their common praxis. This is most obvious in the action of the mass media which essentially addresses vast series of serialities most of which are indefinite and completely powerless in the face of the powerful groups that control and dominate the media. The most important action of groups on series is the kind Sartre calls 'other direction' or 'directed seriality'. Other direction is a term borrowed from David Riesman's book *The Lonely Crowd* and it brings us squarely to the issue of fascism. Political propaganda works on the same principle as advertising, that is, of generating an illusion of what Sartre calls 'totalised seriality'.[20] The series can do nothing, it is dispersed and inert, but the magic of advertising lies in the group's ability to 'exploit seriality by pushing it to an extreme so that recurrence itself will produce synthetic results'.[21] This sentence, obscure as it sounds, comes in a section that will end by discussing anti-semitism and pogroms. By 'recurrence' Sartre means the perpetual flight that characterises the milieu of the Other (collective objects like markets, inflation, rumour, public opinion, and ideology, where serial action is both indeterminate and circular). The form of conditioning contained in the work of organised groups on series is one where the means used is to 'manipulate the practico-inert field to produce serial reactions that are retotalised at the level of the common undertaking, that is to say, reshaped and forged like inorganic matter. And the means to this means is to constitute the serial as a false totality for everyone'.[22] 'Recurrence, controlled from outside as a determination projected from everyone, through Others, into the false totality of a common field, and, in reality, into pure reflexive flight' is what Sartre says he means by other-direction.[23] In politics the advertiser's phantom unity of consumers fixated on the illusion of a totalised seriality (as if the unity of a flight was a real unity) finds its precise counterpart in mass mobilisations based on the manipulation of series and seriality. Manipulated seriality is the heart of fascist politics. Here in India the techniques of other-direction take a panopoly of forms from sustained communal propaganda to communal mass mobilisations. If the mass element in fascism is its distinctive feature, even more distinctive is the way this mass is put together, constructed and mobilised, through what Sartre calls the 'systematic other-direction of the racism of the Other, that is to say, in terms of the continuous action of a group on a series'.[24]

The pogrom then is a special case of this 'systematic other-direction', one in which the group 'intends to act on the series so as to extract a total action from it *in alterity itself*'.[25] The directing group is careful 'not to occasion what might be called organised action within inert gatherings'. 'The real problem at this level is to extract organic actions from the masses' without disrupting their status as a dispersed molecular mass, as seriality.[26] So Sartre describes the pogrom as 'the passive activity of a directed seriality',[27] an analysis where the term 'passive' only underscores the point that command responsibility is the crucial factor in mass communal violence, since the individuals involved in dispersive acts of violence are the inert instruments of a sovereign or directing group. Thus for Sartre the passive complicity that sustains the mass base of fascism is a serial complicity, a 'serial responsibility', as he calls it,[28] and it makes no difference, in principle, whether the individuals of the series have engaged in atrocities as part of an orchestrated wave of pogroms or simply approved that violence 'in a serial dimension', as he puts it.[29] In both instances, what is involved for him is 'impotence and an inert identification with the criminal', an identity in alterity which makes all of them responsible.[30]

In *The Origins of Totalitarianism* Hannah Arendt writes that 'totalitarian movements use and abuse democratic freedoms in order to abolish them'.[31] But in Italy and Germany the fascist movements emerged less to use/abuse democratic freedoms than to reverse the process of democratisation that flowed from the post-war crisis and create movements for the overthrow of still precarious emerging democracies. The distinctive feature of India's fascism is that it has had to grow in a society where the mass of the population remains committed to democracy and no agenda for the overthrow of democracy can ever be affirmed overtly in those terms. Thus Arendt's characterisation of fascist movements using/abusing democratic freedoms to abolish them is, paradoxically, more true of India than it ever was of Europe.

In India fascist tendencies are currently at work in two forms, one direct, the other more insidious. The more direct form consists chiefly in the mobilisation of a communal mass base which fluctuates in intensity but is clearly seen by the RSS as the organic strategy, and the one most directly linked to its ideology of extreme nationalism. That ideology was not a product of the RSS specifically, since the Hindu Mahasabha played an equally seminal role in forging its main elements. I'm referring of course to the fanatically extreme nationalism that was embodied in different ways in Savarkar and Golwalkar and encapsulated India's version of a fascist utopia ethnically cleansed or purged of its 'alien' elements. Everyone knows that both propagandists were deeply influenced by the Nazi extermination of the Jews and took that as their model for the way Muslims would have to be dealt with, in principle anyway. But mass communalism and sustained communal propaganda have been supplemented by more insidious subversions of democracy that combine the elements of a war of position with a war of movement. Thus progressive control of the media by the extreme right which includes the mainstreaming of the extreme right by the media, so that overtly communal elements are repeatedly projected as normal and innocuous (note the repeated presence of hard-core RSS elements on the prime time talk shows of channels like NDTV and CNN-IBN) and the BJP's relentless parliamentary agitations, consciously calculated to induce a breakdown in the functioning of parliament and project that as the bungling of a corrupt and ineffectual government, both have the character of a war of position, that is, a protracted war of attrition against India's democracy that legitimises fascist politics and creates a dispersed revulsion against 'the parliamentary system'. A vital part of this trench warfare has been a widespread infiltration of the state apparatuses, a molecular penetration of the police, the bureaucracy and the intelligence agencies, which creates a state within the state, and one that is barely camouflaged when investigations into the criminal activity of the RSS underground (into the RSS cadre who have drifted into groups like Abhinav Bharat) are sabotaged by the state itself, or when the police are overtly implicated in communal carnages such as the explosion of violence led by the Shiv Sena in Bombay in January 1993. The war of movement on the other hand takes the form of a strategy of tension, a term invented by the Italian Left to characterise the spate of bombings and assassinations perpetrated by neo-fascist terrorist groups in the late sixties and seventies (from 1969 to 1980). Many were false flag bombings that were blamed on extra-parliamentary left-wing organisations, the way the RSS bombings are blamed on Muslims. About the Piazza Fontana bombing of December 1969 which was initially blamed on the anarchists, the neo-fascist activist Vincenzo Vinciguerra stated, 'The December 1969 explosion was supposed to be the detonator which would have convinced the political and military authorities to declare a state of emergency'. The Bologna railway bombing of August 1980 was one of the most horrific in this series of neo-fascist terror strikes, killing 85 people and injuring some 200. In *Godse's Children* Subhash Gatade has shown how the investigations into similar attacks in India have progressively revealed a unified or coordinated network of conspirators, all implicated with the RSS, with Indore as a key centre of this underground.[32] That the RSS outsources the strategy of tension and publicly disowns it is of course mere subterfuge, not vastly more credible than its disowning of Godse himself.

Although fascist nostalgia is not a major characteristic of the extreme Right in Europe today, and a sort of electoral fascism is more widespread (appeals to racism and xenophobia to mobilise electoral support),[33] the Sangh parivar is in some ways a purer version of the political culture of a more traditional fascism. The pogroms in India have far exceeded in scale anything that Germany saw in Weimar or the Nazi period (short of the mass extermination of the Jews when the Nazis finally turned to the 'final solution'). The culture of communalism is also at least as widespread in India as anti-semitism ever was in Germany, especially after the war. In Republican Germany only one region, Bavaria, acted as 'a cauldron of radical Right insurgency',[34] the crucial base that allowed Hitler and the Nazis to survive when there was a general retreat of the nationalist Right in the mid twenties. In India, by contrast, RSS-controlled governments have been in power in different regions at different times and Gujarat in the past ten years has been a microcosm of what the rest of India would look like if fascism ever took over completely. What the RSS has never had and always seemed to discourage was a leadership cult. With the repeated acclamations of Modi as the next prime minister this seems to be changing now, for it is the first time this political sector has found a figurehead around whom to build a Führer cult. Kershaw points out that the Hitler cult was the 'crucial adhesive' of the Nazi movement, its 'integrating mechanism'. Hitler was, as he says, 'the sole, indispensable force of integration in a movemnent that retained the potential to tear itself apart'.[35] This cannot be said of the Sangh parivar, since Modi's rise to what *he* would like to see as absolute mastery and the abject submission of everyone else grates with a political tradition of collective control divested of any fanatical cult of one individual. Since electoral fascism is a major part of their strategy, however, they may well be willing to make tactical concessions in this direction, unleashing a dynamic that no one can foresee at the moment. Finally, whereas German capital was split in its political allegiances, and Thyssen was wholly exceptional in joining the Nazi party whereas 'the more liberal factions of industry continued to support the Chancellor Heinrich Brüning' (this in 1932),[36] in India by contrast the last few years have seen a spate of well-publicised bear hugs between our captains of industry and Modi, in a display of feigned servility that shows that industrial capital at least is ready for fascism if large and overwhelming sectors of the Indian people most likely are not.

As you know, the Supreme Court was forced to intervene to transfer cases out of Gujarat. In the Best Bakery case Justice V.N. Khare even stated he had no confidence in the Gujarat government. He was quoted as saying, 'I have no faith left in the prosecution and the Gujarat government'. There could scarcely be a more scathing indictment of the brazen subversion of the justice system that soon came to characterise the whole way in which *this* state government manipulated the machinery of the law, fabricated or suppressed evidence, eliminated potential witnesses, and even concocted a whole series of encounter killings to create the impression that the Chief Minister's life was constantly under threat from potential assassins. Internal assassinations such as those of Haren Pandya or Sunil Joshi have been one of the cruder ways in which the right-wing seeks to evade legal scrutiny. The spinelessness of the judiciary and its overt or covert sympathies with the extreme Right was a major part of the story of the success of German fascism. We have not reached that state of judicial disintegration yet, and luckily we still have a Supreme Court that is beyond the direct reach of regimes immersed in criminality, even if its Special Investigation Teams can be subverted.

More insidious, however, is the inert grip of ideology. Much of the drive behind the emergence of a more repressive, authoritarian state in India is fuelled by a muscular nationalism that is now characteristic, in serial inert ways, of a large section of the urban middle classes, the media, the intelligentsia and capital. The Left has simply refused to campaign against this deluded form of patriotism which, because it imagines India as a global power, would rather have crores of rupees spent on defense and the nuclear industry than on constructing a viable public health system or affordable homes for the mass of people or even programmes to eradicate malnutrition. It is this nationalism, the pure self-delusion of a country that imagines it can be a major capitalist power on the back of mass deprivation and overt oppression, that has the potential for military conflict, a peculiarly destructive one when combined with that 'continuous invocation of a threatening "other"' that Sumit and Tanika Sarkar ascribed to the new organised Hindutva of the 1990s.[37] The slogan 'India First' rearticulates Golwalkar's mystical nationalism, the hyperorganicism of the nation as some sort of super-individual, as an animate being, but it does so in the idiom of big-power chauvinism, of the race for global hegemony, against the looming background of a potentially huge military-industrial complex that domestic capital is starting to whet its appetite for. For Golwalkar nationalism meant the dissolution of the individual in a larger whole. Gandhi therefore accurately described the RSS as a 'communal body with a totalitarian outlook'. Today those ideas have re-emerged in more sanitised and potentially more destructive ways. But where is the opposition to them? Where is the political culture that says, 'Fascism shall not pass'?

Endnotes

1 See Otto Bauer, 'Fascism', in Tom Bottomore and Patrick Goode, eds., *Austro-Marxism* (Oxford, 1978) pp. 167–86.

2 See Rosenberg, 'Fascism as a Mass-Movement', pp. 19–100 above.

3 R. G. L. Waite, *Vanguard of Nazism: The Free Corps Movement in Postwar Germany 1918–1923* (Cambridge, Mass., 1952).

4 Waite, *Vanguard of Nazism*, p. 39.

5 E.g., Jane Caplan, 'The Historiography of National Socialism', in Michael Bentley, ed., *Companion to Historiography* (London, 1997).

6 Edouard Husson, *Une culpabilité ordinaire? Hitler, les Allemands et la Shoah* (Paris 1997).

7 Translated as Karl Jaspers, *The Question of German Guilt*, tr. E.B. Ashton (Westport, Conn., 1948).

8 Jaspers, *Question of German Guilt*, p. 25.

9 James Sheehan, 'National Socialism and German Society: Reflections on Recent Research', *Theory and Society*, 13 (1984) pp. 866–7.

10 Ian Kershaw, *The Nazi Dictatorship: Problems and Perspectives of Interpretation* (London, 2000) p. 103.

11 For the references to Kershaw, etc., see Chapter One above, p. 13, nn. 38–39.

12 Tim Mason, *Social Policy in the Third Reich: The Working Class and the 'National Community'*, tr. J. Broadwin, ed. Jane Caplan (Oxford, 1993) p. 282.

13 Jean-Paul Sartre, *Critique of Dialectical Reason, Volume One*, tr. Alan Sheridan-Smith (London, 1976) pp. 716ff.

14 Simone de Beauvoir, *Force of Circumstance*, tr. Richard Howard (Penguin Books, 1968) pp. 378, 381.

15 de Beauvoir, *Force of Circumstance*, pp. 396–7.

16 Sartre, *Critique*, p. 638.

17 Sartre, *Critique*, pp. 635–6.

18 Sartre, *Critique*, p. 636.

19 R.D. Laing and D.G. Cooper, *Reason and Violence: A Decade of Sartre's Philosophy* (London, 1971) p. 162

20 Sartre, *Critique*, p. 644.

21 Sartre, *Critique*, p. 643. The passage reads, 'The principle of the new *praxis* (propaganda, agitation, publicity...campaigns, slogans, the muted orchestration of terror as an accompaniment to orders, "stuffing people's heads" with propaganda etc.) is to exploit seriality by pushing it to an extreme so that recurrence itself will produce synthetic results (or results capable of being synthesised). The sovereign will rethink seriality in practice as a conditioning of indefinite flight, in the context of a total undertaking which is controlled dialectically'.

22 Sartre, *Critique*, pp. 649–50.

23 Sartre, *Critique*, p. 650.

24 Sartre, *Critique*, p. 652.

25 Sartre, *Critique*, p. 644.

26 Sartre, *Critique*, p. 654.

27 Sartre, *Critique*, p. 653. 'Seriality – though it may cause lynchings or pogroms – is not a sufficient explanation of, for example, the active anti-semitism of the German petty bourgeoisie under the Nazi régime. Now some highly ingenious recent studies have shown that anti-semitism as a historical fact has to be interpreted in terms of the systematic other-direction of the *racism of the Other*, that is to say, in terms of a continuous action of a group on a series...every act of violence was irreversible, not only because it destroyed human lives but because it made everyone an other-directed criminal, adopting the leaders' crimes in so far as he had committed them *elsewhere* and as an other in an other. Conversely, the acceptance of the sovereign's acts of violence, as an *hexis* in the milieu of other-direction, may always, through the transcendent action of the directing group, be reconverted into a pogrom,

as the passive activity of a directed seriality.' (pp. 652–3)

28 Sartre, *Critique*, p. 654.

29 Sartre, *Critique*, p. 757.

30 Sartre, *Critique*, p. 761. 'After 1848...employers were a curious historical product of the massacres for which they were collectively responsible without actually having committed them' (p. 767).

31 Hannah Arendt, *The Origins of Totalitarianism* (New York, 1985) p. 312.

32 Subhash Gatade, *Godse's Children: Hindutva Terror in India* (New Delhi, 2011).

33 The best recent study is David Art, *Inside the Radical Right: The Development of Anti-Immigrant Politics in Western Europe* (Cambridge 2011).

34 Ian Kershaw, *Hitler1889-1936: Hubris* (London, 2001) p. 212.

35 Kershaw, *Hitler*, pp. 260, 267.

36 Dick Geary, 'Employers, Workers and the Collapse of Weimar', in Ian Kershaw, ed., *Weimar: Why Did German Democracy Fail?* (London, 1990) p. 104.

37 Tapan Basu and others, *Khaki Shorts and Saffron Flags* (New Delhi, 1993) p. 113.

Postscript

Fascism: Essays on Europe and India was published a little over a year before the fateful Lok Sabha elections of May 2014 which brought the BJP and its allies to power following an intense media campaign and blitzkrieg of election rallies, all dominated by the seemingly formidable and largely media-driven figure of Narendra Modi. Although the BJP polled only 31 per cent of the votes, the *lowest ever of any party winning the Indian general elections*, and its allies a further 7.5 per cent at best, the opposition to the BJP was badly fragmented. The 60%+ anti-BJP vote was thus widely dispersed and ineffective. The result of the Bihar assembly elections shows that this state of fragmentation is not an inevitable feature of parliamentary politics in India and *can* be tackled in the face of a fascist threat.

What has emerged in the eighteen months that the BJP has been in power is an increasingly overt assertion of the power of the RSS, whose proclaimed vision for India is to make it a Hindu state with or without the trappings of democracy. This is the first government of independent India where the RSS is openly in charge. Having gained power, it now seeks to expand its own power and entrench itself even further. In the long term the most dangerous aspect of this seizure of power will be the wholesale takeover of educational institutions, the rewriting of school and university textbooks, and the attempt to purge the Indian past of its non-Hindu, cosmopolitan strands.

A more immediate violence dominates the present. The essays in this book that deal with India suggest that communal mobilisation is the 'organic strategy' of the RSS. This view has been vindicated by the way the present government's parent (the RSS) and their sprawling network of Hindu organisations have been encouraged by the BJP's victory, *and* had the freedom, to mount hate campaigns[1] that have led to a spate of lynchings and contributed decisively to the sort of political 'climate' where outfits operating in the shadow of the RSS can openly assassinate anti-superstition campaigners like Narendra Dabholkar. Venom-spewing figures from the ruling party who have been conspicuous in these hate campaigns have had a field day in the past year and a half, since neither Modi nor other BJP leaders seem to care that hate speech is a crime and the hate campaigners in their ranks are openly stoking the flames of communal violence. The structured duplicity that characterises Modi's regime reflects both the division of labour within the Sangh parivar between 'state' and 'movement', government and mass base, Modi and the RSS, but also repeated reminders to Modi about who he owes his position to and *who ultimately calls the shots*. The primacy of the RSS (as 'movement') has meant the emergence of a pattern of low-intensity communal warfare that may well spread to new parts of the country in a drive to communalise India. It is possible that before Modi's term expires the RSS will have succeeded in transforming the Northeast into a new cauldron of communal violence unless the resistance to this is created from now. Communal conflagrations are carefully organised episodes of violence and every round of ethnic cleansing drives Muslims and Christians into relief camps where they fester with no hope of ever returning to their villages. This pattern, driven by the RSS and its vision of an India where the minorities become second-class citizens, is creating legacies of hatred at the ground level that pile up like the blood-soaked debris of India's failing democracy.

It is Modi's silence about the recent spate of violence that has attracted most attention both from the 'liberal' media and from the government's critics within the intelligentsia. India has just seen a remarkable groundswell of protest among writers, film makers, historians and scientists, and the government's response, characteristically, has been to attack and vilify the protesters, denouncing them as 'leftists', 'Communists', agents of the Congress party and even agents of an 'international conspiracy' hatched to defame the country! As if this infantilism was not enough, in a characteristic trope of fascist politics the aggressor emerges as the victim, Modi himself is said to be the object of 'intolerance', and every discourse about the growing climate of authoritarianism and hate politics in the country is converted into a sign of the illiberal nature of the opposition. 'Liberal' in the BJP's lexicon seems to mean a willingness to *submit to* (be 'tolerant' of) a deeply authoritarian political culture, one that polices how we think, what we read or how we express ourselves and our eating habits as much it does the clothes women wear, one's freedom of worship (or the freedom to reject all worship) and, crucially, sexual partnerships. Meanwhile, in rally after rally across the state of Bihar Modi himself is scarcely 'silent', he fuels communal phobias with references to the 'Darbhanga module' (subtext: Bihar's Muslims are terrorists, potentially) and to the incumbent chief minister of the state (who has now won a third term) having designs to deprive *Dalits, Mahadalits* and OBCs of reservations meant for them in favour of Muslims. Wearing his election hat, the prime minister of the country has no compunction pitting one community against another on the basis of pure falsehood. This is the same political figure who, in his official avatar, is on his best behaviour as he interacts with world leaders like Obama (recall that he had mocked Obama unconscionably while campaigning in April 2009) and with royalty in Britain!

At another level, the past year has seen a gradual disenchantment with Modi and his government in business circles (key funders of Modi's campaign), fuelled both by the BJP's defeat on the Land Acquisition front and by the growing sense of a paralysis at the level of government. The leadership cult that was the BJP's main strategy in the Lok sabha elections has thrown up a style of governance (post election) characterised by massive centralisation of power in the hands of their 'leader' coupled with a serious lack of expertise at the level of the PMO; hence paralysis. But resistance within the bureaucracy may well be a second factor. The economy was a major area of the campaign Modi had mounted in the months preceding the general election and this is where the sense of disquiet among his elite supporters has been most visible. At the end of July a major business daily could write: 'India has...shown its steepest decline in a decade over the last year in AT Kearney's FDI confidence index, dropping out of the top 10 for the first time since 2002' (*Business Standard* 29 July, 2015). Manufacturing remains sluggish, there has been no major inflow of foreign investment into manufacturing in spite of innumerable 'summits' and international trips. For the present regime propaganda matters vastly more than policy, growth figures are reworked to sustain the illusion that India is actually doing well economically when the world economy is in recession and exports are falling, credit-rating agencies are lambasted if their warnings about growing 'intolerance' seem damaging to the country's image ('anti-national'), and domestic businesses realise that there is a charmed circle of industrialists who gain vastly more thanks to their closeness to the prime minister than most of them are ever likely to.[2]

More disturbingly, Modi's government, driven by an extreme version of its one-sided commitment to capital ('neo-liberalism'), is quietly engaged in dismantling even the minimal welfare provisions introduced by the two previous governments, witness the attempt currently underway to sabotage the functioning of MNREGA by withholding funds scheduled for wage payments under the scheme; or the slashing of the country's public health budget from its appallingly low levels to an even more shocking one percent of GDP, which risks plunging India into major health disasters, even as pulses, a major protein source for the poor and middle class, become unaffordable for the mass of the population.

One aspect not taken up in these essays is the way what Wilhelm Reich called 'organised mysticism' is used to mobilise mass support for political figures like Modi. Reich used the term to refer to religious ideologies and their patriarchal-authoritarian hold over the masses. These themes are of pivotal importance to the nature of the emerging fascism in India, not least because of the light they throw on the repression and control of sexuality. Moreover, the spate of killings of rationalists starting with Dabholkar shows how deeply invested in these ideologies the right-wing in India remains. 'Godmen' like Ramdev and Asaram Bapu are publicly associated with support for the BJP. Indeed, in Modi's case a major role was played by the Hindu leader Asaram endorsing Modi's political ambitions. In 2006 the then Chief Minister of Gujarat repeatedly invoked the 'blessings' (*ashirvad*) of this religious scamster whose ashram would soon become embroiled in scandals involving rape, murder and black magic, and who would himself be arrested a few years later on charges of sexually assaulting a minor. It is hard to imagine any other major democracy in the world electing a prime minister with these past connections! Yet elected he has been, thanks to the role of the Sangh parivar in building a 'mass base' through decades of molecular work (a labour of fascism) and deploying that base decisively for electoral purposes. As the preface and introductory essays in this book have shown, fascism *only succeeds as a mass movement*. 'Ideology' plays a major role in that process but ideology here has to be understood as a *material* force grounded in what Reich saw as the 'psychic structures' moulded from childhood by family, 'tradition' and the repression of sexuality in the young.[3] These are not aspects of fascism developed in the essays above but they deserve much more attention, especially in India.

A final word: there has been a lot of talk about the Congress Party reinventing itself to be able to recover its loss of ground. The same of course should be said of the Left parties which are now close to extinction as national parties. But parties can only reinvent themselves to the extent that they engage in a learning process. In the case of Congress today, it lacks any serious grassroots presence that can counter the mobilising thrust of the RSS. But it also has to confront the hard reality that much of the blame for the return of the BJP and for the current state of India's democracy lies with earlier Congress regimes. As Kershaw said about the Nazis, fascism always taps 'the rich vein of raw anger… opened up by the perceived failure of democracy amid mounting crisis'.[4] In India this is obvious at three levels. The terrible culture of impunity that has allowed the BJP to get away with the Gujarat massacres is a direct legacy of the Congress leadership's refusal to prosecute those within its ranks responsible for the horrific anti-Sikh violence of 1984. Failure to carry through prosecutions where they were due legitimised the use of mass violence as a means of political consolidation, a strategy that was fully exploited by the Sangh parivar. It is this that has created the bind that every time Gujarat 2002 is brought up the perpetrators are able to counter that with '1984'. Again, successive Congress administrations showed a singular incapacity in dealing with hate speech and fascist mobilisations (they allowed the Shiv Sena to flourish in Maharashtra, allowed the demolition of Babri masjid, allowed the Bombay pogroms of 1992/3, and so on). Most spectacularly, UPA1 simply failed to make any effort to bring Modi to book on grounds of command responsibility for the violence of 2002. Second, the culture of venality that grew up in UPA 2 in particular was a key factor in throwing the Indian middle class into the hands of the BJP. Even if much of the rage and rhetoric against corruption was artificially constructed by the absurd computational exercises of the CAG, the perception that Congress had allowed ministers and allies to get away with massive scams in coal and telecoms fuelled a surge of revulsion that played straight into the hands of the radical Right. Corruption, of course, is more deeply embedded in the bureaucracy than it is in the political class, but it remains the most powerful weapon parties can use to engineer each other's downfall. And finally, at the most basic level of all, the failure of the secular parties (the Communist Parties included) to make any serious headway in confronting the backlogs of deprivation in the country (widespread malnutrition and landlessness, mounting unemployment and lack of access to public health being the chief among these), inequalities that are also largely related to caste but not confined to it, has provided fertile ground for the right-wing to exploit the accumulated underlying sense of deprivation and injustice. This is of course *equally* true of the Left parties where they were in power at the state level, notably in West Bengal, and failed to build popular capacities. This backlog of failure is why 'development' has become such a powerful abstraction, one so effectively exploited by Modi, even if in practice he has a dilettantish fascination with new technologies and no conception of economic management beyond exhortations to capital (most often, *foreign* capital) to invest.

Having said this, it would be a mistake to write off the Congress either as a party without a future or as one irredeemably compromised by its failure to uphold secularism. What the remarkable success of the Grand Alliance in Bihar shows is that *all* secular forces have to be able to work together to defeat fascism in India. This includes the Left parties, which stayed outside that alliance and which, as noted, have never been closer to extinction as national parties than they are today.

8 November 2015

Endnotes

1 The main ones have been 'love *jihad*', *ghar wapsi* (forced conversions), the beef ban, and scaremongering about Hindus being demographically drowned out by the minorities. UP and Karnataka have been bastions of much of this hate campaigning.

2 An extraordinary public display of this partiality was the way the SBI chief was pressured into announcing a loan of $1 billion (the biggest ever for any private business) for one of the least viable projects thought up by any Indian industrial magnate, Gautam Adani's Australian coal-mining project (in the Galilee Basin in Queensland) which none of the major international banks were willing to touch. It is inconceivable that the announcement would have been made without pressure from Modi.

3 See Wilhelm Reich, *The Mass Psychology of Fascism,* Chapters 1 and 2; the best translation of Reich's classic is the one by Theodore Wolfe, available here: http://www.relatedness.org/Mass_Psychology_of_Fascism.pdf

4 Kershaw, *Hitler*, p. 332.

India today
Reasons for concern

The following statement was read out on the occasion of Romila Thapar's Dr. Ashgar Ali Engineer Memorial Lecture at the K.C. College auditorium in Bombay on 26 October 2015. It was read to an audience of over 600 before Professor Thapar delivered her lecture.

The BJP's victory in the Lok Sabha elections of 2014 has ushered in an unprecedented attack on India's democracy and injected new elements of intolerance and authoritarianism in the lives of people living in the country. Behind the mask of a developmental regime promising rapid industrial expansion and millions of jobs for the mass of unemployed youth, we've seen instead a hideous explosion of the cultural politics of the Extreme Right, overt acclamations of a *Hindu rashtra*; a wide-ranging takeover of educational and cultural institutions by the RSS; a rampant culture of violence targeting freedom of expression, freedom of religion, intellectual freedoms, even the freedom of the young to love; a calculated drive to communalise voters in North India with hate campaigns that have led to the horrid lynchings at Dadri and Udhampur; a shocking subversion of the judicial system through a concerted drive to secure the release of elements indicted on fake encounter and terrorism charges; fabrication of evidence to crush a handful of individuals who have campaigned for justice for the victims of the Gujarat violence; and of course the brazen murder of anti-superstition crusaders.

The fabric of India's democracy is today being torn to shreds. This is the first government in independent India where the RSS is overtly in command. We are further away from both Nehru and Ambedkar than ever before, from Nehru's contempt for the RSS as a harbinger of fascism, and Ambedkar's vision of a casteless India. (It's worth recalling that in December 1947 Nehru wrote: 'We have a great deal of evidence to show that the R.S.S. is an organisation which is in the nature of a private army and which is definitely proceeding on the strictest Nazi lines'; and again in December 1948, 'The R.S.S. is typical…of the type of organisation that grew up in various parts of Europe in support of fascism'). In this brief statement I'd like to draw your attention to three strands of this wide-ranging assault on democracy that merit particular concern.

The most troubling aspect of the state of Indian democracy remains, as always, the *appalling culture of impunity* that has evolved since the anti-Sikh pogroms for mass crimes that target minorities with the explicit backing of leading political figures. It is appalling that politicians known to be complicit in large-scale communal violence have escaped legal retribution and are not even seen to be seriously threatened by legal sanctions. The fatal omission here in India's criminal justice system is a clear and robust concept of command responsibility. Even hate speech cannot be combated legally without having to seek the consent of the executive, a preposterous Catch 22.

Majoritarian notions of democracy

These sustain the new cultures of intolerance by giving them a seeming legitimacy. 'You have hurt my sentiments' is the fiction used to justify both violence and intolerance. The so-called sentiments that are said to be hurt are manipulated, serial devices akin to the Nazi 'stab in the back' theory that was used to justify the attacks on German democracy in the 1920s. Majority and minority are not organic realities, they are serial identities, false manipulated constructions that have no existential reality beyond the manipulations themselves. Any minority constructed by majoritarianism will by the nature of its situation be and feel marginal and insecure. What is affirmed here is a fundamental lack of equality, a huge black hole at the heart of our democracy.

Organised mysticism and cultures of gullibility

Dabholkar, Kalburgi and Pansare were active in combating the organised mysticism and cultures of gullibility widespread at the 'popular' level. How can any modern democracy flourish if the supposedly 'popular' cultural base is one steeped in various forms of *promoted* mysticism and credulousness? These enterprises have both an ideological and an economic dimension. They are run by religious entrepreneurs who have every stake in keeping the mass of the population in a state of abject subjugation. They exploit the poor and they reinforce a pervasive cultural domination over them. Witness the latest example of this cynicism, Ramdev's exhortation to the poor and the middle class to stop eating pulses since the prices have gone through the roof.

If we have a Prime Minister who, as one distinguished writer says in a recent interview, 'is not doing anything to stem the rising tide of hatred', it's worth asking why. The liberal media hankers for a liberal Prime Minister, one who will intervene decisively to crush the extremist fringe and refocus the country's attention where it matters. But the fringe/Centre binary is seriously misleading in one sense at least. The Hindu Right is not a fragmented movement but one deeply unified at the ideological level, even if it speaks in different voices, through different organisations, and works at a multiplicity of levels. What the media are therefore asking for is for the Prime Minister to repudiate the ideology that spawned him. When Gandhi described the RSS as a 'communal body with a totalitarian outlook', he nailed a description that remains as valid today as it was in the forties. Of course, Modi is not Bhagwat, he incarnates that wing of Hindu nationalism that seeks to position itself as modernising India without secularism and without constitutional democracy. The vast mass of citizens in this country have to ask themselves whether that is the vision of India they seriously subscribe to.

Jairus Banaji

A very select reading list

Background

Alan Kramer, *Dynamic of Destruction: Culture and Mass Killing in the First World War* (New York, 2007)

Martin Kitchen, *The German Officer Corps 1890–1914* (Oxford, 1968)

R. G. L. Waite, *Vanguard of Nazism: The Free Corps Movement in Post-war Germany, 1918–1923* (Cambridge, Mass., 1972)

Dick Geary, 'Employers, Workers and the Collapse of Weimar', in Ian Kershaw, ed., *Weimar: Why Did German Democracy Fail?* (London, 1990)

Anton Kaes, *Shell Shock Cinema: Weimar Culture and the Wounds of War* (Princeton/Oxford, 2009)

Anthony Kauders, *German Politics and the Jews: Düsseldorf and Nuremberg, 1910–1933* (Oxford, 1996)

Ian Kershaw, *Hitler 1889–1936: Hubris* (Penguin Books, 2001)

Social base

J. Noakes, *The Nazi Party in Lower Saxony, 1921–1933* (Oxford, 1971)

P. H. Merkl, *Political Violence under the Swastika:581 Early Nazis* (Princeton, 1975)

Michael H. Kater, *The Nazi Party: A Social Profile of Members and Leaders, 1919–1945* (Cambridge, Mass., 1983)

Detlef Mühlberger, *The Social Bases of Nazism, 1919–1933* (Cambridge, 2003)

Divisions within German capital

Henry Ashby Turner Jr., *German Big Business and the Rise of Hitler* (New York/Oxford, 1985)

Alfred Sohn-Rethel, *Economy and Class Structure of German Fascism* (London, 1978)

Reinhard Neebe, *Großindustrie, Staat und NSDAP 1930–1933. Paul Silverberg und der Reichsverband der Deutschen Industrie in der Krise der Weimarer Republik* (Göttingen, 1981)

Nazism and women

Claudia Koonz, *Mothers in the Fatherland: Women, the Family and Nazi Politics* (London, 1988)

The Nazi state

Franz Neumann, *Behemoth: The Structure and Practice of National Socialism* (London, 1942)

Tim Mason, 'The Primacy of Politics – Politics and Economics in National Socialist Germany', in S. J. Woolf, ed., *The Nature of Fascism* (London, 1968); repr. in Mason, *Nazism, Fascism and the Working Class: Essays by Tim Mason*, ed. Jane Caplan (Cambridge, 1995) 53–76.

Tim Mason, *Social Policy in the Third Reich: The Working Class and the 'National Community'* (New York/Oxford, 1997)

Detlev Peukert, *Inside Nazi Germany. Conformity, Opposition and Racism in Everyday Life* (New Haven, 1987)

Claudia Koonz, *The Nazi Conscience* (Cambridge, Mass., 2003)

The Holocaust

David Bankier, *The Germans and the Final Solution: Public Opinion under Nazism* (Oxford, 1992)

Ruth Bettina Birn, 'Revising the Holocaust', *The Historical Journal*,

40/1 (1997) pp. 195–215

Christopher R. Browning, *Nazi Policy, Jewish Workers, German Killers* (Cambridge, 2000)

Christopher R. Browning, *Ordinary Men: Reserve Police Battalion 101 and the Final Solution in Poland* (Penguin Books, 2001)

Karl Jaspers, *The Question of German Guilt*, tr. E. B. Ashton (New York, 1947)

Enzo Traverso, *Understanding the Nazi Genocide: Marxism after Auschwitz*, tr. Peter Drucker (London, 1999)

Fascist parties today

David Art, *Inside the Radical Right: The Development of Anti-Immigrant Parties in Western Europe* (Cambridge, 2011)

The Extreme Right in India

Des Raj Goyal, *Rashtriya Swyamsevak Sangh* (New Delhi, 1979)

Marzia Casolari, *In the Shade of the Swastika: the Ambiguous Relationship between Indian Nationalism and Nazi-Fascism* (Bologna, 2011)

Jyotirmaya Sharma, *Terrifying Vision: M.S. Golwalkar, the RSS and India* (New Delhi, 2007)

Tapan Basu and others, *Khaki Shorts and Saffron Flags: A Critique of the Hindu Right* (New Delhi, 1993)

Some classic films on fascism

Alain Resnais, *Night and Fog* (1955)

Luchino Visconti, *The Damned* (1969)

Bernardo Bertolucci, *The Conformist* (1970)

Pier Paolo Pasolini, *Salò, or the 120 Days of Sodom* (1975)

Theodor Kotulla, *Aus einem deutschen Leben* (1977)

Alexander Kluge, *The Female Patriot* (1979)

Helma Sanders-Brahms, *Germany, Pale Mother* (1980)